Crazy Dave

N A T I V E VO I C E S

Native peoples telling their stories, writing their history

Crazy Dave

BASIL JOHNSTON

MINNESOTA HISTORICAL SOCIETY PRESS

Native Voices

Native peoples telling their
stories, writing their history

*To embody the principles set forth
by the series, all Native Voices books are
emblazoned with a bird glyph adapted
from the Jeffers Petroglyphs site in southern Minnesota. The rock art there represents one of the first recorded voices of
Native Americans in the Upper Midwest.
This symbol stands as a reminder of the
enduring presence of Native Voices on
the American landscape.*

Publication of Native Voices is supported
in part by a grant from the St. Paul
Companies.

Published in 2002 by the Minnesota
Historical Society Press

www.mnhs.org/mhspress

Published by arrangement with
Key Porter Books. Originally
published in Canada by Key Porter
Books, Toronto, 1999.

Manufactured in the
United States of America

10 9 8 7 6 5 4 3 2 1

⊛ The paper used in this publication
meets the minimum requirements of
the American National Standard for
Information Sciences—Permanence
for Printed Library Materials, ANSI
Z39.48-1984.

International Standard Book Number:
0-87351-423-8

A Cataloging-in-Publication record
for this book is available from the
Library of Congress.

*I*t wasn't until recently that I decided to write about my uncle David McLeod as I and others remember him, but the idea had been imbedded within me for years, undeveloped.

He was part of my growing up, part of my life for five years, and he left a lasting impression on me and those who knew and loved him. His soul-spirit still wanders the Big Meadow and the grove of poplars in the back of what used to be Grandmother's property, where he used to cut wood and talk to the Little People. He himself is now in the world of spirits, but he won't let us forget him. He often appears to me through others to remind me not to forget him.

Each time I saw Wiarton's own tall, lanky, retarded individual with a quart basket over the crook of one arm, gathering empty beer bottles and cigarette boxes to keep the Ontario highway clean and tidy a mile or so north and south of the town, I thought of Uncle David. When I saw a similarly deprived man sweeping the sidewalk of Oxford Square in London, Ontario, I remembered Uncle Dave. As I watched some men and women from "Daybreak," in Richmond Hill, Ontario, washing and cleaning bus shelters in and around town, or receiving Holy Communion from Father Bill Scanlon or one of his associates, happiness on their faces, I recalled Uncle David.

Around 1938 my father left us. Mother was broken-hearted, Grandmother angry and distraught. Shortly after the dissolution of our parents' marriage, the Indian agent, Fred Tuffnell, and the priest, Father Labelle, decided that my sister Gladys and I should go to the residential school in Spanish, Ontario, but Gladys rolled in a patch of poison ivy and broke out in a festering rash that sent her to bed and thus escaped committal to residential school. In her place came our younger sister, Marilyn, four and a half years of age.

In mid-winter of 1944, my father, Rufus Johnston, recently returned from service overseas as an anti-aircraft gunner, obtained my release from the residential school to which I had been sent five years earlier so that I could complete the full grade eight program in Cape Croker, then go on to high school. Six months later I was in Regiopolis College high school in Kingston, Ontario. Once again, I had been sent away from home. In mid-March 1945, lonesome, I returned to Cape Croker, to my mother and family.

Within weeks I was uncomfortable. I felt crowded, boxed in, as I had often felt in residential school. There was not enough room for five people in Mother's rented house, and not enough food.

I then went to stay with my grandmother, not permanently but for a few days. Going to Grandmother's, staying a week or two, then returning to my mother's became my practice, albeit an irregular one. I had no fixed address, no occupation.

Most evenings, as soon as supper was done, Uncle David and I left the house and Grandmother, he to go his way, I to go mine. He to go to "the other side," I to go to the church corner to loiter there with Ernie, Bunky, Kenney, Wildore, sometimes Ronnie and Paddy, to discuss the war, exercise our command of our ancestral language, and of course, discuss girls. Other times we drifted to Resime's place to talk to Shirley, Merzy, Joan, Helen, and Mary. When we had two or three nickels to spare, we went to "the other side" to play pool. Otherwise, we had little to do.

Bored? I don't know if we were bored or not. But we counted the months to our sixteenth birthdays so that we would be old enough "to register," without knowing what the term really meant or what obligations it entailed. We had a vague notion that registering at the post office was the first step leading to enlistment in the armed forces. We'd heard that registrants were required to declare their aspirations. We all agreed that "technical engineer" would be the most impressive. Service in Canada's armed forces would bring adventure, travel, money, respect. Better than anything Cape Croker could provide. There'd be something to do. On those evenings when it rained, I remained bound indoors with my grandmother. Silently I cursed the heavens for preventing me from going out. Meanwhile, Uncle David played cards or the organ. I stewed and fidgeted.

As for Grandmother, she sat down, as she did every evening, in her rocking chair in front of the window that faced the south and the limits of our world, the ramparts of the bluffs of the Niagara Escarpment, six to seven miles away. I now believe that my grandmother welcomed the rain, and even prayed for its advent so that she would have some company, even mine.

She rocked gently back and forth in her rocking chair, looking toward the bluffs and the world outside her own house. Nothing, it seemed, could disturb Grandmother's equanimity, not storms, calamities, explosions, or Uncle's insufferable organ playing which lasted as long as two hours. She gazed upon those bluffs without getting tired. She had learned to live with what life and fortune had doled out to her.

She looked as if she could do without companionship. But, as our people say, "What you see is not what is. Don't be taken in by appearances." Grandmother longed for company. She was lonesome, but she would never admit it.

I didn't realize it then, but the rains were doing both my Grandmother and me a favor. She had me to talk to; I had her to pass on to me what she knew. That I should be confined with her was meant to be. So far as I know, Uncle Walter and I were the only ones in our family to whom Grandmother related the family history.

My instruction in a part of the Anishinaubae history began with a simple inquiry born out of curiosity as to why my surname and her last name were different, and why Grandfather Norman did not live at home with her.

"Grandson," she said, "Norman is not your grandfather. Ed Johnson was your grandfather. He died long before your time." And Grandmother told me about my real grandfather, about an aunt and two uncles who had passed away many years before. And she told me about other people; her grandmother, Misqua-bunno-quae (Red Sky Dawn), and her flight from Wisconsin; the troubled times for Indians in those days a hundred years before; and more. As to why

Grandfather Norman was living apart in his own house, Grandmother would not say.

While my grandmother talked, I half listened, my mind and spirit elsewhere, accepting her stories as no more than fairy tales such as those told by John Angus or C.K. Jones. At ages fifteen and sixteen I wasn't much interested in the history of the family, or of the Cape Croker people. There were things far more relevant, and so my grandmother's stories rested in the depths of my memory, along with thousands upon thousands of other useful and useless bits of information that are accumulated every day and form part of one's learning. I squirreled away my grandmother's stories somewhere in my memory. Sometimes they well up to the surface uninvited; more often they remain anchored to their resting places deep in my mind, indifferent to my pleas to come forth.

During the years that all of us went to the residential school in Spanish, we were given to understand that the Roman Catholic Church's teachings on spiritual matters represented the only way of looking at life, the afterlife, and any other kind of life. There was but one God; "Him only shalt thou serve and worship." Attending God were legions of angels and saints in heaven; on earth roamed devils and guardian angels; in purgatory, a halfway house, were the departed who were being cleansed by fire before admission into heaven and the Divine Presence. There was hell as well, inhabited by the wicked. To believe in Weendigo, Little People, Nana'b'oozoo, Manitous, and Thunder Birds, and to offer tobacco to trout, beaver, bears, partridges, corn, and blueberries, bordered on idolatry, pantheism, and paganism, deserving of eternal damnation. What I learned of Christian doctrine cast some doubt on my grandmother's teachings, and, of course, on my heritage.

I'm tempted to say that I regret that I didn't listen more closely to my grandmother. To say so presumes that I might have benefited far more than I did, and done something far more useful than I was able to accomplish.

How much my grandmother told me I cannot say. Certainly far more than I've managed to retain. But I never forgot her breaking the news to me that there are realities in the world other than the physical, that every being and thing has an unseen principle of life. I didn't think of life and being in those terms then; only later. This my grandmother taught me even before I went to school in Cape Croker. Unforgettable too is the lesson that she passed on to me in my teenage years; that is, to know who I was by getting to know my people's history. When I must have seemed inattentive to her, she reminded me sharply that "You'd better get to know where you came from. It's the only way you're going to get to know yourself." Until my grandmother told me about things, I had given them no thought. But they have stayed with me and have become part of my outlook and perception.

My grandmother died in the late fall of 1946. My father, who had not come back to Mother as we had hoped, left the reserve, as did many other men, to work in lumber camps that provided a steadier income than did fishing. They now wanted a monthly paycheck such as they had received in military service. Besides, "Fishing is done; pulpwood cutting is done."

In the fall of 1947 I too left the reserve, encouraged to return to school by Frank Nadjiwon.

Back to Spanish I went, to enroll in the high school program that the residential school was then offering. I graduated in 1950, went on to university, and worked in business for seven years before going to teacher's college and teaching high school in North York, Ontario. In 1970, because of my work in the native community in Toronto, I was seconded by the Royal Ontario Museum (ROM) to initiate a native program in its Department of Ethnology and in the larger community around Toronto and southern Ontario. When my leave of absence from the North York Board of Education expired, Dr. E.S. Rogers of the ROM asked me to stay on as a permanent staff member. I agreed.

In my capacity as teacher in the Department of Ethnology, I traveled frequently and widely in southern and mid-Ontario. I read widely—boring ethnological stuff. Wherever I traveled, people told me stories and offered me explanations not recorded in ethnographic texts. In the years since leaving Cape Croker, I doubt that I had given Grandmother's stories two seconds of thought.

It wasn't until thirty years later that I was reminded of her account of the exodus of the Pottawatomi from Green Bay, Wisconsin. In

1976 I paid a visit to Jane Rivers of Wikwemikong on Manitoulin Island, Ontario, a dear friend and gifted storyteller, now deceased. After our talk, Rivers took me to call on Phillip Pitwaniquot, a well-known local historian and raconteur. He startled me by telling me about the flight of Pottawatomi from Green Bay to Canada and other parts of the United States ... a long time ago, a story remarkably similar to the one my grandmother had told me. At that moment, thirty years after my grandmother's passing, her story, which had rested unrecalled in my memory, rose to the surface of my mind. Her story now acquired meaning and credibility. Two years later, Dan Pine of Garden River, Ontario, told me much the same story. Whether Pitwaniquot and Pine knew each other I'm unable to say, but neither one knew my grandmother.

In a general way, history bears out my grandmother's account of the dispossession and dislocation of the North American Indians, not only in Wisconsin, but elsewhere.

My grandmother and many others, as Indians, were victims of those cataclysmic times, 1750–1850, of which she spoke. Her own grandmother and their kin fled Wisconsin sometime in the early 1830s to seek sanctuary, peace, security, and beauty in another part of Anishinaubae-akeeng, which extended from Minnesota to the Gatineau Valley in Quebec, north and south of Lake Superior. But the dream of peace and plenty was snatched from them. In 1854, the Saugeen-Nawaush peoples, who had taken in the Pottawatomi refugees from Wisconsin, were forced and cozened into surrendering a vast tract of land, and were driven and penned into two small reserves, one at Saugeen on the Lake Huron side of Bruce Peninsula, the other at Naeyaushee-winnigum-eeng (Portage Point), now Cape Croker, on the Georgian Bay side. The Saugeen-Nawaush were isolated from each other and from their new neighbors who were settling into the surrendered lands.

Around 1980 I began to dally with the idea of writing a series of stories about some of the misadventures of Uncle David. I did write three or four episodes, but suspended the project to devote time to "more important" works, a questionable assumption.

More important! Uncle David less important! Yes, he was a story in himself. But, as our people would say, I wasn't ready. Yet he kept recurring in my mind. The more I thought about him, the more he reminded me, in certain respects, of the place and situation of the North American Indian in Canadian society. It was assumed that Uncle David didn't know much about anything, or what he knew didn't count; what North American Indians knew didn't amount to a jar of jelly beans, and did not have any larger relevance. As long as Uncle David stayed where he belonged and didn't bother anyone or interfere with anyone's business, neighbors could put up with him; and as long as North American Indians kept the peace and didn't rock the boat, society could tolerate them. Uncle David didn't belong in the community. He wasn't one of the normal human beings; he was dumb and couldn't talk; didn't and couldn't understand. He didn't belong in the society of sensible people. He belonged in some institution where he could learn to perform simple tasks and operations. Some day he might have learned to help himself and earn a place at the bottom of the totem pole, or the ladder.

Indians didn't belong in Canadian society. They were wild. They were more at home in the forest and in the open prairies, with bears and gophers. Some even believed that Indians came from somewhere in Asia. They didn't understand or practice Western European traditions. They belonged in an institution where they would be supervised, tolerated, and modified before they could be admitted into the larger civilized society.

Reserves ostensibly were created to protect the Indians from the encroachment of settlers and unscrupulous speculators, swindlers, and other riffraff; to wean them from their traditional pursuits and pagan beliefs and practices; to groom them for farming and the trades, for the exercise of self-government and democracy, and for conversion to and espousal of Christian beliefs; and to earn them a place among the citizens of the country.

Indians, it was taken for granted, were as children in the understanding of and exercise of civilized institutions, and needed the guidance and the protection of a Great White Father and a Great White Mother to nurture and tutor them to the point where they could look after themselves and their communities, like their more accomplished neighbors. When the Canadian government undertook to look after the Indians, it declared our ancestors to be "wards of the state," needing the patronage of the federal government. In 1876, to carry out the fiduciary duties it had assumed, the Canadian government consolidated several acts that had been passed years earlier for the benefit of Indians into one statute known as the Indian Act. It conferred considerable power and authority upon the minister of the department responsible for Indians at that particular time. At various times, Indians came under the Department of the Interior, the Department of Mines and Resources, Citizenship and Immigration, and currently Northern and Indian Affairs. The Great White Father didn't know where to put Indians, like orphans shunted from one foster home to another, unwanted. No wonder decisions were so long in being made.

But before I could start to write, I needed to know more about David and Grandmother, and the history of the community. For one thing, I knew little of what went on at home while I was in residential school. Other than "this is to let you know that we are fine and hope you are the same. So-and-so got a baby and so-and-so died," I knew nothing else. Nor did I know what went on in my community, or what happened to David from 1947 to 1954 while I was going to school. A good thing for me that my other uncles, Walter, John, and Stanley; my mother, Mary; my sisters Ernestine and Janet; and my cousins Berdina, Rose, and Ray, lived on the reserve during those years, knew Uncle David intimately, were familiar with the goings-on, and were able to fill me in on what I didn't know.

What I knew of the past history of Cape Croker came in fragments, in disjointed bits and pieces from C.K. Jones, Sr., Peter Nadjiwon, Oliver Johnston, and other people of my grandmother's generation whom I had the good fortune to know.

There were many events and incidents that took place in the mid-1930s through the late 1950s during Uncle David's lifetime of which I was not aware. Fred Jones, George Keeshig, and Edwin and Isabel Akiwenzie told me what they knew.

I knew most of the people on the reserve in the late 1930s and the mid-1940s. I saw them at fall fairs, dances, weddings, and funerals; I fished and lunched with fishermen. I visited them, listened to their stories. As a penniless spectator watching billiards, I not only kept my eyes on the game, but kept my ears open to stories about our neighbors, kin, and friends. It was through anecdotes that I became better acquainted with C.K. Jones, Sr., C.K. Jones, Jr., Liza, Budeese, CFRB, Kitchi-Low-C, Levi Chegahno, Elastus Sky, Elias Chegahno, Percy Pitwaniquot, Jonah Chegahno, Fred Tuffnell, Father Oscar Labelle, S.J., Miss Burke, Rev. Burgess, Dr. Wigle, and many others.

I could not have had a better informant than my Uncle Walter, who knew the goings-on in the reserve. He had served the band council as secretary for over fifty years. Still, despite his familiarity with the history of the people, and his intimacy with Grandmother, there were many details of which he was unaware.

And so I began the story of Uncle David, except that I didn't get too far. I then realized that I could not write only about David, but had to include my grandmother in the narrative as well. Uncle David depended on her almost completely. Grandmother looked after him, worried about him, subordinated her life to his so that he could lead his life and existence as well as he could. She, too, needed someone. She needed David, not to the same extent that he needed her, but she needed him. She needed company. She needed someone to care for. For years he was her chief contact with the outside world, bringing her the news in his own private language. From David's accounts Grandmother derived a hazy, fragmented picture of what was going on in the community. But what she learned from David was no worse than what Mary Jane and other reporters represented as fact and the truth.

Whatever David may have been to others, some of the neighbors on the reserve referred to him as Crazy Dave. But he was Uncle David to me, maybe not so much by choice as by training and the fear of having my ears pulled if I were to refer to him by any other name. He was, at various times in our relationship, friend, enemy, playmate, antagonist, companion, traitor, a Judas and Brutus combined. In thinking about my Grandmother Rosa (pronounced Rose-auh by nearly everyone on the reserve), a poor woman, I began to understand how she could daily look at those bluffs in the distance and even see beyond them, and how she could tolerate life's storms with equanimity.

This is a story of my Grandmother Rosa and her son David, who was born with Down syndrome, then called Mongolism. He had a shambling walk, slanted eyes, and a thick tongue, and he babbled in his own language.

This is also a story, albeit sketchy, of a native people attempting to regain a little of what they once had in abundance: freedom, equality, independence, land, pride, justice, dreams, and the chance to show and to say, "This I can do." They failed to regain a single inch or ounce of what they once had, mainly because of the Indian Affairs Branch and the Indian Act, but partly because of their implicit trust in the promises made by the government that it would look after them, and because of their own petty jealousies and suspicions.

The Indians have a story to illustrate this facet of their character:

On the morning of their fishing expedition, an Indian and a White Man caught crabs, which they were going to use as bait. As they caught the crabs, they put them in pails.

"Guess that should be enough," the Indian observed when his pail was half full.

"Think so?" the White Man rejoined, doubtful as ever that he'd had enough of anything.

"Yeah. We can always get some more if we run short."

"Never thought of that," the White Man remarked, looking into his pail, which was half full. "Maybe we should have a bite to eat before we go out," he added, as usual hungry for something.

"Good idea," the Indian agreed, reminded of his own empty stomach. He set his pail of crabs down next to the boat, then turned to go.

"Aren't you going to put a cover on your pail?" the White Man asked in alarm. "Your crabs might get away."

"Nah!" the Indian scoffed. "Just like us Indians, them. Firs' one tries to get out won't get too far. Others will pull him back 'fore he goes two steps."

To those already mentioned, family, the deceased, I add the names of kin, friends, neighbors, and acquaintances who shared what they knew of the principals in David's and my grandmother's lives, and of the past of Cape Croker. Alfred (Indian Act) Jones, Norman McLeod, Maggie Desjardines, John Angus, Christine Keeshig (Grandmother's sister), Gregor Keeshig, Francis Nadjiwon, Antoine Akiwenzie, Henry and Verna Johnston, Joe and Irene Akiwenzie, Tom Jones,

Lillian Nadjiwon, Norman Jones, John and Mary Louise McLeod, Victor (Ching) Johnson, all deceased; George and Alexandria Keeshig, Fred Jones, Edwin and Isabel Akiwenzie, Wilmer and Barney Nadjiwon, Winona Arriaga, Ross and Dorothy Johnston, Ernest Nadjiwon, Eugene Keeshig, Charlie Shoot (Akiwenzie), Donald Keeshig, Delina Johnston, Ron and Lila Johnston, Gordon and Stella Johnston, Ross and Ella Waukey, Philomene Chegahno, and Ross Whicher of Wiarton, Ontario. I thank you. Without your help, I could not have written this story. I hope that I have written it as well as you expected and the story deserves. If not, it wasn't for lack of trying.

To Beverley Slopen, my agent, thank you for persisting in asking, "When are you going to write about Crazy Dave?"

To my family, my lovely Lucie, and Babes (Miriam), Tibby (Elizabeth), and Geoffrey; our grandsons, Joel, Jason, and David, thank you for your love and support.

To Barbara Berson, my editor, thank you for your guidance. I hope the book reflects a bit of what you hoped for.

To Anna Porter, a gracious lady and friend, thank you for your faith and support.

Finally, to the reader. *Crazy Dave* is not meant to represent the complete story of David McLeod or the history of Cape Croker. Rather, it is a sketch of a mother and her son impaired by Down syndrome, and it is but a glimpse of the community and its politics and the times that served as the little world in which David tried to do what others did, and tried to be what others were, but could not be.

The stories and opinions I have used as sources for this book will not be found in the band council minute book, or in the diaries of the clergy, or in the archives of the *Wiarton Echo* or in the *Owen Sound Sun Times*, but are stored in the memories of the older generation still living.

randson! Listen! I'll tell you what my grandmother told me," Grandmother said to me one night as I stared gloomily at the rain beating on the window and pounding on the roof. I wasn't really interested in Grandmother's stories about the past, but I didn't have much choice. Of all the stories that Grandmother told me, I remember one only because it matched the stories that John Angus, of our community, told. Thus began my first lesson in the history of our people, yet I didn't put much stock in it.

When the White People came to this land they told our people that they were looking for another land, another people to trade with so that they would have better lives. They said they were poor, they had no land, their king owned everything and everyone; they couldn't come and go without their master's permission; they couldn't keep everything they grew in the fields, but only what was left over after their masters and priests made off with what they wanted; they couldn't talk to "their betters," and their women couldn't give medicine to their sick children without risk of being accused of witchcraft and being burned alive.

Some of our people couldn't believe what these strangers said, but others did and felt sorry for them. These strangers were poor; they needed sympathy. They didn't even know how to hunt. Our ancestors took pity on them and gave them a hand. Besides, they were few.

Soon our ancestors regretted that they had opened their arms to these strangers. Shipload after shipload of White People flooded the land, fulfilling the old prophecies of their coming. At first these aliens were friendly and peaceful, but within a hundred years of their coming, they were fighting and killing Indians in the east and taking their land.

Some of our young men went to the east to help our kindred people. Many didn't come back; many came back wounded; some were no longer able to keep themselves but had to depend on their neighbors for handouts. The survivors described the weapons of the aliens and their armies.

Still our people didn't believe these stories. The White People! They were still far off, as far away as the moon. Hmph! Perhaps the Indians to the east didn't know how to deal with these intruders. Now, if they were to encroach upon the lands of the Indians south of Lake Superior, the warriors would strike out like coiled rattlers, or badgers, to drive off trespassers and keep them at bay. Such raids had always been enough to keep other Indians in check.

However, our people didn't know the White People. The aliens from Europe were not like Indians. They were greedy, greedy beyond belief. They wanted land. They bought land, and if they couldn't buy it, they stole or killed for it. And they were never satisfied; they wanted more. They were as greedy as our Weendigo that craved and fed upon human flesh. No matter how much this monster ate, it could never sate its hunger. It had to have more, yet more was never enough. The people from Europe were the Weendigo incarnated in the flesh; they wanted land, all of it, and *more*.

But unlike our Weendigo, which could be checked and even killed, this Weendigo from the east was indestructible. It fought.

If the White People couldn't buy or steal what they coveted, they took it by war. They would risk their lives, they would kill; and they made war not in short, swift raids, as did our people, but in crusades that they prosecuted until the enemy was destroyed and his land taken.

They were accustomed to war, as if it was in their blood. They took pride in their armies, in their commanders, and in their victories. Their kings wanted land, war, glory, power.

Because of their kings' avarice, European countries were in a perpetual state of war, with only periods of truce interrupting the bloodletting. Every king had a standing army ready to go to war. To the kings human life meant little, if anything.

Over the centuries of wars the White People developed an arsenal of weapons and tactics. With only bows and arrows, spears and clubs, and raw courage, the Indians were no match against White People, who had firearms and whose numbers grew ever greater.

Even though the Indians were outnumbered and outgunned, they often outfought and inflicted stinging defeats on the White People's armies. By the time Pontiac and, later, Tecumseh called for a united resistance to the White invasion to defend life, liberty, and land, it was too late. The White People were firmly entrenched along the eastern seaboard and were settling into Shawnee and Miami lands in the Ohio Valley and even farther, into the Midwest. They didn't have enough land; they needed and wanted more.

The White People came to Wisconsin and asked to buy the land around Green Bay. If they could buy the land, the American delegation proposed that the Pottawatomi Anishinaubaek relocate in Indian territory to the southwest, on the other side of the Mississippi; for the sale of their homeland, the Pottawatomi would receive payment and the protection of the American government. However, if the Pottawatomi refused to sell their land, settlers and speculators would confiscate it as they had done to other Indians and the American government would be powerless to help the Pottawatomi.

Our ancestors protested that this land was their home; it belonged to their forebears and it belonged to their descendants. They could not abandon it as birds abandon their nests when they have raised their young. It was not an easy matter to uproot one's home and life and transplant it in another place. The Indians loved the land that the Creator had allotted to them. They could not part with it.

Take it or leave it, the American delegation said.

Our ancestors were crushed; they were angry. They were told to leave their land, their homes, to make way for aliens who coveted the land but did not love it or respect it for its own sake. Had they been numerous they would have laughed at the demand and told the deputation to leave, but they were without power or the means to refuse.

They thought about the offer and the consequences. Then they sent a delegation to Indian territory to assess the land that would be their new home if they were to accept the White Man's proposal. On its return the delegation reported that no Anishinaubae could ever live in a land that was flat and had few rivers and lakes.

Even after the delegation had described the Indian territory, the Pottawatomi Anishinaubaek were divided in their thinking. They disagreed, as they had always done. Some were in favor of staying and standing up to the White People in defending the land that Kitchi-Manitou had given them; others were in favor of accepting the government's proposal and making a new home in Indian territory with other Indians. Still others were in favor of striking out for another part of the Anishinaubae nation's vast territory that extended north and east into Canada, and settling there among their kin and own people.

For this latter group the only question was "Which way?" North or south? Nearly all preferred the northerly route skirting the west and northern shores of Lake Michigan, then through the Straits of Mackinac and on to Canada, the route that some of their ancestors had taken in the trading missions and raiding routes. At the last moment a small party of fifty or sixty people, made up of six families, the Nauwaudjiwons (now Nadjiwon), Migwans, Nashkewes, Menominees (now Rice), Pitwaniquots, and Taubissungs (now Toby), changed their minds. There were too many people in the main group, at least 500, too many canoes, 150 to 200. There might not be enough food along the way.

These six families decided to go south, spend the winter in the Chicago area and continue their flight come spring. Men and women, young and old, children and infants, took with them their clothing, their sacred articles, and their weapons. Despite taking little baggage, the band could not move fast; it could travel only as fast and as far as the old and the very young could go. Besides, the men had to hunt and fish along the way.

They frequently prayed, "God! Have pity on us. Zhawaenimishinaung Kizhae-Manitou."

When this group arrived in the outskirts of Chicago they came upon a dozen or more Indians whose tribal origin the refugees could not determine. They were hanging from gibbets, lynched, it was presumed, by White People. What the refugees didn't know or weren't aware of was that Black Hawk, a Sauk and Fox Indian, was stirring up the country against Indians by his resistance to White encroachment.

The refugees immediately abandoned plans to winter in Chicago. They went on as far as their strength and endurance could carry them, as far as Bad Bird (Matchi-Binaesheewish) in southern Michigan. Winter set in and bound them where they were. They were forced to ask the people in Bad Bird, also Anishinaubaek like themselves, for sanctuary and for permission to hunt rabbits and small animals in order to survive. The Bad Bird Anishinaubaek felt sorry for this bedraggled, dispirited little band, and allowed them to pitch their camp in their village and to hunt, trap, and fish with them until spring.

In this part of the country there were deer, birds, and fish aplenty, yet the Bad Bird people were not much better off than the refugees. No longer were the Indians here free to go hunting and fishing whenever they needed food, as they once had been in the habit of doing. Since the White People had taken the land, they would not allow Indians to enter upon their private domains to hunt or fish for survival. They acted as if they owned the animals, birds, fish, and insects. It didn't matter to them that people were hungry; "Let them hunger." Still, the Indians slipped out of their reserves to pursue and kill deer on the sly to keep from starving.

It was during that winter that Grandmother's grandfather died, along with two children.

In the late spring the Green Bay refugees resumed their flight. With several of their hosts serving as their guides, they made their way across lower Michigan, avoiding towns and large settlements along the way.

They crossed the St. Clair River at Algonac on logs and homemade rafts under cover of darkness. They'd heard that there were many Pottawatomi people like themselves on Walpole Island, among whom they'd find peace and rebuild their lives. There would be no need to go any farther.

But when they asked for asylum they were turned down. As much as the chiefs, headmen, and people of Walpole Island sympathized with them and would have liked to have admitted them into their community, there was not enough land for fifty more people. Besides, the Ojibway and Ottawa Anishinaubaek objected to the admission of more Pottawatomi into their midst.

The refugees asked where in Canada they might start life afresh and once more dream. Their hosts pointed to the land of the Saugeen-Nawaush Chippewas of Bruce Peninsula, owners and proprietors of a vast tract of land that would fulfill their dreams and needs.

The Saugeen-Nawaush Chippewas were the most fortunate of Indians, owning more land than their fellow Ojibway. Everyone envied them. They had more than enough land for themselves, and more than enough of everything else. The Walpole Island Indians assured the refugees that the Saugeen-Nawaush would welcome them, for they were a generous people. "Tell them," their hosts said, "that the Walpole Island people sent you."

In mid-summer the little band, refreshed and heartened, resumed their trek northward along the western shores of Bruce Peninsula up to the mouth of the Saugeen River. From there they struck inland to Owen Sound, then known as Great Sturgeon Bay, the principal town of the Saugeen-Nawaush Chippewas.

When they met the chiefs and headmen of the Saugeen-Nawaush Chippewas, the refugees' spokesmen told them that they had been dispossessed of their lands in Wisconsin and were seeking asylum, and that the Walpole Island people had recommended the Saugeen-Nawaush Chippewas as hospitable and generous. But the request was not granted as readily as the Green Bay refugees had been led to believe it would be. For a while, based on the cool reception they received, the refugees thought they would be asked to leave. Over and over the refugees were asked why they had left their homes, why they hadn't gone to Indian territory. As Pottawatomis, they didn't belong. But finally, after much debate, the Saugeen-Nawaush Chippewas agreed to admit the refugees on condition of good behavior.

At last, after a year of wandering, the refugees came to a land that was as described by the Walpole Island Indians. Its waters were alive with fish, its forests swarmed with bear, deer, wolves, rabbits, and beaver; its skies throbbed with the beat of the wings of partridges, pheasants, geese, and ducks; its meadows were lush with berries, fruits, vegetables, nuts, and medicines.

They thanked Kitchi-Manitou for the good life.

Yet they were uneasy. There were people in Owen Sound who didn't want them there and turned their heads if they chanced to meet them or, if they spoke, made snide remarks about intrusion and taking up someone's place. To be cold-shouldered by their own kindred, many of them Pottawatomi like themselves, hurt the refugees more than it would have had the snub come from strangers. They *did* belong. As Pottawatomi Anishinaubaek they belonged to the land, in whatever part of the entire breadth of country that Kitchi-Manitou had given the Anishinaubae peoples.

But the sense of brotherhood, sisterhood, of having right of place in the land was changed. So much for traditional Chippewa hospitality. It was an empty boast, a self-congratulatory benediction.

For some, the resentment was too much. The Migwans family moved to West Bay on Manitoulin Island; the Menominees moved on to Honey Harbour, Moose Deer Point, and Parry Island, later changing their surname to Rice; some Pitwaniquots and Nashkewes moved to Wikwemikong on Manitoulin Island, while the rest hung tough in Owen Sound among the Saugeen-Nawaush Chippewas. The Nauwaudjiwons, too, stayed to plant their roots in the cold earth and, blending in with their hosts, abbreviated their name to Nadjiwon. The Taubissungs, after a short stay, moved to Beausoleil Island and then to Honey Harbour, where their name was shortened and anglicized to Toby, after which their national origin could not be deduced from their name.

The refugees had come to Canada to escape the depredations of the White People, and they warned their hosts of what to expect from their White neighbors and their government. Their hosts believed not a word.

But within twenty years of the arrival of the refugees from Wisconsin, the Saugeen-Nawaush Indians were pressured to surrender their homeland in its entirety and to migrate to Manitoulin Island, which was envisioned by the colonial government as Canada's very own Indian territory. The lieutenant governor did not ask the Ottawa Anishinaubaek if they would make way for transplanted Indians.

If the Saugeen-Nawaush Indians were to sign a treaty surrendering their lands, the colonial government promised that the Crown would compensate, protect, and bring the Indians to that state of education where they could look after their own affairs.

The Saugeen-Nawaush peoples were now subjected to the same strong-arm tactics as were applied to the Green Bay Indians to surrender their lands. They were outraged. In 1848 they wrote to their fellow Indians in Burlington, asking them to take up arms with them and to beat off the White People; they themselves were ready to take up clubs and spears and knives. There was no answer from their allies. Along with the Beausoleil and Couchiching peoples, they sent a delegation to London, England, to appeal to Queen Victoria for her intervention. Her Royal Highness was too busy to see the delegation.

In 1854 the Saugeen-Nawaush Indians gave in, surrendering the greater part of their homeland, Bruce Peninsula, retaining only a reserve north of Southampton on the Lake Huron side, another at Cape Croker on the Georgian Bay side, hunting grounds at Willow Creek, and numerous islands and shorelines.

With their marks on the parchment the chiefs and headmen were forced to surrender not only their homeland but everything that went with it. They lost what Pontiac and Tecumseh had predicted they would lose: freedom, independence, rights, dreams, duties, heritage, institutions.

By the Treaty of 1854, the Saugeen-Nawaush peoples became dependents, wards of the Crown, as children who need a father to protect, feed, teach, and, if necessary, punish them.

Thereafter an agent of the Crown would act as protector-guardian of the Saugeen-Nawaush people until Her Majesty's children had reached that state of education and sophistication where they could take their place among the other subjects of Her Majesty. There were short cuts to the lofty status of citizenship. Anyone who wanted citizenship needed only to renounce his or her birthright by way of "enfranchisement." *Voilà!* An Indian became "white" and carried a "blue card" to prove it. An Indian woman gained all the rights, privileges, and duties of full citizenship the moment she whispered "I do" in marriage to a White Man. For the rest, the Crown would look after the Indians until the Indians grew up and were able to look after themselves.

The treaty embittered everyone. The chiefs and headmen resented the duplicity and the bullying tactics of the colonial negotiators, and blamed one another for weakness and for surrendering too much. Ordinary men and women suspected that some of the chiefs and headmen had taken money under the table.

Since the resignation of David Van Dusen as tribal interpreter in 1848, after several years of service in this capacity, the Saugeen-Nawaush Indians had been at a serious disadvantage in dealing with "their" superintendent in Owen Sound.

It was during this time when an interpreter was most needed that three brothers, Lamourandiere by name, stopped over in Cape Croker on their way to Killarney, Ontario, where they had intended to settle and go into a business partnership. All three were half-breeds who spoke, read, and wrote English, French, and Chippewa-Anishinaubae. The chief and band council were not about to let these brothers slip through their fingers. Cape Croker had greater need of such men and their talents than did Killarney. To persuade the Lamourandiere brothers to settle in Cape Croker, the chief and head-men offered them band membership, land, and permission to marry one of the local princesses.

For the brothers, the decision to abandon their original plans and to become full-blooded Indians, members of the Cape Croker band, was not an easy one. Finally, after weeks of weighing all the pros and cons, Fred Lamourandiere accepted Cape Croker's offer, stayed, and was inducted into band membership. His brothers continued on to Killarney.

As the only trilingual Chippewa in Cape Croker, a formidable man who could deal with White People nearly on their own terms, Fred was appointed band council secretary.

Not long after settling in Cape Croker, Fred Lamourandiere married a local princess. From this marriage were born Christine, Louis, and my grandmother, Rosa.

*A*t her baptism in 1876, Rosa was given a "White, Christian" name, a practice that was becoming more common among Indians. Receiving a White name was in keeping with the changing times and consistent with her lineage as the daughter of Fred Lamourandiere. Rosa, her sister, Christine, and her brother, Louis, were three-quarters Indian, one-quarter White.

For their lineage Rosa, Christine, and Louis were called "Weessaukitae," scorched or part burned, to refer to their half-darkened complexion. Half-breed! But they weren't the only ones on the reserve to be less than full blood. When Rosa came to understand the term she was instantly provoked into fury; she would coil her five-foot, one hundred-pound form and spring at the provocateur. The other boys and girls soon learned not to call her names.

While Rosa earned the respect and silence of her eight- and nine-year-old playmates, she drew complaints from the parents of children whose teeth she had jarred and rattled. "Your daughter been pickin' on my daughter, Fred! Would you have a word with her?" neighbors grumbled. Fred had several words with Rosa, several times. "But Dad!" Rosa argued, "I don't like anyone calling me names .... I'm just as Indian as anyone else!" When these fatherly talks and threats of strappings failed, Fred asked his mother-in-law to speak to Rosa. "Daughter is much too ready to fight. Too thin-skinned! She's causing bad feelings."

Great-grandmother took Rosa aside. She didn't scold her or threaten her as her father had done. Instead, she pointed out that anger was a gift not meant to hurt others but to keep one from getting hurt. "Kitchi-Manitou gave you too much, more than what you need or is good for you. Unless you do something, you keep this temper in check, you'll never live at peace within yourself or with the world and other people."

Rosa promised her grandmother that she would try to bridle this temper.

What an odd way of looking at anger. It was more curse than gift. Giving too much! Didn't Kitchi-Manitou know how much people needed? Did Kitchi-Manitou also give too little? Why not give the same amount to everybody?

There followed many questions, many unanswerable, others easily explained.

"Are there good gifts?"

"Yes," her grandmother assured her.

"And what are mine?" Rosa asked.

"I'm not sure. But you have many. You will have to find them. You can start looking now."

Rosa began then. What could she do? What did she want to do? What did she want to be?

Meanwhile, their father was teaching her brother, Louis, to read, write, do arithmetic, and to farm, preparing him for life in the modern world. The old ways and the old days were gone.

As their father led Louis over the lessons in English, French, and Ojibway, Rosa and Christine listened and looked on. Alone, the sisters practiced the language of the "civilized."

Hearing the two girls speaking the English they had picked up, their mother sniffed, "What do you want to know that for?"

"Well, Louis is learning it," the girls rejoined. "Why can't we learn it?"

"Because Louis has to learn it. You don't have to. You're to learn other things—sewing, cooking, washing, keeping the house clean. Nobody's going to marry girls who can't look after the house and kids, or plant gardens and can berries."

Fred Lamourandiere's son and daughters were being groomed and primed to live like White People.

Later, when Rosa began to notice boys, she even dreamed of

romance, of being swept off her feet by a prince and living happily ever after. Just like the heroines in the stories her father sometimes told her and Christine. So romantic, not like the Indian way. Except that Rosa couldn't think of any of the young men on the reserve as prince-like or so prepossessing as to set her heart aflutter. Maybe the boy of her dreams would come from some other village beyond the line of bluffs. Like all young girls, Rosa dreamed.

She wasn't going to allow her father to choose a husband for her, as he had done for Christine, who had to marry their father's choice, Jay Double U (John Wesley Keeshig). No! She'd run away before that ever happened.

Sometime during her sixteenth year Rosa's father began to bring Ed Johnson's name into their conversations in obtuse ways. "Nice young man ... a good worker. He's going to make some young woman happy and lucky ...."

Until she asked her parents why they kept bringing Ed Johnson's name into their discussions, Rosa didn't know that her parents and Ed's parents had already made a pact for her to marry Ed. Ed wasn't her idea of a prince. Her skin didn't tingle when he spoke to her at church.

When her father told her that she was already pledged to Ed Johnson, Rosa cried and screamed at her parents for giving her away to a man she didn't like. She accused them of not caring for her. Finally, she sobbed that she was leaving and that she would never come home.

That same afternoon, Rosa packed her clothing and moved out of her parents' home and into her maternal grandmother's home. But Rosa received less understanding and sympathy than she had hoped for and expected. "Your parents know better than you do what kind of man will best look after you and your children. Listen to your parents!" her grandmother told her. Several days later, her grandmother sent Rosa back to her own home, contrite, but not contrite enough to admit the error of her ways and to agree to marry Ed Johnson.

It took two years for Rosa to give in to her grandmother's words and wishes to control her temper and pride and to do what her parents wished. She agreed to accept Ed Johnson ... for better or for worse.

Two more years went by before Ed Johnson was ready to marry Rosa. This was in 1896.

"You're so lucky!" girlfriends and neighbors told Rosa. Only twenty and she had married the most eligible young man on the reserve. He wasn't a prince, nor did he set Rosa's heart on fire. He didn't sweep her off her feet, but he was solid, reliable, and industrious.

A year later Rosa gave birth to Adolphus. For the first time in four years Rosa felt lucky and happy. But her happiness was short-lived. Baby Adolphus died within a month of his birth. It was her Ed, her parents, and her grandmother who comforted her during her mourning and her grief.

Her Ed was a prince. Quietly, without her knowing it, Ed had swept her off her feet. She cried on his shoulder, making it a little easier to bear her loss and to accept life's setbacks. She had to live up to her grandmother's expectation to be strong. "Your life will improve," her grandmother told her again and again.

And it did. In 1899 Rosa gave birth to Elizabeth. The baby lived for less than six months, giving Rosa six months of happiness and then leaving her months of bitterness. It was God who was at fault. God didn't want her to be happy.

"Don't blame God," her grandmother warned. "Maybe you wanted that baby too much! You made it afraid that you wouldn't let it go when the time came to live its own life. And … so the baby left. Don't be too angry. Don't be too sad. It's not good for you. You have to learn to take whatever life has to offer. You'll be better off for it."

Rosa tried, but it was hard to suppress the bitterness and the sorrow that had settled within her soul and to look on life with equanimity while her sister and the other women in the village prospered. When she became pregnant for the third time, Rosa cried for joy, but she also cried in fear. She wanted the child to survive more than anything else. Yet she could not want the child too much. She tried to be collected, but could not. She wanted to give a gift to her Ed, yet was afraid that her gift might be taken from her.

In 1901 Rosa brought a boy into the world. His name was supposed to have been Raphael in honor of one of the archangels, but the name, with three consonants that did not exist in the Ojibway language, was unpronounceable. The Ojibway could manage two consonants, but not three. Raphael became Raffeous and then, finally, Rufus. After Rufus came Bobby (1903) and Walter (1905).

Rosa's well-wishers had been right. Ed was a good man, a strong man who hunted, fished, trapped, gardened, and harvested apples, pears, butternuts, and berries. He and his family weren't going to be caught short during the winter. Ed looked to the future and prepared for it. He wasn't going to be caught needy in his old age when his strength gave out. He built an addition to the homestead that he used as a general store, selling a few staples and dry goods: tea, lard, sugar, baking powder, flour, tobacco, and candies. With Ed and a family, it was easy to live at peace with oneself and with the world. Rosa's parents had made a good choice for her.

Life for the next generations was going to be better than it had been for Ed's and Rosa's generation. The government built a school on a knoll less than one hundred yards from the Ed Johnson homestead, and hired a teacher. Around the same time the Catholics built a church and appointed a resident priest. Not to be outdone, the Protestants constructed a Methodist church and installed a minister to preach the true way to the non-Catholics. Indian Affairs constructed a council-dance hall and a fine stone mansion to serve as an agency and a residence for the newly appointed Indian agent, out of the Saugeen-Nawaush monies. Finally, two roads were slashed from the reserve through the woods to the outside world. No longer did the Indians have to paddle, row, sail, or walk to get to Wiarton. The outside world was now a horse's trot away.

The signs boded well for the future, as favorable as the bright setting sun augurs a good morrow.

In the evenings Ed would read the sun, the clouds, and the winds, and listen to the call of birds and tell Rosa what the next day was going to be like. Ed always looked further than the next day. As he patted Rufus on the head he predicted that "Someday you're going to read and write and speak English better than me."

Ed was strong, strong as an oak, and indefatigable. At the end of a day, as he once did, he could carry his working companion on his shoulders with two fifty-pound bags of potatoes tucked under his arms for a distance of half a mile. In late summer of 1907 Rosa whispered to Ed that they were going to be parents again. She hoped that their child would be a girl, a sister for their sons, the one who would look after them when they were old. Rosa wanted to share the good news with the entire village, but a little echo, the echo of her grandmother's voice advising her to keep her longings in check, held her back. But Ed, under no such restriction, told his friends, who spread the news. He too wanted a daughter.

One evening in late October, after he had been cleaning, smoking, and salting the fish that he and his partner had caught in nets earlier in the day, Ed complained that he was tired. "Ed! You've been working all day. What did you expect? You're not as young as you used to be. You're thirty-seven now. You should expect to be tired. You need a good night's sleep. Tomorrow you'll be ready to work again."

"Yes," Ed agreed. "It must be age coming on, catching up to me." A couple of weeks later Ed complained again. "Rosa! I'm tired. I didn't work all that hard to be tired."

By December Ed could not work beyond mid-afternoon. He was spent. Reluctantly he agreed to have one of the local medicine people come to check him over. But the medicine person could not say what was wrong with Ed Johnson. He intimated that Ed's condition might have been brought on by the Bear-walker. Ed's condition deteriorated even further.

After Christmas a doctor was summoned from Wiarton to examine Ed Johnson. His diagnosis was leukemia. Nothing could be done for Ed. He was finished. Through January and February, Ed wasted away, until the end came on March 10, 1908.

For Rosa, the winter of 1908 was one of prolonged agony, watching her husband slowly pass away. When she cried, Ed reached out, shook his head, and wheezed, "Don't, Rosa! You must be strong!" Her sister, Christine, who kept watch with her at Ed's deathbed, bade her, "Don't, Sis! It will make your baby sad." It was a struggle for Rosa to keep her grief and her fear under control, to try to be calm for the baby's sake as well as for her own.

With Ed's death, Rosa had nothing, no one except three boys and another child on the way who would want everything and need everything. For them, too, their father's passing wrenched their lives. Rufus cried for the first time. Life had snatched his father from him just when he was getting to know him. Bobby cried whenever his older brother cried. Walter asked, "Where's Daddy?" Rosa could say nothing, do nothing except draw her sons into her arms.

In the days and weeks that followed, thoughts of tomorrow and the next year interposed themselves in her memories, trebling her grief. She tried putting them out of her mind but could not. Poor Rufus! Bobby! Walter! And the baby! Rosa sold the remaining stock in the store until the shelves and the bins were empty. Somehow she would have to carry on, hide her grief and bury it.

For the boys, forgetting their grief was easier. At least it seemed easier for them to get over their sense of loss. They had friends galore who came to the house every day to play: John Bucket (Akiwenzie), Chittum (Fred Lavalley), Enoch (Taylor), Aesop (Andrew Akiwenzie), Alvin (Waukey), kids who'd make anyone forget anything, almost. They had the entire neighborhood and the nearby woods to play in, but they preferred to play in the vacant shop.

There the fire started, set by kids playing with matches. Rosa, Rufus, Bobby, and neighbors managed to rescue a few pots, pans and dishes, a mattress, and a dining-room table before the fire destroyed the house and everything in it, including the tin can that contained the family savings: $500, maybe $600. Rosa and her sons now had no place to live.

Christine, who lived in a fine two-story house not more than seventy-five steps away, took them in. For the grown-ups, living together in one house was cramping. For the children, communal life was the way they were meant to live, sharing the same beds and whispering late into the night with their cousins, Pont (Gregor), Vestie (Sylvester), and Virginia.

Neighbors and kin brought food and clothing to help both Rosa and Christine. Even before the charred remains of the house had finished smoldering, C.K. Jones, the hereditary chief of the reserve, convened the band council to discuss helping Rosa. It decided to sponsor a "wood-cutting bee" and a "house-building bee" to put up a two-story dwelling, thirty feet by thirty feet, on a vacant, unclaimed twenty-five-acre lot in the Naeyausheeng district, a mile north of the Catholic neighborhood. In addition, the band council voted to give Rosa and her family relief.

John was born in May 1908.

By the end of the summer the house was finished and Rosa and her children were ready to move in. A pipe-smoking teamster volunteered to move them to their new home in Naeyausheeng.

"You're going to be like them Iroquois that used to live up this way," the teamster remarked, referring to a group of Mohawks—Montours, Diabos, and other families whose names have now been forgotten—who came to Cape Croker as landless, statusless Indians from Quebec, seeking asylum. In a spirit of magnanimity the Cape Croker Chippewas admitted the homeless nomads to membership, allocating them some land at the farthest north end of the reserve, now known as Benjamin's Point. Here the Mohawks cleared land, farmed, and prospered, outdoing the Chippewas who were still fishing and logging. In a fit of envy the Chippewas asked the Mohawks to leave. The evictees found asylum in Oshweken, among their own kindred. "You're going to be like a hermit ... at least no one will bother you," the teamster observed.

"I don't have any say," Rosa sighed. "I've got to take what's given to me."

As often as the pipe went out, every second minute or so, the teamster knocked it on the side of the wagon and relit it with a match that he flipped over his shoulder.

Halfway to the new home Rufus and Bobby, who were running alongside the wagon, cried out, "Fire! Fire! The wagon's on fire!" The teamster and Rosa turned around in time to see hungry little flames licking at the mattress. The teamster and Rosa, with Walter in her arms, abandoned ship and chucked the burning cargo overboard before the horses noticed the blaze, panicked, and bolted.

Rosa and her boys were now poorer than before, the poorest of the poor in Cape Croker.

After unloading the table, pots and pans and inspecting the new house that consisted of two large rooms, one upstairs and one downstairs, Rufus and Bobby gathered grass, hay, straw, and cedars for their bedding.

It wasn't much, but the log house, whitewashed inside and out, was everything. Rosa looked out the south window; to her left and to her right were poplar woods; one hundred and fifty yards to the south was the concession roads intersection; just beyond was a large, seventy-five-acre meadow; and in the distance, seven miles away, were the bluffs of the Niagara Escarpment. There were no immediate neighbors.

Rosa and her boys lived alone just outside the Catholic neighborhood, out of sight, out of hearing. The neighborhood wasn't far by any means, no more than a twenty-minute walk, but with baby John, three-year-old Walter, five-year-old Bobby, and seven-year-old Rufus to care for and a house to look after, Rosa may as well have lived ten or even fifty miles away. She was chained, as it were, to her new home and to her heartaches.

She wasn't much better off than those people who were ostracized from their communities for committing offenses that threatened to tear their community apart were they to stay. Banishment from their community, family, friends, and neighbors was the worst form of punishment a society could impose on such people. They were outcasts, undeserving of friendship, goodwill, or a helping hand.

In those first few months, and in that first winter, there was not a day that Rosa did not feel like an outcast, unwanted by both men and God, especially when memories of her Ed oppressed her most heavily.

Rosa longed for her sister to come to her house to visit, but Christine, with three boys and a baby girl, was no more able to detach herself from her family than Rosa was able to get away from hers. Once every six weeks or two months Christine was able to spare two or three hours in the evenings. For Rosa, Christine's visits were precious.

From time to time woodsmen and cattle-drivers passed by. About the only time they stopped in was to seek shelter from the rain, or to take a short rest after working all day in the woods.

Once a month the chief, C.K. Jones, came by buggy to ensure that Rosa had enough food and fuel. C.K., then in his mid-fifties, seldom lingered for more than fifteen minutes, long enough to find out what Rosa needed in the way of supplies. He then had someone make a delivery. Carrying out his chiefly duties enabled C.K. to boast: "The Catholics can accuse me of a lot of things, but leaving them hungry is not one of them."

Rosa's other guest was Father Cadot, the Ojibway-speaking parish priest. The Catholic congregation feared and respected Father Cadot. God was with him.

Father Cadot wasn't going to fail God, himself, or his flock. He would have accepted martyrdom, as his predecessors had done, if martyrdom was in store. As it was, Father Cadot didn't have to face hostile Indians, only distances, high winds, thunderstorms, blizzards, and hunger. His mission extended from Cape Croker and Saugeen to Byng Inlet on the north shore of Georgian Bay, about forty-five miles south of Sudbury. For even the strong and the hardy, the trip was formidable at any time. Yet Father Cadot, 5'4", weighing one hundred and thirty-five pounds, made the journey many times. To get from Cape Croker to Collingwood, the nearest railway station seventy miles away, took Father Cadot and his horse two days. From Collingwood to Byng Inlet, the priest traveled by train and on foot. When he had to go to Christian Island, Father Cadot sometimes paddled there aboard a canoe. In winter, not even blizzards could deter the missionary from delivering the good news to Saugeen, forty miles away on the Lake Huron side of Bruce Peninsula; the storms merely delayed him overnight in Hepworth a couple of times. Nothing could stop Father Cadot from doing his duty.

Him, Rosa would have preferred not to see. He made her nervous. She didn't know what to say or do in his presence; he knew so much more than anyone else, and he was more spiritual than any man or woman, a messenger of God's word.

Father Cadot was a Jesuit and, as such, was regimented and punctual. On the last Friday of each month when he was home at Cape Croker, he came to see Rosa. Rosa's only calendar was the moon, the old Indian way of keeping time. It misled her at first because there were thirteen months by this means of reckoning time. After she was caught unprepared for Father's visits a few times, Rosa turned to Rufus, who was starting school, to keep her posted on the days and dates.

"What day is it, Son? Is it nearly the end of the month?" she asked Rufus nervously, frequently.

A couple of days before the last Friday, Rosa scrubbed the floors, wiped the windows, polished the stove, washed the clothing and the bedding, and bathed her boys. She wasn't going to be caught unprepared by a man of God. She didn't know much about them except what she had observed and heard in church. Super-critical they were, seeing every imperfection and condemning it. No, Rosa wasn't going to give Father Cadot a chance to criticize her house or her house-cleaning.

As she watched the priest tether his horse to the main gatepost, she hissed a warning to Bobby and Rufus to "behave, or else your little buns will be smarting."

But Father's first visits weren't as unpleasant as she at first believed they would be. He spoke highly of Rufus, "A good student, a good Catholic boy, one of my best servers. Keep up the good work, Rosauh! I'll remember you in my prayers and I'm sure that God will reward your efforts." Father Cadot put Rosa at ease.

Though Father Cadot had said nothing to disturb Rosa, he unsettled her with his mention of prayer. He may not even have mentioned prayer. Not long after he left, Rosa's conscience began to bother her. What bothered her was her practice of offering tobacco in thanksgiving whenever she picked plants or roots or cedar boughs. It was a pagan practice that smacked of pantheism and violated the First Commandment. Rosa worried that she would be condemned for performing what was looked on by most of her people as an act of respect for God's creations.

Rosa did what Father Cadot had told her to do. She prayed every night for her boys and for herself, for forgiveness, compassion, and strength.

In the case of her boys her prayers were answered. They were healthy. Rufus did well in school, coming home with unbelievable stories of cows jumping over moons, cats in boots, fish granting wishes, wolves blowing down pigpens. The White People had strange beliefs.

Before winter was over, Rufus badgered his teacher, Miss Moffat, into allowing him to enroll in the music program as a trumpeter. Then he badgered her into letting him take the trumpet home "to practice," promising that he would guard it with his life. What Rufus really wanted to do was to show his mother what he was learning at school.

As soon as Rufus got home and had taken his coat, hat, and boots off, he took the trumpet out of its case. He blew several notes over several bars, mostly squeaky sharps and flats. There was an immediate outcry. "Let me try! I wanna blow the trumpet!" Both Bobby and Walter bawled, reached out and stamped their feet. "No. You're too small. I can't let you!" Rufus refused. As he held the trumpet away from Walter, Bobby reached out, and grabbed the instrument. The boys yelled, they wrestled for the trumpet. They fell to the floor … on top of the trumpet. Metal crunched. The squabbling abruptly ended.

"It's broken! … You broke it," wailed Rufus.

The bell of the trumpet was bent. Rufus spent the rest of the evening in tears, trying to straighten it out. It was useless.

On the way to school Rufus hid the trumpet in a culvert. At school he told Miss Moffat that he'd forgotten it, promising to bring it to school the next day. But after Rufus failed to bring the trumpet back to school as he had promised for three days in a row, using forgetfulness as an excuse, Miss Moffat threatened to go to the Johnson homestead to retrieve the instrument. Rufus confessed that the horn had been damaged. While telling Miss Moffat about the accident, Rufus took extra pains to emphasize that it was his brothers who were at fault.

"Not only did you damage the instrument but you tried to lie your way out of taking responsibility, you ham-handed little oaf." Rufus never forgave Miss Moffat for calling him a "ham-handed little oaf" in front of the whole class. Her, Rufus could not forgive; Bobby and Walter, he eventually forgave.

At the end of the month following the struggle for the trumpet, Father Cadot came to Rosa's house for his visit.

As soon as he sat down, Father Cadot brought up Rufus's damaging the school's trumpet. But it wasn't Rufus's carelessness that bothered Father Cadot as much as his attempts to put the blame on his brothers instead of accepting responsibility as a man and facing the punishment he deserved.

"Well, it wasn't entirely Rufus's fault," Rosa said in defense of her son, and she explained what had taken place on the evening that Rufus brought home the trumpet.

"That may be," Father Cadot conceded, "but Rufus shouldn't have lied or hidden the instrument. You and I must teach that boy to accept responsibility. Now is the time to do that, while he's still young. I'd like you to speak to him about owning up to things."

Father took a long sip from his teacup. "You'll be starting school come this fall, won't you?" he asked Bobby, who was standing near-by. He patted Walter on the head. "Now, you listen to your mother and say your prayers. That's a good boy. I hope to see you in church one of these days." Then, turning to Rosa, he added, "You'll bring them to church soon, won't you? Winter's over; you should be able to come to mass once in a while. I realize that it must be difficult for you with four boys, but you must try. It will do you a world of good and ... you will please God."

"Yes! I'll try," Rosa promised. Not being able to attend mass bothered Rosa.

Twice she tried in May, but both times something happened to abort her efforts. The first time, Bobby and the family dog, Quebec, could not be found when Rosa was ready to leave. They returned half an hour later, too late for church. The second time, the boys pushed Walter into a water-filled ditch while they were roughhousing with each other. Rosa sent Rufus and Bobby along to church alone. She went back home with Baby John.

On his next visit, Father Cadot once more brought up the subject of attendance at mass.

"Were you to make an effort, even once a month, your example would mean far more to your children than all your words. You're young, and by managing your time better, you should be able to come to mass."

"I have four boys to feed ..." Rosa braked her temper, "and to control."

"I know that it must be difficult," Father broke in, "but you must make an extra effort."

"I have no extra effort to put out," Rosa argued. "I've put out my all ... you don't know how much work there is ...."

"Mrs. Johnson! You don't have much choice. As a Catholic you are to come to church on Sundays." And Father walked out.

Rosa was unsettled. She didn't need Father Cadot to remind her that she should go to church. On top of that, she was angered by Father's insinuation that she wasn't organized and that she was holding back. If only Ed were alive to help her. She prayed for God's forgiveness.

Rosa welcomed visitors, but her visitors—the chief, the priest, the occasional passerby—were not the kind she looked forward to.

She longed for someone to talk to, for someone to talk to her, not to remind her of her obligations or simply check up on her needs. She wanted someone to laugh with, put ideas to, confide in, swap stories with, someone whose presence would give comfort, hope, security, faith, trust, inspiration.

Rosa was grateful, but all the help she received only served to remind her of her utter helplessness. She was no more able to look after herself than a child, completely dependent on handouts. Unable to say or think, "I earned this. I made this for myself. I can do this. I can do this for myself." Rosa was afraid to look any of her neighbors in the eye, and she resented the Indian agent and the priest's visits that were more like snooping missions.

It was always the same. "Do you need anything?" the priest asked in Chippewa. Rosa felt like vomiting each time Father Cadot asked the question. Of course she had "need." The boys needed new shoes, new socks, new underwear, new shirts, new hats, new coats. But she wasn't about to say yes, for it was akin to begging.

Sometime during this period, the Johnson family name was slightly altered by the band council secretary, who sandwiched a "t" between the "s" and the "o." Johnson became Johnston. No one noticed the change. It squatted, acquired squatter's rights, without once giving offense. The "t" neither lessened nor added to Rosa's misery.

-ʘ-n early July, Rosa heard and then saw wagons clatter by on the road in front of her house. It was Isaiah Pitwaniquot and Joe Jones with their teams. She wondered where they were going with their loads of lumber.

Rufus and Bobby were off at once to follow the wagons. They paid not the least attention to their mother's cries to "get back here, mind your own business." Not five minutes later she heard the clatter and the clash of boards and timbers as the teamsters discharged their cargo in the vacant lot across the road, just east of her house.

A half an hour later the wagons rattled by, heading back to the main village. Behind them ran Rufus and Bobby, who went as far as the corner before coming back.

"What's going on across the road?" Rosa asked the boys the moment they stepped into the house.

"Isaiah and Mary Jane are going to build a house," Rufus answered. "Now, me and Bobby can have Alvin (Alvin Waukey, Mary Jane's son by her first marriage) to play with."

"Mary Jane! The girl who called me half-burned!"

For that insult, Rosa had smacked Mary Jane. The village wits had had a field day with the incident. Stories soon circulated saying that Rosa's punch had stunted Mary Jane's nose. But Mary Jane was born with a snub nose that flared and twitched as she talked, as if it were trying to catch some scent in the air. She was one of the community's leading gossips, according to hearsay. "A regular blue jay," Rosa mused, and she wondered how they'd get along.

Within a couple of days Rosa heard the sound of hammers and the clang of boards.

Why Isaiah and Mary Jane would be building a house in her part of the reserve puzzled Rosa. They already had a nice home and farm in Sidney Bay. Where Rosa lived the land wasn't fit for gardening, and was next to bone dry in the summer. Even the frogs kept their distance.

On her first visit to Naeyausheeng to look over the construction of her new home and the site, Mary Jane called on Rosa.

"Eeeeyoooh! Rosauh! Good thing that you're up here, otherwise I'd have no one to talk to except Isaiah and the dog. Gets tiresome to be talking to the same people all the time."

"I'm so thankful," Rosa replied in kind. "I thought that I'd never have a neighbor. It's been so long since I've had a visitor that I feel that I've forgotten how to talk to other women. Always children. And they don't talk. But why on earth did you choose Naeyausheeng? So far from everything, everybody?"

"Eeeeyoooh! It's that Isaiah. Wants to start a farm for Alvin. Says that when we're old, Alvin will look after us. He gave that house to Percy in Sidney Bay. I tried to talk that man out of it but you can never tell that man nothing. You know how men are. We already have a house and that was good enough," Mary Jane rambled on.

Though it had been years since their fight, Mary Jane had changed little. Her eyes brightened and dimmed as she talked, and she talked quickly as if she might forget some detail if she did not deliver the story in one breath.

Since their childhood days and their teenage years, so many things had happened to them. Mary Jane had gotten married and given birth to Alvin. Her husband had died. She had remarried, becoming the wife of Isaiah Pitwaniquot, a widower. Other than that, Rosa knew little of Mary Jane; she was almost like a stranger.

Mary Jane talked on about the future farm, animals, the soil, and what housework she and Rosa could jointly do. For a small woman, petite like Rosa, five feet tall and one hundred pounds or so, Mary Jane had enormous energy and ambition.

Mary Jane talked on, looking over Rosa's shoulder as if trying to see if there was something taking place behind Rosa that was newsworthy. She talked as if she and Rosa were old friends, longtime neighbors. Bygones were bygones. Life in Naeyausheeng was a fresh start for both.

In early September, Mary Jane, Isaiah, and Alvin moved into their new home, a modern two-story clapboard house with a parlor, a dining-living room separated from the kitchen, and three bedrooms on the second floor. Rosa envied Mary Jane.

It was spring 1911. Such a relief for Rosa to have the boys playing outside instead of cutting loose and squabbling in the house. Alvin Waukey was with Rufus, Bobby, and Walter. They were playing follow the leader. As the eldest, Rufus was in the forefront, leading his followers over ever increasingly difficult obstacles. He led them up the side of the porch, over the roof, and jumped down the other side.

"Stop climbing on the roof; someone will get hurt," Rosa shouted at the boys.

"Alright," the boys agreed.

Walter, the last to jump down, cried out as he landed and clutched his foot.

"Get up! Stop crying like a baby," Rufus growled.

Bobby ran into the house, crying out, "Walter's hurt his foot."

Rosa went out to see. Walter had stopped crying and was now sitting on the ground massaging his foot. Rosa examined Walter's foot, kneading it here, now there. It wasn't swollen too much, nor discolored too deeply. No more than a sprain she thought, and Rosa warned him, "Don't jump off the roof again."

But Walter's foot did not heal; he was lamed for life.

Once she settled into her new house Mary Jane called on Rosa almost daily, sometimes a couple of times a day. She wanted Rosa to know what was going on in the reserve. There was no question in her mind that Rosa would be itching to know.

"Eeeeyoooh! Rosauh! Did you hear that Chibwaush (Norman McLeod) bought some land just up the road and is going to build a house? Rosauh, before you know it our part of the reserve is going to be like Wiarton, with people huddled together like pigeons."

A year and a half later Norman McLeod moved into a little log house that he had built as temporary lodging. He told Isaiah that he intended to build a home just as fine as the one Isaiah had erected. Mary Jane had not been making up stories.

To Rosa, Norman McLeod meant little; he was just another relative, just another young man who had left the reserve to seek work outside and, after having been absent seven or eight years, had come back home.

What she noticed about Norman as he walked by on the road in front of her house every morning and evening was his height; he was not much taller than she was. An overgrown elf, she thought, but a cheerful one, his lips ever puckered, whistling some tune, yet ready to break into a smile.

When Rufus, Bobby, and Alvin were on the road playing some game and spoke to Norman, he'd stop and talk and even play with them.

Before too long, Rosa's sons invited Norman into the house. "Can he stay for supper?"

After that Norman began to stop by uninvited for short visits to rest his legs. Soon Norman's need to rest his legs became more frequent, daily, the rests longer and longer, till 9 p.m. or until Rosa drew attention to the time and reminded him that he had work to do the following day.

Before Norman began calling on her after supper, evenings had been dreary. Rosa looked forward to Norman's visits. With his wit and knowledge of the world outside, he kept her amused and informed.

They compared backgrounds. He wasn't quite sure whether his roots were in Alberta or somewhere near Hudson Bay. Rosa believed that Norman was boasting when he said that his family name had some connection with Fort McLeod. More likely he came from some obscure place in the north.

Originally his family name was Pitwaniquot, but an Indian agent changed it one day when annuity monies were distributed. One of Norman's ancestors drew up to the table, along with his family. Through an interpreter, the agent asked the Indian in front of him what his name was. "What did he say? What does that mean?" the agent inquired of the interpreter. "Coming Cloud," the interpreter answered. "Write down McCloud," the agent instructed. And so, with an order and a stroke of the pen the Pitwaniquot family was given an anglicized name. More recently, McCloud was amended to McLeod, giving the name a Scottish flavor.

And Norman told Rosa that, while working on ships and on the railroads, he had gone to Toronto, Detroit, and Chicago, where he saw immense stone buildings and automobiles. So much more interesting than Mary Jane's humdrum stories, but almost as far-fetched.

The next spring Norman brought trilliums, dandelions, crocuses, and lilies that he'd picked on the side of the road. As he handed Rosa the bouquet, he planted a kiss on her cheek.

The first time Norman conducted this ritual, Rosa accepted the flowers but stammered, "Don't" to the kiss, a protest that was muffled by her hand, which she clapped to her mouth in astonishment and embarrassment. The kiss she didn't want and, though Norman's declaration, "You're pretty," pleased her, she didn't believe him, for she had never regarded herself as pretty. Her nose had a ridge on it, and was a little too wide at the nostrils. Her mouth was slanted, her lower lip was too thick. Her eyebrows were too thin. No, she wasn't pretty, not as pretty as some other girls.

One "Don't" would have been enough for others, but not for Norman. He continued to bring flowers and to whisper sweet nothings. Rosa didn't know what to do.

Not knowing how to end the attentions Norman was paying her, Rosa mentioned her difficulties to Mary Jane.

"Eeeeyoooh, Rosauh. That's awful! Tell him you don't like him. Throw him out. Tell him not to come back. That's what I'd do." Mary Jane sniffed defiantly, then added after a brief pause, "You know, Rosauh, people are starting to talk."

Rosa's face burned.

The next time Norman came around, that is, the very next day, Rosa said, "I don't think you should come to the house anymore. You should look for a younger woman, more your own age. I'm ten years older than you are … and I've got four boys … and people are starting to talk."

"But Rosauh! I love you. I don't care for anybody else. Your boys can be my boys. As for talk, I don't care! We've done nothing to be ashamed of."

"Well, I do!" Rosa interjected. "I don't want people saying things about me that aren't true. I don't want the priest hearing about it. You never know what he might do."

"Who told you that, anyway?" Norman asked, knowing full well the source.

"Mary Jane!"

"*Her!* Why would you believe her? She's one of the worst gossips in the whole reserve. She can't mind her own business ... Rosauh! ... Will you marry me?"

"No! Go home!"

Telling Norman to go home should have ended his visits. Rosa's meaning was quite clear, or so she thought. Except that Norman paid no attention to her. He merely adjusted his visits. Instead of staying two to three hours as he had done in the past, he remained for a few minutes, just long enough to chat with the boys and to help them cut wood and carry water.

At first Rosa said nothing to Norman about his continued visits. What made saying anything to him difficult were her boys. They liked Norman. For her part, she didn't dislike Norman. He was an affable young man. She didn't want to hurt his feelings by telling him to stay away.

It wasn't until several weeks had gone by that Rosa asked Norman why he didn't court other women, young women.

"Because I love you," Norman declared once more. "I've been coming around for months. In all that time not once did you tell me that I was unwelcome. It was only after that Mary Jane told you people were talking about us that you told me I shouldn't come around. She's nothing but a troublemaker. You shouldn't listen to her ... Rosauh! I love you," Norman repeated.

"Norman! Stop talking nonsense! I like you, but I don't love you."

"But, Rosauh, my *pet*," Norman rejoined, emphasizing the term "pet" to fluster her, "does love have to make sense?"

Rosa had no answer for that remark. Even if she had had one, Norman would have had still another comment to make. He could be exasperating in argument. Say one thing and he'd turn it about. It was no use arguing with him; his mind was too quick, he was too well spoken. He knew what to say; she didn't. Rosa terminated the discussion with an exasperated "Aaaah!" that came from deep within her throat.

Rosa's "aaaah" was an expression that carried with it a tone of annoyance, akin to "cut it out," nothing else. It was best to cut it out, say no more before the "aaaah" took on rancor and articulation. As far as it went, the expression represented a moral victory for Norman. As he stepped out the door, he turned around and said, "Don't be too upset with me, Rosauh. I can't help it if I care about you." Then he went out.

That night, much as she tried, Rosa couldn't keep Norman or his words out of her mind. He was pleasant, hard-working, good-natured. If only he were closer to her age, if only he weren't a cousin. Rosa checked her train of thoughts and feelings when she realized that she was indulging in girlish fantasies. She thought of loving. She thought of Ed. And she cried for Ed's arms and his companionship. She was alone. Love: Was it supposed to make sense? The thought confused her.

The next evening she saw Norman turn the corner and come up the road, whistling, a saw slung over his left shoulder, an ax in his right hand. Rosa hoped and expected him to come in, the next moment hoping that he would not. When he passed by without coming in, she was relieved, sort of. Nor did Norman drop in during the next few days, though he looked longingly, it appeared, at the house. On Sunday he stopped on the road to wait for the boys, whom he was in the habit of escorting to church. As usual, Norman was dapper, wearing a new cap, a suit, shirt, tie, and shiny black shoes. No wonder there were many young women, according to Mary Jane, who wanted to snare him. The thought nettled Rosa. In turn, the feelings that the thought roused unsettled her. She shouldn't feel that way about Norman, for she didn't love him. Yet the thought of other women upset her. It made no sense.

Later in the week Father Cadot paid Rosa a visit. With his craggy features and shaggy black beard drooping down to his upper chest, the priest looked as Moses must have looked as a young man: stern, ready to erupt and dash the stone tablets upon which were etched the Ten Commandments. Father Cadot could speak in tongues, French, English, and Anishinaubae. No one could put a thing past him.

Usually amiable, Father Cadot wore a scowl as he tethered his horse and buggy to a fence post. He looked like a wrathful Moses having come upon his people in the desert worshiping idols. Even his walk was petulant.

His knock was petulant as well.

"Come in, Father .... Sit down."

Father Cadot declined the invitation. He came right to the point: "Rosauh! I'm disturbed. I have it on good authority that you're seeing Norman McLeod ... and that he's been seen leaving your house later in the evening than is respectable. It's causing talk. Worse, your boys may learn things that they ought not."

"What do you mean?" Rosa bristled.

"You know very well what I mean," the priest fired back. "Either you stop seeing this man, who is too young for you anyway, or you marry him. Better that you stop seeing him ... and start coming to church. You may well find your boys in some residential school otherwise." Father Cadot snapped out the words, spun on his heels, and stomped out.

As the priest got on board his buggy, Rosa, who had found her voice, shouted at him. "Lies ... they're all lies. That's all you listen to. What do you know about friendship? What do you know about loneliness?" Rosa fumed. She'd never go to church again ... not as long as that priest was there.

Soon after this confrontation Father Cadot accosted Norman on the road in front of the church. He gave Norman a stern lecture, at the end of which he delivered an ultimatum. "Either marry the woman or stay away from her. But better that you court someone your own age."

This was not the first time that Father Cadot would have forced a courting couple to marry. He and his predecessor, Father Artus, S.J., were old hands at this sort of thing. A couple had but to court too long for the priest's liking and he would storm to the young swain and issue an ultimatum: "Get a license or I'm reporting you to the magistrate."

Maybe the priest was right; perhaps it was better for him to find someone his own age. Norman tried to forget Rosa, but could not.

In the meantime, Rosa was going through similar mental and emotional turmoil.

Before venturing another visit, Norman let a month slip by. Mary Jane noticed that Norman had suspended his visits, and remarked to Rosa that it was "all for the better." Norman walked by the house every day without slowing down. But one Sunday, after walking the boys home, Norman came to the door with them. At the door he asked, "Mind if I come in?"

"What's holding you back?" Rosa asked.

Norman went in. He began talking as if there'd been no intermission in their relationship. Rufus and Bobby ran out and across the road to play with Alvin. With only Walter and John present, too young to understand or to care what was said, Norman told Rosa that Father Cadot had spoken to him about his visits and that he had tried to do the priest's bidding but could not carry it out any longer. "I love you, Rosauh! Will you marry me?"

Rosa nodded, "Yes."

When Norman told Father Cadot that he and Rosa were going to be married, the priest was delighted. Most people were glad for Norman and Rosa, and wished them well; others were uneasy about the kinship, but weren't sure enough to object. They left it up to Father Cadot's better judgment to decide whether Norman and Rosa were too closely related.

Everyone was happy, except for Rufus and Bobby. They didn't want Norman as a father; he would be usurping their real father's place. He didn't belong at their mother's side. As a visitor, the boys accepted him; as a stepfather, no. They didn't come right out and say they didn't want Norman marrying their mother, but they discussed it with their friend Alvin. Rebellious as they had been, they now became even more rebellious than before, not so much at home but at school. The teacher reported them to the priest, the priest reported them to the village constable, the constable reported them to the chief, the chief reported them to the Indian agent.

Nineteen hundred and thirteen was a bittersweet year for Rosa. She and Norman got married. Later that spring the boys' fate was decided when Rufus told his teacher to "go to hell," a sentiment that was echoed by Bobby.

Clearly Rosa had no control over her boys and if something were not done to control their behavior, Rufus and Bobby would come to no good. Better that they be sent to a residential school. Besides, sending them to a residential school was in keeping with the government's policy to "un-Indianize Indians."

One of the first residential schools in Canada was built and opened in 1825 on the Wikwemikong reserve in Ontario. It operated as a day school in its early years, and was meant to Christianize the Indians. For the Indians of Manitoulin Island and elsewhere in Ontario, the school was a good thing. Indian youth would receive an education and would deal with their White neighbors on equal terms. They'd also learn trades. Indian parents clamored for the admission of their children. Dormitories were added to the school to provide residence for youth from other reserves. The school became a residential school.

In the late 1880s integration became the popular philosophy. Reverend Wilson, a principal of one residential school, boasted that "not a word of Indian is heard from our boys after six months." The more Reverend Wilson thought about mixing up the races, the warmer he got. "Yes!" he preached, "Indians and Whites should become one in language, one in pursuits, tastes, ambitions, and hopes ... we want them to become apprenticed out to White People and to become, in fact, Canadians."

Soon after Rufus, Bobby, and Walter arrived at the residential school in Wikwemikong on Manitoulin Island, the institution burned down. Another school was constructed in Spanish, Ontario, a village better suited to wean Indians away from their heritage by virtue of its greater remoteness from Indian communities.

John was still too young to be ripped from his mother and his home. But with three boys taken from Rosa, an old wound was reopened. Death had taken her first two children, now life had taken three others, leaving her with one. Life had given her Norman and hope, and then had snatched Rufus, Bobby, and Walter from her.

"I'll get them back for you," Norman promised, giving some hope to Rosa's spirit.

Soon after they were married Rosa discovered that Norman had paper and pencils and books, and liked to read. Evenings after supper Norman opened his trunk, from which he took one of several books that he kept, and read silently by the coal oil lamp. Other than her father and Ed, Rosa had not seen another person read books or write on paper. Norman even received letters that were delivered to the priest's residence. Rosa thought her husband was one of the most clever men on the reserve.

"What are you reading?" she asked him the first night that he opened a book and turned over a page.

"Poetry."

"What's that?"

"It's ..." Norman paused, scratched his head. It was hard to explain poetry, for there was no form quite like it in Chippewa-Anishinaubae culture. "It's like our sacred chants ... except that poems are longer and they're not sacred ... they're about love, beauty, sadness ..." And then, after another moment's reflection, he added, "Maybe these subjects *are* sacred."

"Do all the White People write poetry? Does everybody write poetry? Do you write poetry?"

"No!" Norman laughed, "only smart people—Keats, Shelley, Byron, Wordsworth, Tennyson, and Shakespeare .... Chief Shaking Spear must have been a Chippewa." Norman laughed again.

"What's good poetry?" Rosa asked.

"It opens up your mind, soul, spirit .... Would you like to hear a poem?" Receiving a nod, Norman opened the book, read a couple of poems, and then recited a couple more.

As Norman read, Rosa's admiration grew. She didn't understand a word, but she was spellbound. "Anyone who could do that has to be clever. Norman should be a councillor," she thought.

"Ed could read and write, but never read poetry," Rosa remarked.

"I'm your husband now; don't forget that!" Norman reminded Rosa, an edge to his voice.

Rosa apologized. She had not intended to slight Norman but to pay him a compliment. Ed was not so easily forgotten, though it had been five years since he had gone on to the next life.

Norman's abilities and accomplishments reminded Rosa of Ed. At the same time she envied Norman his ability with books and paper. It made her feel backward, unable to be part of his world. She wanted her mind, soul, and spirit opened up. "Can you teach me to read, write, and talk the 'White' language?" she asked Norman one evening.

The lessons went on sporadically for several months until Norman's laughter and corrections of her pronunciation and syntax put an end to Rosa's attempts to become literate. Norman was the last person to hear Rosa speak a word of English.

Just how much English Rosa understood no one could say, but she did occasionally pick up a newspaper and linger over the printed page a little longer than an illiterate might. Perhaps she did not want to speak the language of the people who had caused her so much grief.

Poetry was not the only thing that Norman read. He had history books and, once a week, he collected old newspapers from the priest. He relayed what he read to Rosa. She knew about the wars in Europe, Africa, and Asia; about trains, planes, and steamships; about the White Man's wars upon the Indians; about canals being built and huge cities with tall buildings and rows of shops; about earthquakes and floods. "Our people are going to have to adjust," Norman often said.

"Yes, they can adjust all they want, but it's going to do them little good," Rosa answered.

"Don't be such a pessimist, my dear," Norman teased. "There's a lot more goodwill out there than you can imagine."

But a pessimist Rosa was not. She laughed easily and readily. Still, no evening passed, no matter how pleasant it had been, without ending in a pall of gloom. "Let's pray for the boys, Norman. Will you write to the boys for me? Will you speak to the chief to get the boys home, Norman?" And sometimes Rosa cried.

Norman could not make Rosa as happy as he would have liked. He wrote letters. He spoke to the priest, the agent, and the chief. Father Cadot assured Norman and Rosa that "the boys are receiving the best of care, and not to worry." These assurances did little to quell Rosa's anxiety and loneliness. If only she could receive a letter, she would go to sleep at night untroubled.

Late that fall Rosa's low spirits were uplifted by the stirring of life within her. There was new hope and Rosa looked forward to giving birth again. Secretly she hoped for a daughter, someone who would look after her in her old age, a sister for her sons.

Rosa and Norman talked about the baby every night. To Norman the baby was a he, a foregone conclusion, taking it for granted that

Rosa wanted a boy as well. The odds were good that the child would be a boy, for Rosa had given birth to five boys and one girl, a good ratio.

And though Rosa spoke of Rufus, Bobby, and Walter, she no longer cried for them. To do so would have made the unborn child sad and uneasy, and grow up to be a melancholy and nervous person. Mothers-to-be were to avoid overexcitement, extremes in emotions. They were to be as composed as they could be. Rosa's serenity was a good sign for Norman; it meant that Rosa was reverting to her true self, the woman he hoped she would be.

Norman's own inherent enthusiasm and good humor were refueled. He started planning a larger house, a two-story building on his property just up the road where he had constructed his cabin. And each time that Rufus's, Bobby's and Walter's names were mentioned, Norman renewed his promise to bring the boys back home. Despite his efforts and plans and letters, Norman could persuade neither the government nor the church to let the boys return.

In the spring of 1914 Rosa gave birth to Stanley. At last she could cry, and she cried for joy as she held her baby, but she also cried in sorrow as she remembered her other sons.

Just months after Stanley was born, war broke out again in Europe. A prince was assassinated in the streets of an obscure town in the backhills of the Balkans. Within weeks, the bigger nations entered the fray, using the Balkan uprising as an excuse to settle old scores with one another, and soon civilized Europe was aflame and crackling with war.

England waded into the conflict to champion justice, civilization, and the preservation of its empire. It issued a call for volunteers from her colonies, dominions, and protectorates throughout the world to come to the defense of king, flag, and the British Empire. Along with a great many Indians from Cape Croker and other reserves in Canada, Norman enlisted in the country's armed forces.

When Norman came home wearing the uniform of which he was immensely proud, he asked Rosa how she liked it. Instead of saying that it was handsome, as Norman had hoped, Rosa was negative. "What are you doing in that thing? You have no business fighting in the White Man's war!"

"We have to fight for what we have," Norman explained. "Besides, you'll have money coming in every month."

"Blood money!" Rosa retorted.

Almost overnight Cape Croker became like a ghost village. Its forests no longer rang with the blow of axes, and its waters did not glint with the flash of oars. Even the seagulls had deserted the shoreline and gone on to Lion's Head and Tobermory. There was no shortage of loneliness and anxiety.

Rosa was once more alone and lonely. She missed her children, she missed Ed, and she missed Norman, all at the same time. Her loneliness and sense of isolation might have been worse were it not for Mary Jane who, now that Norman was away, came over much more frequently to call on Rosa.

Mary Jane brought news that she gleaned from various sources: her husband, her son, passersby whom she accosted. She wanted to find out what was going on in Rosa's life and world. She couldn't hold the news within her; it was meant to be passed on.

When Mary Jane delivered news, anything that she thought Rosa would be eager to hear, she reported it as if she herself had been at the scene. "Eeeeyoooh, Rosauh! Agent's been drinking again. Your priest caught him with a bottle right on his desk. When your priest told McIver that drinking wasn't right, the agent swore at him and swung at him. Father Cadot just got away. Now he's writing to the government, tattling on the agent.

"Eeeeyoooh, Rosauh! I knew it. I just knew. I could feel it in my bones. And I told you when I first moved up here. People would come up here to live. Bert Ashkewe and Ida are going to build up there at the corner. Be a regular village. People living so close together we'll be able to see and smell all their dirty laundry.

"Rosauh! Your priest is gone again. I don't know why he don't stay here and look after his church and his people like our minister .... If he stayed home and watched, his people might behave the way he wants them. Instead, he just goes off, like that. He must have money."

All these stories and the particulars she edited with her own style, perceptions, and biases.

"He has such a big mission," Rosa explained. "Cape Croker,

Saugeen, Christian Island, Beausoleil, Parry Island, Shawanaga, Byng Inlet."

When Mary Jane came to visit, Rosa could guess from her neighbor's pace whether the news was going to be good or bad. A brisk pace meant that the news was of a lighter variety; a more deliberate pace represented a heavier message. Rosa could also tell from the aroma that clung to her clothing what Mary Jane had been doing; whether she had been baking bread, boiling berries, or making quill boxes.

Mary Jane wore a tam, as did most women in Cape Croker, a red sweater, an apron, and, underneath the paraphernalia, a print dress with red, white, and yellow flowers on a navy-blue background.

They were discussing dreams one day when Mary Jane told Rosa that she had recently discovered that she had the gift of knowing events before they happened. She couldn't say whether she had had this gift all along, or had recently been infused with it. Rosa had heard of seers but had never known one. Now she stood face to face with one.

Had anyone else but Mary Jane told her that she could foresee the future, Rosa would not have doubted her for an instant. But Mary Jane's words were questionable. Her accounts of events, past and present, were too wild for belief.

To humor her neighbor, Rosa asked her to tell her about Norman and her boys in Spanish.

"Need some tea with lots of leaves," Mary Jane explained. Rosa brewed a pot with an extra handful of tea leaves pitched in.

When the tea was well steeped, Mary Jane took the pot, shook it, and revolved it four times so the leaves would be well stirred before settling on the bottom. Then she filled two cups, one for Rosa and one for herself. They drank the tea while discussing Isaiah's "room-tism" and Alvin's threat to run away and become Catholic. After Rosa finished her cup of tea, Mary Jane solemnly turned the cup upside down on the saucer and revolved it four times, a sacred number. A moment of silence passed before Mary Jane drew the cup and saucer to her. She turned the cup right side up and held it at different angles, studying it intently.

She squinted as if she couldn't see clearly enough. "I can see lots of men, lots, and they're all walking together; they're going someplace. They're alright. Your Norman is alright. Over on the other side I see lots of boys. They're alright, too. Nobody is sick. One of your boys will be coming home soon, too, and another one after that. I can also see someone leaving, but I can't tell ... and there's something else, not too good, but I can't tell what it is, it's ... it's so blurred."

Rosa listened without putting any stock in what Mary Jane foresaw in the tea leaves. Still, she told Mary Jane that she felt better. Even the leaves were arrayed for and against her.

The next year, 1915, the Indian agent carried out the government's policy of weaning Indians from their Indianness by weaning John from his home, all the way to Spanish; he was the tea-leaf figure going away.

In 1917 Rufus, sixteen and eligible to leave residential school, was released from Spanish. Rufus came home a man, 5'9". Bobby and Walter, not yet sixteen, remained behind. Almost the first thing Rufus did after returning home was to get roaring drunk with Alvin Waukey and John Bucket, on wine that they filched from Bob Nadjiwon. When Rosa took issue with him, Rufus retorted that he was celebrating his release from prison and beatings that he would not have been subjected to had she not sent him to Spanish.

"I never sent you there. I never wanted to let you go there. I tried to keep you ... How could you think of such a thing?"

Rufus didn't answer her. Then he asked why she had gotten married, as if she ought not to have done what she did.

Rosa reeled under the accusations. She tried to explain that it was not her that had sent him, Bobby, Walter, and John away, but it was useless. As for Norman, Rosa could not get Rufus to accept that she had married him because she loved him.

Within weeks of coming home Rufus talked about going away, joining the army. He didn't have a sense of belonging, acting and thinking as if he were an intruder. The residential school had alienated Rufus from his family and village. Two months later, he left Cape Croker.

Rosa had little chance, little time to get through to Rufus, if in fact she could have. When Rufus got something into his head, he would not let it go; no one and nothing could shake or pry it loose. And Rosa feared that Bobby, Walter, and John would turn out to be like Rufus, cool and distant and suspicious of her.

When Rosa told Mary Jane how changed Rufus was, insensitive and unloving, Mary Jane nodded and declared, "That's why the images in the teacup were blurred."

One morning just before Christmas, Mary Jane came across the road in her deliberate, worried gait, even though it was cold. "Eeeeyoooh! I'm sorry to hear about Norman. ... What happened?"

"What happened?" Rosa gasped. "What happened to Norman? Who told you? When? Where?"

"Didn't you hear? Didn't they tell you?"

"No! No! No! Tell me!"

"Norman was wounded!"

"Oh, my God!" Rosa slumped to her chair, weak. "Who told you?" Visions of Norman broken and torn flashed in Rosa's mind. A one-legged man. A bedridden man. An armless man, a blind man, a deaf man, a useless, broken man. "Bad?" she asked.

"I don't know how bad, but the minister read it in the Owen Sound paper, and he told Alvin. All the paper and the minister said were 'wounded in action.' I don't know what that means."

"Oh my God!" Rosa exclaimed once again. "How can I find out?"

"I'll send Alvin down to the priest to find out if he has any news."

But the priest didn't have any news either.

In 1918 a car stopped on the road opposite Rosa's house; she looked up from her work, uneasy. Then she saw Norman struggle to get out of the car with the aid of crutches, like a decrepit old man.

She rose quickly when she realized that it was Norman and, taking Stanley by the hand, went out to meet her husband. Rosa laughed and cried at the same time. Norman hobbled; he wasn't broken, bedridden, blind ... it didn't matter. She offered Norman her arm.

Norman held her and he, too, cried as she clung to him. "I missed you," he told her. "I'm going to be alright. I won't be able to run, but I'll be able to walk."

They clung to each other while Stanley tugged at his mother's skirt.

"Norman! This is your son, Stanley."

"My goodness! What a big boy!" Norman remarked as he picked up Stanley, who recoiled and squealed. He shrank from his father, a stranger.

"What's wrong with him?" Norman asked, setting Stanley back down.

"He's just making strange, but he'll get used to you. What happened? How did you receive your wound? Does it hurt?" Rosa wanted to know.

"I just got shot. There's nothing special about it. A lot of other boys and men got shot, some a lot worse." As for pain, Norman explained that his wound felt as if there was a grain of sand or salt around his knee, or even a splinter or thistle imbedded in his knee. Doctors removed bone chips from his knee but were unable to remove all of them. Because of his wound Norman was to receive a pension for life.

Rosa accepted Norman's explanation as to how he had been wounded. Nothing unusual about it. In war, killing and wounding were daily occurrences. Nothing heroic about it.

Norman may not have regarded himself as a hero, but to the boys and the old men and the women, he was like the other returned soldiers, brave men deserving of honor and respect, like warriors of old. As the boys and men asked Norman to describe how he had received his wound, they imagined him charging toward the enemy into a hail of bullets, holding his rifle with the bayonet like a spear, with two hands.

He dodged the questions by saying that he didn't want to relive "hell" again. But the real reason Norman was reluctant to describe how he had been wounded was that he was afraid that if Veterans Affairs learned how he had received his wound, it might revoke the $16.76 pension it had granted him.

Only years later did Norman disclose how he came by his wound. He, Peter Nadjiwon, and Gregor Keeshig were pinned down by enemy fire in a small, shallow trench they had dug. They had only to raise their helmets above the level of the trench to draw a hail of enemy fire. They gallantly held out not only against the enemy but against their bladders and bowels until dark. When darkness covered the battlefield and only flashes from cannon fire and shell bursts illuminated the sky and earth for brief moments, Peter, Gregor, and Norman drew lots to decide who would leave the trench first, second, and last to relieve themselves. Peter and Gregor went first and second, respectively. Meanwhile, Norman held his crotch, squirmed, and tightened his rectum to keep from leaking and breaking loose.

When Gregor returned, Norman clambered out. Just as he squatted twenty feet away, the enemy opened fire. Norman scrambled back to the trench on all fours. His pants were unfurled around his ankles. He clawed his way back like a baby. At the lip of the trench his pants snagged on a root. He felt a sting in his knee as if a bee had lanced him. He yelled. At the same moment, Peter and Gregor pulled him into the trench. Norman could not recall whether he had relieved himself.

"I wasn't 'wounded in action' in the ordinary meaning of the word," he explained. "I was wounded in the course of going to the toilet. Goddamn Germans!"

The wound didn't bother Norman too much or too often, only when the weather was going to turn sour. "I could be a weather forecaster," Norman often said afterward, "but nobody wants another forecaster."

The White People signed a truce on November 11, 1918. Over the winter months the soldiers from Cape Croker returned from service. But it wasn't until spring that the community came back to life. Its woods rang with the thud of axes and the crash of falling trees. Its roads crunched under the heels of passersby. Lamps burned later into the night. The loneliness and apprehension that had hung over the village like a heavy fog moved off.

Husbands and wives, boyfriends and girlfriends made plans for the future. Young men who had enlisted when they were eighteen, seventeen, or even sixteen, and who had spent four years learning how to kill and cowering in trenches in fear and loneliness, now had to make the great leap forward into the world of earning a living by work. They were all expected to resume what they had been doing, as if there had been no interruption.

Norman and Rosa also made plans. With his injured knee that throbbed even when he split a few sticks of wood for the stove, Norman was sure he would not be fit enough to swing an ax or saw wood all day long. He and Rosa talked about farming. Farmers may not have had much money, as so many claimed, but they always had something on the table for every meal; they never had to run to a neighbor to borrow some potatoes or tea. Instead, it was the other way around. Neighbors went to farmers for potatoes, turnips, cabbages, whatever they needed to keep them going, pledging their twenty-five-acre lot, if they had one, for the loan. Besides, farming fell into line with the Great White Father's plans for the Indians. Rosa agreed.

Talking about dreams and planning for the future was the easy part. More difficult was winning Stanley's trust and affection, and fulfilling their dreams and plans.

At first Stanley cried and shrank from his father each time Rosa offered him to Norman. "What's wrong with the boy?" Norman asked. "He's just making strange," Rosa explained. "He'll get used to you." Even after Stanley grew accustomed to Norman, he did not fling his arms about his father's neck, as children of four are wont to do on occasion as a sign of affection, and as Norman would have liked. Rosa did what she could to help Stanley overcome his distrust of Norman. "This is your father. Don't be afraid of him." At best, Stanley eventually allowed his father to take him into his arms.

"It's that war," Mary Jane explained when Rosa mentioned Stanley's antipathy toward his father. "Makes everybody strange."

Now that the war was over and Cape Croker had come back to life, there was much more news for Mary Jane to report than during the past few years; news that was much more interesting than someone's "art-rightus" or "room-tism": the awful flu of 1919, who was in a family way, and who had received a visit from the Bear-walker.

By early spring, Norman's knee was throbbing less. He could split wood at home without wincing each time he swung an ax. Before the pulpwood cutting season was finished, Norman put in a couple of weeks in the bush with other men. His knee held up, though it was slightly swollen and tender at the end of the day.

When he was at work, Mary Jane visited Rosa, bearing the latest news and just as often old news that she told as if it were fresh. No couple could come together in a tryst; someone was bound to see them. No one could operate a still; someone was sure to smell the spirits. No one could go on a dream quest; someone would get wind of it. The next day rumors would be rife around the reserve. Few could keep what they saw or heard to themselves. "I saw so-and-so at such-and-such. Thought that no one would see them ... but I saw them. Ha! ha! ha!"

When Mary Jane heard the stories, she was mortified, and had to denounce the conduct. Otherwise, if she said nothing about debauchery or moonshining, she might be seen as condoning immorality. By expressing "Eeeeyoooh!" to her listener before recounting the scandal, Mary Jane was showing that she was opposed to turpitude.

To some, particularly men, the occasional exercise of carnality was amusing; to Mary Jane it was scandalous, the beginning of the corruption of the entire reserve. She told Rosa about two enterprising women from Owen Sound who set up shop in a tent in Little Port Elgin "to mattress men who cared to be mattressed." She told Rosa about the ambush that certain young men were preparing for Budeese (Bob Nadjiwon) for stealing their girlfriends. Men! Never satisfied with one woman. Always looking for someone else.

"Just like that Chittum (Fred Lavalley) and Flossie (Mrs. Mike Lavalley) seeing each other at Sweet Corner. I don't know what this reserve's coming to, Rosauh. Wasn't like that in the old days.

And that old C.K. now going around holy as a priest. Won't talk to his brother Tom for marrying that Nellie woman just because she's Catholic. At least she can talk Indian. He wasn't so holy a few years back when his wife died. Got a housekeeper right away ... a white girl, at that. Didn't even think of an Indian woman. Good thing the council kept an eye on old C.K. and made him marry that Zetella girl. And his son Stinker married his father's sister-in-law, Liza. Imagine that. How are C.K. and his son related besides being father and son? And Peter Nadjiwon married that Charlotte ... you know ... sister to Zetella and Liza. Heard that Father Cadot might throw him out of church. You know, Rosauh, no one can trust the men."

To Mary Jane, lying was almost as abominable as lust, a degree or so less wicked. But she didn't preface her remarks about falsehood with the traditional "Eeeeyoooh!" Lies, especially John Angus's lies, didn't deserve emphasis. "Of all the liars on the reserve, John Angus was the worst, telling children that he worked for Santa Claus in California ... and all the kids believed him. Not only is he a liar but he left his wife, or rather, she threw him out. Now he's got no home ... serves him right.

"It was partly her fault for letting John come and go as if he were young and single. That's why I keep my old buzzard close to the house. Every woman has got to watch her man, Rosauh."

Rosa passed these gems, extracted from the local romantic scene, to Norman as they sat at supper. The stories fit Norman's sense of humor and the absurd. The new kinship between C.K., Sr. and C.K., Jr. kept him guessing. And he predicted, from the growing number of Indians marrying white women, that some day the half-breeds would outnumber the full-blooded. "They won't bother learning the language, just like those Penn sisters. The language will die out; Indians will give it up."

Norman cautioned Rosa, "Don't pay too much attention to Mary Jane; don't take her too seriously. She can be a troublemaker, my pet. I don't want you to be part of it."

Though she didn't realize it, Rosa was probably better acquainted with what went on in the reserve and the larger world that most people in Cape Croker.

In early spring of 1919, Norman petitioned the band council for a loan to buy a cow and two piglets as starters for a future farm. The request was readily granted. There were few on the reserve more deserving of help and support than Norman McLeod. None had his qualifications; Norman was fluently bilingual, and he could read, write, add, and subtract.

A few weeks later a cow and two piglets were delivered by breeders from Purple Valley, a neighboring village. Norman and Rosa were busy. They erected an enclosure for the animals. Norman framed and set a foundation down for a new home on his property. As the fruit trees blossomed he and Rosa planted vegetables, for which Norman built a root house of gravel.

Come winter there would be an ample supply of food at hand.

Bobby came home at the end of June. He'd been away for seven years. He was Rufus all over again for Rosa. He had gone away as a little boy, come home as a man. He had gone away lovable and loving, returned hard and remote. But at least Bobby helped Norman on occasion.

Farmers could not have asked for better weather that spring, with just the right amount of sunshine and rain for their crops. The farmers agreed that it looked like a good harvest. And it might have been had it not been for the tent caterpillars that swept through the forests and clearings and gardens, devouring every leaf and shoot and stalk in their paths. They stripped Norman's apple, plum, cherry, and lilac trees and devastated his garden. The gray mass crawled on, vanishing a few days later as mysteriously as it had appeared.

As Norman surveyed the devastation, his hope and faith were severely shaken. Rosa, more accustomed to setbacks, shored up Norman's sagging spirits. "You've survived war, you can survive this. We'll have enough meat."

The piglets, which were to provide a litter of piglets the next year, would have to be slaughtered to make up for the shortfall in food caused by the tent caterpillars. The piglets thrived. From the time of their arrival they were allowed to roam free and forage for themselves, exercised considerable resourcefulness in finding food, and adjusted their tastes according to the fare offered by Mother Earth, eating leeks, fiddleheads, and wild rhubarb. Soon after they settled in to their new home, the piglets made their way into the neighboring woods, where they found a creek bed. There they dug and scraped until they struck trickles of muddy water. The two piglets grew and got fat.

Better than humans, they must have sensed something in their keeper's makeup that showed that Norman was a bumbler. Still, the pigs came running when Norman called them: "Coosh! Coosh! Coosh!" Even among pigs, hope springs eternal.

At the beginning of September, Bobby left home. He was going to look for Rufus and work with him.

Rosa prayed for her sons every night: "Great Spirit, keep them well!" When Norman returned from the priest's house, where mail for the Catholics was left by the mailman, Rosa asked him if there was any word from Rufus. "No, nothing," was the answer she received each time she asked. After a while she was afraid to ask. Eventually, she quit asking. Still, she continued to pray for Rufus; she prayed that he had lived through the terrible flu that had killed so many people earlier that year. Unknown to Rosa, Rufus was working in the lumber camp at Christian Island and had not even suffered so much as a headache during the epidemic.

So when Bobby said that he was going to look for Rufus and work with him, Rosa was doubtful. Even if Rufus was alive, it would be next to impossible to find him. He could be anywhere. Still, she asked

Bobby to tell him to write. "Tell him I pray for him every day .... I'll also pray for you. Please write."

Bobby promised.

In the fall Norman summoned his pigs from the woods and locked them in a pen he had constructed near the site of the future new home. For the slaughter he borrowed a barrel, a vat, ropes, pulleys, and assorted knives and scrapers. Finally, he cut and assembled a large pile of logs.

"Shouldn't you get someone to help you?" Rosa asked.

"No! We can do that on our own. Don't have to pay a man or share the meat with him." As for the water he needed to boil in order to scrape the bristles off the pig, Norman had to import a whole barrel from Isaiah's well. The property he had bought and chosen for his homestead was one of the few areas on the reserve that did not have a known water supply.

The day began well. The two pigs, now quite fat, came lumbering to their execution at the first call of "Coosh! Coosh! Coosh!" expecting a handout. The execution of the first pig was swift; a quick draw of the knife across its neck and the deed was done. Pig number two, seeing his companion slain mercilessly, made for the woods.

While they were scraping the bristles off the pig, Rosa asked how Norman was going to keep the salt pork since there was no second barrel in sight nor one at home. Norman suspended his scraping and scratched his head, not knowing what to do. He'd forgotten this detail in his planning.

"Do any of the poets say anything about looking ahead?" Rosa inquired.

Norman let the remark pass without comment. He was thinking. Finally, after some moments, he asked, "Do you know how to smoke or dry meat?" With a shake of her head Rosa answered, "No." Preserving meat in the old way was a lost art.

To keep the meat from spoiling, Norman and Rosa roasted the pig. After a week of eating warmed, cold, and shredded roast pork three times a day, with still two hundred pounds of meat remaining, Rosa couldn't stand the thought or the sight of pork. "Give it away!" she snapped, almost throwing up.

For Norman the next few days were just like the old days as he went from neighbor to neighbor trading roast pork for fish and vegetables.

The farming setback that he and Rosa suffered didn't dampen Norman's spirit for too long. He was an optimist. "If it hadn't been for the war, my pet, think of where we'd be," he was fond of saying. Norman's spirits were boosted even further when he and Rosa learned that her nausea was not caused by the thoughts of roast pork but by pregnancy. And just as uplifting for Norman was Stanley's growing acceptance of him as someone special.

It was in high spirits that Norman went to the band council later the following spring to ask for another loan to give his stalled farming career a boost. "Gonna roast more pigs this fall?" some of the councillors kidded Norman, but they granted his request on the condition that he not slaughter his pigs as he did the previous fall. However, when the Indian agent, who was not at the council meeting, reviewed the minutes, he turned down Norman's application.

When C.K. Jones, the chief, told him the bad news, Norman erupted. He spewed forth a shower of expletives that shocked even old C.K. "A snot! A good-for-nothing snot!" he fumed. "A drunken snot."

He was still smoldering when he stepped into the house. "That goddamned snot turned us down. I didn't fight in the war to be treated as a dog."

By now the monies that he and Rosa had set aside were dwindling, and they had nothing to show for their efforts. They were still paying off the loan for the cow and the pigs they had acquired the previous year. At the rate that their money was slipping away they'd soon have nothing in their savings. They had to postpone further work on their new home. With the birth of a child expected in the new year and Walter's return from residential school imminent, Norman's pension might stretch from month to month.

Until then Norman had never been short of money. He had never asked for credit at a store. To him and to many others, only people who were too old, too lazy, too improvident, or too sick asked for credit or relief. For an able-bodied person to ask for help was unthinkable, like asking for alms, charity. This Norman would never do.

Without telling Rosa, Norman decided to moonshine as a way of avoiding indebtedness. For Indians to have anything to do with spirits, either as producers or as consumers, was a federal offense punishable by either fine or imprisonment, or both. To hold his head up was worth the risk to Norman.

He brewed what was known in the local trade as a "batch of mash," made from bran, the main course for pigs, left over from the previous year. When the batch was brewed, he invited several of his friends to sample his product. "Damned good stuff," they all agreed. It was the seal of approval that Norman needed.

To keep his business under wraps Norman decided to limit the patrons to his most trusted friends, and the frequency of the drinking sessions, which he referred to as "reunions," to once a month.

A few days prior to the first official party, Norman told Rosa that he and several of his comrades were going to have a "reunion" at the future homestead. "Funny place for a reunion!" Rosa commented, to which Norman replied, "Well! Can you think of a better?" And that ended that.

After church on Sunday Norman extended whispered invitations to his preselected customers. "Come on up to the new place next Saturday evening. We'll have a reunion. I'll make some mash. Don't tell anyone else ... after 6 p.m."

On Saturday morning Norman went to inspect his still and his brew to ensure that "the batch" was ready and well-proofed. Even before he entered the woods Norman heard a commotion in the vicinity of his still. He sucked in his breath, in dread and in anger. Thinking that some good-for-nothings had chanced upon his "product" and were helping themselves, Norman broke into a run; he forgot about his bum knee.

But instead of a bunch of idlers were raccoons squealing and fighting, two perched unsteadily on the rim of the barrel, two more sprawled on the ground as if asleep or dead. Norman picked up a stick. "Get t'hell out of here," he roared, as he swung at the first raccoon and sent it toppling over the side of the barrel. He swung again and sent the second raccoon tumbling to the ground.

In the still a raccoon was swimming in the spirits, trying but unable to get out. When Norman tried to collar it, the raccoon snarled and bared its teeth, ready to sink them into its rescuer's hand. Norman clubbed it. Then he fished the raccoon out and pitched it to one side.

Norman studied the brew. His first impulse was to tip over the barrel and dump the contents, except he wasn't strong enough to budge the barrel. And then when he breathed in the aroma that made his nostrils twitch and his throat and lungs burn, bringing tears to his eyes, he did not have the heart to chuck out such fine spirits, his investment. Norman's avarice overcame his scruples. Who was to know that raccoons had washed themselves in the spirits?

While Norman was mulling over the morality of serving contaminated spirits, his eyes and mind dwelt upon the sight of the six raccoons stretched out on the ground. They would make fine roasts. Norman gloated as he bludgeoned them. He got back at them; there was nothing like revenge and then some.

Norman bore his kill home to Rosa, who crinkled her nose. "Mmm! They smell funny! Where'd you get them?"

"Yes! I noticed that, too," Norman agreed. "They smell as if they must have been feeding on sour apples or even berries, last year's crop. I wouldn't worry about it if I were you. Just skin and clean the little poachers. I'll give you a hand later, when I come back."

Shortly after 6 p.m. Gregor Keeshig, Peter Nadjiwon, Muggs (Morgan Johnston), Fred Lavalley, Edgar Jones and his wife, Andrew Taylor, Bert Ashkewe and his wife, and Kitchi-Low-C arrived at the site of the unfinished homestead. Norman soon lost whatever scruples he may have had about the quality of the brew. No one got sick. In fact, all of his guests were lavish in their praise of Norman's brew and his brewmaking talents.

Around 8 p.m. Isaiah drifted in and joined the company as if he had been invited. The guests assumed that Norman had invited him, while Norman took it for granted that one of his guests had invited the old man. Norman was a bit put out by Isaiah's coming, not because he had any objection to the old man himself, who was as welcome as anyone to a party, but because he was married to the loudest magpie in the whole district.

Norman was as gracious and attentive a host as the occasion demanded. "Another cup?" he kept asking over and over. Another cup, another nickel. He himself did not drink. When asked about his abstention, Norman explained that he was suffering a mild case of indigestion. "Too bad," his guests commiserated, "you don't know what you're missing."

Throughout the evening the returned soldiers relived memories of training camps; of marches; of drilling at home with pikes in Sidney Bay instead of reporting to camp; of ocean crossings and seasickness; of bullying officers, English bully beef, French girls, mud, French girls, trenches, French girls, and of course, how Norman had received his wound. "He farted so damned hard, he woke up the Germans. They got mad at him for interrupting their sleep, so they shot him. And stink, too …!"

When Isaiah didn't return home when he should have been back by her calculations, Mary Jane put on her tam and slipped a shawl over her shoulders. Halfway to Norman's half-finished homestead, she heard loud, happy voices, male and female, in the distance. She could see the pale glow of a campfire in the woods in back of Norman's. Why there? Why not in the yard? Funny kind of man that "Rosauh" married. Mary Jane bristled and accelerated her pace.

The party got louder and happier. The returned soldiers forgot the war, discussed their dreams. They were dreams that would never be fulfilled; council was too weak, and the agent was too strong, too much of a snot. Pont (Gregor Keeshig) lamented, "They never told me that my wife had died while I was overseas; none of them, priest, minister, agent, chief. Goddamned bastards!" After they aired their broken dreams, they sang songs.

Mary Jane entered Norman's property by the gate, passed the framework of the house-to-be, and made her way to the woods and on toward the partying place. She crossed the clearing gingerly to keep from stepping into groundhog holes and breaking a leg. At the edge of the woods, unable to find the trail that led toward the glow of the campfire, Mary Jane felt her way forward with her feet over stumps, roots, depressions, humps, keeping her arms in front of her to ward off limbs and branches.

As she entered the clearing she saw Norman and her Isaiah, their arms entwined around Ida's waist. Norman was breaking into

"Mademoiselle from Armentières, shame on you." Isaiah was beaming.

Only when she strode into the clearing to take hold of Isaiah by the ear did the company notice Mary Jane. Words, laughter, and song were choked in their throats.

"Tau! Hau!" Ida, the first of the company to recover her composure, remarked, "Why don't you stay? Come and join the fun."

"You won't have so much fun if the chief and council and the agent hear about this," Mary Jane shot back as she led Isaiah away.

"You're just a forlorn, wrinkled old buzzard. Take your prisoner home like a bad little kid."

The words "wrinkled old buzzard" rang and echoed in Mary Jane's ears. "That hummingbird, flitting here and there," Mary Jane thought, but the term wasn't strong enough to hurt. Her mouth and lips quivered, but no sound came out. She knew what she wanted to say, but for the first time Mary Jane was speechless. Being unable to think of a retort burned her to frustration with herself, and with everyone else. Besides that, those two women would tell the whole reserve that she treated her husband like a "doormat."

Mary Jane was seething. She bit her tongue to avoid saying anything to Isaiah. Let the worm squirm. He wasn't man enough to say no to wine or to bad company. He deserved to be led away like a child. That Ida and Kitchi-Low-C! Let them gloat and puff for the present; wait till Judgment Day.

But the thought that Ida would someday burn in hell didn't produce as much comfort as Mary Jane might have liked. Mary Jane couldn't dismiss Ida's face, all powdered up, her lips rouged so that she might look "white." But she wasn't fooling anybody except herself; she was no more pale-faced than any other woman on the reserve. A couple of smacks on her cheeks would bring her down a few notches on the totem pole, where she belonged.

She'd get even with that Ida and those others, those Catholics.

"How was the reunion?" Rosa asked Norman when he came home later that evening.

"It was a good reunion until that Mary Jane came over to fetch Isaiah ... I don't know who invited him; he never served in the army.

Anyway, Mary Jane came over. Just came over, took Isaiah by the ear, dragged him off as if he were a disobedient little boy. And he never said a word. Poor man … And how did you fare with the raccoons?"

Rosa told Norman that other than the smell of sour something, the meat was fresh.

A week after the reunion, C.K. Jones came by Rosa's house looking for Norman, who was at Little North Bay, cutting pulpwood.

"Any special reason?" Rosa asked.

"Well!" C.K. drawled in his thin, raspy voice. "I just wanted to have a word or two with him about the reunion that he held on his property last week. Now, don't you go getting worked up. There was nothing serious, just a bit of drinking, no drunkenness and no fighting. I just don't want word that Norman's got a still in his backyard reaching the agent's ears. It's that Mary Jane making a big to-do about nothing just to get back at Ida for calling her a wrinkled old buzzard. My daughter-in-law, Kitchi-Low-C, told me about it. Anyway, let Norman know."

Rosa was mortified. Norman was moonshining! She was a moonshiner's wife. She'd heard about wine and moonshine, but never in her life had she taken a drink, and now people would think of her on the same wavelength as they thought of people who didn't belong to Father Cadot's Christian Temperance Union. A reunion was nothing but a cover-up for a drinking bout.

Rosa tried to follow C.K.'s advice to keep her head level, telling herself that it was no more than a small still, soldiers getting together in comradeship, drinking a little. She would have remained on an even keel except that other voices hinted that "the agent might come" and "the priest could make trouble" and that they might take Stanley away from her as they had taken her other children. "Say something, do something," the other voices insisted. "If you don't, women from the outside might come to the next reunion just as those women had come to Little Port Elgin and set up their mattresses in tents on the beach. You wouldn't want that to happen, would you?" The thought stirred up ripples of fear. These in turn stoked the embers of the Lamourandiere temper.

When Norman came home that evening, Rosa was smoldering, ready to erupt. Even before he stepped into the house she let loose a salvo of invective. "You bumbling bumblehead!" she spat, forcing Norman to step back. She pressed her verbal attack: "You liar, you tell me there's a reunion, nothing but a glorified drinking party. Now everyone's talking about us .... You can't do anything right, can you?" She heaped scorn on all of his efforts: gardening, farming, building. Norman was born to fail, born without common sense ... learning poetry and history instead of something useful.

During this diatribe that lasted a good half hour Norman said nothing, though at first he felt like giving it back to Rosa word for word. Except that he knew better than to provoke her even further. Rosa's outburst reminded him of thunderstorms that split the skies with bolts of lightning and bursts of thunder and then, having spent themselves, moved off. Better to sit still and wait out the storm.

Rosa's rage subsided. The storm was over except for the sporadic boom. Rosa, hands on her hips, stood in a pugnacious manner as if daring Norman to say a word.

Finally, after several moments of suspended speech, Norman asked tentatively, "Are you done? You don't have anything more to say?"

"Yes! I'm done!" Rosa answered testily and, baffled by the query, asked, "Why?"

"Because," Norman began, "you don't realize how eloquent you are. Never have I heard such oratory. So completely was I spellbound by your delivery that I don't want you to stop .... You can outdo the priest, the minister, C.K., and even Wilfrid Laurier ... you'd turn enemies into friends." That was as far as Norman got. Rosa reached for the broom.

Reading her mind, Norman sprang forward to wrest the broom from her. Stanley, who had been looking on only steps away, grabbed his father's leg and hung on. Norman pulled on the broom. Rosa let it go. Norman spun, pitched sideways. He cracked his head against the wall. Then he slumped to the floor.

Rosa gasped and the next instant was kneeling on the floor cradling Norman's head. Over and over, between sobs, she whimpered, "I didn't mean it ... I wasn't going to hit you ... I just wanted to scare you!" When she noticed blood on Norman's head, Rosa nearly fainted.

"Stanley! Water! The facecloth!"

Stanley, standing a step away, wide-eyed in fright, was gone and back in an instant with a facecloth. Then he stood to one side and watched.

Rosa bathed Norman's face and temple until his eyelids flickered and his eyeballs rolled about unfocused in their sockets.

"Tau! Hau! Rosauh!" Norman exclaimed slowly and in a tone just above a whisper. "For a small woman you've got as much wallop in your fist as the kick of a horse ... I think you broke my skull!"

"I didn't hit you!" Rosa protested.

"No! Dad! Mom didn't hit you," Stanley broke in, coming to his mother's defense. "You fell down by yourself. You hit your head here," he said, showing his father where he had struck his head.

Rosa continued to wash Norman's head.

Norman looked up mischievously at Rosa. "I should get hurt more often to get this kind of attention." Then, after a few moments he added, "You know, Rosauh, I don't think there's another couple on this reserve that can stand up to us."

Rosa had to laugh in spite of herself, and she forgot Norman's failures and foibles, regretted that she'd been angry with him. He was a good man, doing the best with the talents and shortcomings endowed on him by the Creator.

They made up; Norman promised to reform, that is, not to moonshine again.

In the morning Norman told Rosa that he suspected Mary Jane of making up stories about the reunion. "Watch her, watch what you say. She can twist your words and your stories and make it look like you made them up. She's bad company, all mouth."

"Don't you speak ill of Mary Jane. She did more for me than anyone else did when I first moved up here. She's always welcome in my house and in my mind. She may gossip, as you say, but she'd never hurt anyone. Don't pick on Mary Jane now, Norman. There are many others on this reserve who lard up their stories and no one calls them gossips. John Angus and C.K., for two. Even if half of what Mary Jane says isn't true, half is better than nothing.

"Be nice to Mary Jane, Norman! She'll be here when the baby's born."

The baby was overdue, forcing Rosa to count the days and to worry. She wanted a daughter, then checked herself to rein in her longing. Mary Jane, as Rosa expected, came over every day to offer what help she could.

When Rosa finally went into labor, the baby was a month late.

"It's a boy," Maggie Bonhomme (Jones), the community midwife, whispered as she handed the baby to Rosa, who glowed in relief that the wait and the ordeal were over. "A strong, healthy boy," Maggie declared.

"A brother for you, Stanley, someone to play with when he gets older and bigger," said Mary Jane, who not only assisted at the birth but also cared for Stanley through the long vigil and the false alarms. "Aren't you glad you have a brother?"

"No!" Stanley shot back. "I wanted a sister like Mommy wanted."

"That's not nice to say," Mary Jane remonstrated. "He'll be your friend and playmate."

But something was not quite right with the baby. Even when Maggie spanked the baby's bottom to startle him into gasping for air on entry into this world, he didn't squall as did every other baby so struck. Maggie spanked him again. There was no reaction except for a shiver. Nor did the baby cry later that day when he was hungry or wet, as did other babies. Such a good baby. He ate and slept without fuss.

Except that the baby, David, didn't utter a cry that day or during the next few days. Rosa waited for David's cry to let her know that he was hungry, that he needed his diaper changed. She constantly had to check him. Nights became nerve-wracking. Rosa didn't have a clock; she slept in fits, woke up in starts, reached for the baby to check if he was hungry or needed to be wiped and changed. If only David would cry, then maybe she'd exact three or four hours of unbroken sleep and rest from the fleeting night.

"You're so lucky," said her sister, Christine, and Ida, who came by to visit Rosa. "I wish my baby slept all night." They told Rosa not to worry about her baby's inability to cry. He'd outgrow it and then ... she'd rue the day. Better that she be thankful for having such a quiet, unfussy baby rather than one that bawled and trumpeted with every minor discomfort, waking up the entire household. Yet, despite these assurances, Rosa was uneasy. Only she, as David's mother, could sense that something was not right.

Had the baby been a girl as Rosa had wished, she would have been named Catherine after one of Rosa's ancestors. But the baby was to be named David, not because it would commemorate one of Norman's forebears as was once the custom, but because the name symbolized so much for Norman: the weak standing up to the strong, the weak overcoming the strong. It was the name of a champion, a boy who had stood his ground, slain a giant, and put the enemy to flight. When his hero became a man, he was appointed chief of all his people. With such a namesake, their son, Norman reasoned, might be destined for an illustrious future.

"Where'd you get all this stuff? A boy of twelve defeating a man, a giant at that? Did C.K. tell you that? Maybe John Angus? Sounds like one of John's stories."

"It's in the Bible."

Rosa looked at their David. Destiny! Greatness! His future was more like obscurity, like that of every other Indian. Inwardly Rosa scoffed at Norman's dreams. What did these matter as long as David was healthy?

A month later Norman and Rosa took their David to be baptized. Father Cadot commended them for their apt choice of a name for their son. It betokened great things; it was the name of the family that begot Jesus Christ.

"David." Norman pronounced the name as it was supposed to be pronounced in English. To Rosa and to most others, unfamiliar with the consonant sounds F, V, R, L, and X which did not exist in their language, David was "Daybit."

When Rosa mentioned, "I wish that he'd cry," Norman dismissed the anxiety with the explanation, "He's just a tough little boy. He doesn't whine with every little hurt. Don't worry about it."

Just like other men, all Norman cared for was toughness and strength. He didn't seem to care about other qualities. Norman didn't see the little things that Rosa observed: the brief smile, almost cheerless; the dull eyes, not quick or sparkling. Norman didn't see beyond the sturdy arms, the strong face.

In the evenings after he came home from work, Norman would make David smile and laugh by tickling him, but this mirth was not spontaneous or deep. It wasn't the kind of mirth that echoed real happiness.

"See, Rosauh! He's a good-natured boy; that's why he doesn't cry."

"If only."

Stanley also liked to hear David laugh. He too would join in the family fun and tickle his brother. Hair, Stanley guessed, could induce laughter as readily as fingers, and so he put his head down on David's bare stomach and shook his hair. David gurgled and laughed; he reached out, took hold of a handful of hair, and pulled. Stanley screamed.

Norman laughed, remarking, "Maybe you'll know better next time to keep your hair out of the baby's reach."

"Tau! Hau!" Norman exclaimed as he pried David's little fingers from Stanley's hair. "This son of ours is strong, Rosauh! He's got such a strong grip." Turning to David, Norman said, "Let's see how strong you are!" And Norman offered his fingers to David, who promptly closed his own around them. Slowly, Norman lifted his son up from Rosa's lap, up over his head, holding him there until David whimpered. Norman let him down. "I do believe that you're going to be the strongest McLeod ever," he remarked in admiration. "And so young!"

At four months David was able to draw himself to an upright position and waddle sideways around the bed and the table by hanging on to whatever support was at hand. There were daily accidents, unavoidable. He pulled chairs on top of him, he upset the washstand with its basin full of water, and he pulled the tablecloth off the table, along with the dishes, but not once did he cry. Other than to look startled when an object fell on top of his head and to hold up a bruised arm, David did not cry out. He was truly a tough child.

In 1921 Walter came home after spending nine years in Spanish. He cried as he embraced his mother. In many respects he was no different from any other sixteen-year-old boy; he didn't or couldn't say "I love you, Mom" or "I missed you." But the tears that trickled out of the corners of his eyes said what his tongue could not.

As she drew Walter into her arms, Rosa's mind went back to that day nine years before, in 1912, when the little boy limped out of the house into the Indian agent's buggy and was drawn away out of her care. They had stolen him from her; they had stolen part of her life. Now a man, 5'10", almost as tall as his father had been, he had limped home. Rosa sobbed quietly for several minutes.

"Is your foot still bothering you?" Rosa asked when she had recovered her composure.

"I can get around," Walter replied, without answering the question. Rosa didn't press the matter any further.

Walter had put his arms around her and cried, something that neither Rufus nor Bobby had done when they got home. He wasn't shy about putting his arms around her now, any more than he was reluctant to shed tears. The nine years of absence and education seemed to have changed Walter little. He used to come to her to be drawn into her arms, and he still would not admit that his foot bothered him.

Rosa looked down at Walter's foot. She saw that a part of Walter's boot had been cut to make room for a growth that had formed on his instep. His foot had never healed from the injury he had suffered while playing. The kind, caring brothers and priests had never looked after it. She didn't pursue the matter of Walter's foot for the moment.

"How's John?" she asked.

"He's doing well," Walter said at once. "I think he's going to be a priest."

"A priest!" Rosa gasped in shock and disbelief. "A priest! Are you sure?"

"That's what John said. He told me not just once but several times, and he spends extra time in church praying and he's always volunteering to serve mass. He knows nearly the whole mass in Latin. Then there are times when he gets into mischief and trouble and says that he hates priests and talks about girls and wants to get married."

Then, remembering that Walter had not yet taken notice of Stanley or David, Rosa introduced them. "This is Stanley, and this is 'Daybit.'" Walter shook Stanley's hand warmly, and then took David into his arms, something his older brothers did not do.

While Walter was getting acquainted with Stanley and was making small talk with David, his mother asked, "Why didn't you answer our letters? Why didn't you write?"

"Did you write?"

"Yes, many times. Norman wrote many times before he went overseas."

"No, we didn't get any letters ... maybe they got lost in the mail."

"But didn't you write? Didn't you think of us?"

"Yes, we wrote but we didn't have any money for stamps."

"You didn't know anything about us, whether we were dead or alive?"

"Yes, we knew. The priests knew everything. They used to tell us when something happened. They wrote to the school. Our prefects used to read us Father Cadot's letters and how you sent us your best wishes and regards. That made being away a little more bearable."

Walter had his own burning questions. He wanted to know where his brothers were. When Rosa told him that they had long gone, "they didn't even stay two months after they came home from school," Walter was disappointed. "I thought that they'd be home and that we'd be together again. We often talked about coming home and never leaving again. We had been away too long. I don't understand why they're gone. Where did they go?"

"Bobby's in Parry Island Indian Reserve working at Depot Harbour loading and unloading boats and trains. Your Uncle Louis is there as well. He writes Christine once in a while. That's how I know."

"What's Uncle Louis doing over there?"

"He moved there with Mary, that's his wife, more than ten years ago. She didn't want to live here anymore. Who can blame her? Mary didn't want to come here in the first place. It was that Father Cadot who brought her here to marry Xavier Nadjiwon, but he drowned at Partridge Point, along with five other men, a long time ago. Then Father Cadot made her marry Louis. She was always lonesome while she was here. And she never got over it, even after she married Louis. She still wanted to go home to Parry Island where she was born, to be with her parents and her relatives, and she didn't want to stay here anymore for anyone, not even Louis. So Louis went with her to Parry Island.

"Louis writes Christine once in a while. He told us a couple of years ago that there was lots of work in Depot Harbour. Your cousin Gregor was the first one to go there. Now there are a dozen men or more from here working and living in Parry Island.

"But from Rufus, not a peep. I would have thought that with all his education he would have written to let me know how he is.

"You know, Son, I think about them, all of you, all the time ... and worry. I don't know if Rufus is alive or not. Maybe he died in that awful winter two years ago (the flu epidemic of 1919) when nearly all the people in the reserve got sick and quite a few died. We all thought that we were going to die. I just hope that Rufus is alive."

"Don't worry, Mom," Walter tried to settle his mother's fear. "Rufus will be alright. It's just that he's thoughtless; he doesn't mean to be."

"I wish ..." Rosa murmured. "I suppose you'll soon be leaving?" she asked, fearing the worst.

"No, I wasn't thinking of it," Walter said in a matter-of-fact way. "I want to stay at home and work."

Walter worked around the house doing chores that Rosa assigned him and helped Norman enlarge the root house, and he cut wood. But this kind of work didn't earn money. Walter had to go to the priest for old clothes; he had to ask his mother for money to finance his smoking habit. At first Walter thought nothing of asking and receiving. Then, after three months, it began to embarrass him. Other young men were already working, earning their keep, helping their parents. But not Walter.

There was farm work around Purple Valley and Lion's Head, and logging at Hope Bay, Little North Bay, and further up the peninsula, but no one would hire Walter. No one wanted a cripple.

After three months of frustration, Walter borrowed $5 from Father Cadot to go to Parry Island. "I'll write, Mom!" he promised as he took his leave.

That fall, Stanley, aged seven and wearing oversized Dutchman's breeches that had been worn by a succession of poor boys, started school. Before the bell rang at 9 a.m. the school wits made fun of Stanley by calling him "meeknoat," in the local vernacular meaning pants, a term borrowed from the French words "ma culotte" and then corrupted. Later, the nickname "Meeknoat" was abbreviated to "Meeks." The abbreviated name reflected Stanley's diminutive size.

"Meeknoat!" The name echoed across the school yard as it echoed across the vault of Stanley's mind. "Meeknoat!" meant more than an article of clothing. Its intonation conveyed other meanings: "Couldn't your mother alter your pants so that they'd fit you?"

Having lived in isolation with no neighboring children to play with, Stanley didn't quite know how to react to the teasing he received. Up to this day his contact with other children was limited to an hour once a week at church. They were then friendly and Stanley wanted to get to know them better, to play with them. Now these same boys who appeared friendly were laughing at him.

In class, Stanley dwelt on learning English to carry out his father's wish. He was a good student, the kind that teachers would like all of their students to be. At recess and during the lunch hour Stanley stood to one side and watched the other children playing ball, his feet itching to run with the players but his pride holding him back.

From the school porch Miss Moffat saw Stanley hanging back. She wouldn't allow him to isolate himself any more than she allowed any other student to set himself apart from the others. She went over to where Stanley stood and gently but firmly pushed him to the playing field. "Now play!" she commanded. For the first few minutes Stanley ran to and fro without attempting to kick the ball, then he threw his heart, soul, and feet into the game. Before the game was over, the other children forgot that Meeknoat was an outsider; he was one of them, he could play.

Play and friendship were infectious. Stanley was infected immediately; he wanted to visit other children and to play.

Soon after Stanley discovered the joys of play, he learned that his mother didn't share his enthusiasm. She refused his requests, "Can I go and play at my friend's place?" She was cross when he came home late from school. "Where were you?" she demanded to know. And she always found some chore for him to do: draw water, bring wood into the house, take the wood ashes out into the field, watch his brother.

"You never let me do anything," Stanley complained. "You never want me to have any fun. All you want me to do is to work, work, work." And Stanley blamed his little brother for his deprivation. His father, too, was at fault.

Stanley sulked because he was forced to work while other boys his age, he thought, were allowed to play without having to perform backbreaking labor. He didn't accept the reason, "It's for your own good." It was more likely to relieve the parents of work, passing on the unpleasant jobs to kids. "Someday you'll thank us for teaching you the habit of labor."

Fat lot of good it did his parents and the other people in the community. They worked six days a week, the year round, and were no further ahead than they were the year before. Most were always in the hole. They worked, made a few hundred dollars, paid their debts, got even, and basked in their debtless world for a week or so. Then it was back to the merchants once more. "I'm a little short of cash. Could you give me some credit until my ship comes in?" Back in the hole again. Crawl out, slide back down. Claw back to the top on hands and knees, drawn back, even pushed back. Start over.

"Anything else? Will that be all?" the merchants asked with smiles. Credit was easy, friendly.

"No! Thanks! That will be all for this time," the debtor declined with a smile as he and his family slid another $5 back into the hole. He smiled as he looked into the face of the merchant, but the smile masked a wish that he had enough money to pay for everything at once. Next spring, he would be $500 in debt. If he cut enough pulpwood, he would liquidate his debt and start all over.

It wasn't supposed to be this way. Farming was supposed to produce a stability to life that hunting and fishing could never bring. There would be no more shortages, no more need. The root houses would be full. To bring about this Utopia, the Indians cleared the woods, plowed the land, and planted grains and vegetables, but no amount of manuring or praying could make the infertile soil yield a hundredfold, much less onefold. They had to fish, cut pulp, trap, hunt, snare, and harvest apples and nuts just to make ends meet. There was even less now, less than in the old days.

In the old days, the men could go up the peninsula or down as far as Durham or Hanover to hunt deer and bring back meat to keep them through the winter. Not anymore. They lost land, freedom, independence. They could no longer come and go as they once did, take from the forests what they needed to feed their families. They were now bound to credit and the stingy soil.

"Give it time," the Indian agent said. "It takes time to train the soil; it takes time for you to get the feel of plants and animals."

During winter, when nothing grew, their need was even greater. Women scrimped to keep their families from falling too deep into a hole as a way of helping their men, who were working at Hope Bay cutting logs. They bought soup bones to give potato soup flavor, then saved the bones for a second pot. At every meal there was bannock, baked, fried, or cooked open face in front of the grates. Potato soup, bannock, salt pork, salt fish. It wasn't until the tugs from the Whicher sawmills in Colpoy's Bay or from the Hyndman Company in Owen Sound towed the booms of logs and pulpwood in the spring that the families saw any money, except that the money wasn't theirs; it belonged to the merchants. The bread-winners and their wives looked at the money, held it, then took it to the storekeepers.

"Here's the money I owe you. Hope we're all square."

The storekeeper extracted the account booklet from a shelf behind the counter, consulted the amount owing, and then took the money and counted it. The debtor looked on, hoping that he had enough to settle his bill, even daring to wish that he'd have money left over. For the storekeeper to declare, "Yes, your account is all squared away" was a relief. "Always a pleasure to do business with you, Mr. Chegahno. Now, what would you like?"

At that moment Mr. Chegahno felt that he was on top of the world. He had climbed and clawed and done without to get out of the hole. He owed nothing, was indebted to no man. It felt good.

But he couldn't resist that "Now, what would you like?" The tone was friendly, genuine. And the loose gravel gave way at Mr. Chegahno's feet and he felt himself slide back down into the abyss.

It would have been worse had it not been for Georgian Bay and the fish. When the pits and the root houses yielded no more potatoes, turnips, and cabbages, and the barrel of salted meat yielded its last pound of pork, the Indians always turned to the waters, even in winter, for their "daily bread."

A bay, someone called the body of water, and the name stuck, Georgian Bay, as if it were an insignificant body of water. But the Indians called it "Kitchi-gummee" in recognition of its size and importance; to the Indians it is indeed one of the Great Lakes.

As often as they turned to the lake, it never failed them. And yet many turned their backs on the lake after World War I. They couldn't resist the bait, the promise made by the agent, and vouched for by the clergy, that farming would provide a better life. Already hunting and trapping were in decline. Just how much longer fishing would last was anybody's guess. Not much longer. Anyway, farming would not be so hard a life.

The lake was the wellspring of the good life for Budeese (Bob Nadjiwon). He was the only man who refused to forsake the old way of life in favor of farming, the modern, civilized way. And it rewarded him with a good life, wine, women, and song; but for the rest of his neighbors it was a life "in the hole."

In the schools the teachers urged their students to learn English in order to get ahead. The catalogs that came into the reserves were illustrated with sketches of the latest styles and new products—stoves, beds, furniture, clocks, watches, purses, washtubs, scrubbing boards—all visible manifestations of the good life, within reach of those who got ahead. Get ahead. Look ahead.

Outside the boundary of the reserve, the nation was forging ahead, tripping over cars, bicycles, tractors, pens, phones, wireless radios, pianos, jobs, money, trains, all chasing the pot of gold. Everybody was getting ahead, the way it should be, the way it was intended to be.

About the only person who objected to this single-minded pursuit and dream on the reserve was Father Cadot. He warned the congregation of the menace of materialism, of the worship of Baal.

Few listened. A little more materialism and they'd be out of "the hole."

Norman, as did many Indians on the reserve, did his business at Carl Whicher's General Store in Colpoy's Bay, going there once a month to shop, usually the day after receiving his pension check. Carl Whicher was a successful businessman whose store and sawmill were thriving. He was getting ahead.

Always amiable, Carl was a good man. A person's religion or color didn't make any difference to him. When he greeted Norman, "Good to see you. Leg getting any better? How's Rosa and the children?" he meant it. "I'd like to congratulate you on your election as councillor. Being chief would be the next step .... You'd make a fine chief, Norm."

"Carl. This salt pork is a cent more this month than it was last time I was here ... and tobacco's gone up. What are you trying to do, put me in the poorhouse while you stash away more money?"

"I wish I was making as much money as people think I'm making. Sorry, Norm, but my suppliers raised the prices on me. I've got to raise my prices as well or else I'll be out of business. I've got to stay ahead in the game."

Carl explained that he could no longer compete with the lumber companies in the Muskokas and that it was just a question of time before he shut his mill down. He guessed that the big mill days in Owen Sound were numbered as well.

"What are we to do then?" Norman asked.

"You have to look ahead, a long way ahead. See what people will need and want. Go into business for yourself. Forget timbering here, it's done. Forget farming, there's not enough land on the Cape that's arable. The way I see it, there's going to be a need for chicken and turkeys, just mark my words."

Norman thought about Carl Whicher's remarks, which took on even more appeal as he dwelt upon them. Chickens and turkeys pretty well foraged for themselves. No need to spend money to feed them. They laid eggs that could be eaten and sold. The way that birds reproduced themselves, he and Rosa would have a large flock in no time. Besides, he'd be independent, no more busting his butt felling and sawing logs. He could get ahead without having to go outside the reserve. When Norman had worked out the details of poultry farming he let Rosa in on what he planned to do.

What a marvelous idea, she thought. Maybe there was a chance that raising birds would bring in a little extra money to enable her to buy clothing for Stanley and food for Baby David.

At the next council meeting, his first as band councillor, Norman joked, "Bring out the dictionaries when I talk." But he didn't say much until C.K. and the council came to the last item on the agenda, designated as "other business." Norman then asked for a loan amounting to three or four hundred dollars to start a turkey farm. Council was impressed with Norman's submission.

"Sorry, Mr. McLeod," the Indian agent interrupted Norman's address. "I cannot approve your application. You're a member of this council and it wouldn't look right for you to receive a loan while some other member may be turned down."

Norman was flabbergasted. There was a momentary silence. Then his temper erupted. He rose up abruptly, sending his chair clattering to the floor. He pointed a shaking finger at the Indian agent. "You donkey's rear end. I went to war so's we can have a better life. But so long as you're here, we'll never have a better life. You're working against us. You're worse than the enemy that we fought against .... I resign."

Norman stomped out of the council hall.

Next month, while at Whicher's store, Norman told Carl that the Indian agent had turned down his request for a loan for starting up a turkey farm.

"Norman!" Carl said, "Why don't you go to the bank?"

"Banks wouldn't lend us any money," Norman rejoined at once.

"How much do you need?"

"I don't know, a few hundred, I suppose."

"Norman! You've got to be more specific than that. Here! Let's do some calculations." And Carl Whicher did some rapid, amazing additions on a sheet of paper, estimating how much a coop and feed would cost. "That's about how much money you would need to get started. Get ten or a dozen birds, a pair of males and the rest hens, and eggs from one of the local farmers. I'll give you credit for the building materials and feed. You must take a few risks to get ahead, Norm. There's a farmer in Oxenden keeps some birds. You might want to see him."

Taking Carl Whicher's advice, Norman went to Oxenden and bought a couple of toms and eight turkey hens and eggs from the farmer, and took them home. The lumber and the wire and the feed were delivered and piled on one side of the site of the coop that would be constructed at a later date. In the meantime, the birds wouldn't need shelter or feed just yet.

Over the next few weeks Norman checked on the hens and the

eggs daily. The toms and the non-laying hens scratched the ground and fed on grass and insects. "What's keeping the poults?" Norman asked himself. One morning he heard the long-awaited "cheep! cheep! cheep!" of little poults and the motherly "chick! chick!" of the hens. Amazing, he marveled, that within minutes of breaking out of their shells the poults could fend for themselves.

A week after the turkey poults were hatched, it rained, a night and a half a day. The following morning when Norman looked in on his flock, he found nothing but little poult corpses in the mud, as pitiful as the corpses of his comrades and enemies lying in the muck on the battlefields of France. He couldn't figure out, nor could anyone explain to Norman, what had happened to his birds.

His hens tried again but the poults did not survive the first rainfall. Shortly after, a fox found the hens and toms. All that was left of the flock were feathers and down.

Norman was now deeper in debt. His only object now was to get out of the hole that he had dug.

"How are the birds?" Rosa asked him.

"All the poults are dead," he answered, unable to look her in the eye.

"How come?"

"I don't know."

A few days later she asked, "And how are the big birds?"

"A fox got them."

"You can never do things right, can you? Why didn't you build a coop for them when you had the chance?"

Maybe she was right, maybe he was one of those born under an unlucky star. Blame the stars.

"How are the birds coming along, Norman?" Carl Whicher asked him when Norman next went shopping. The question made Norman squirm, reminded him of his failure.

"I had some bad luck, Carl. All the poults died, right after a heavy rain last month."

"Sorry to hear about that, Norman, but I heard that turkey poults are allergic to rain. Your poults must have got wet and drowned. Better luck next brood."

"Thanks, Carl," Norman acknowledged Mr. Whicher's good wishes. He said nothing about the hens.

He had been looking forward to buying some new clothes for Rosa, Stanley, and Baby David, but he could not. He didn't want to go another penny in the hole. Instead, Norman went to the church to rummage through some old clothes that still had some wear left in them, and therefore some respectability. He, Norman McLeod, had to make do with what other people would have no more to do with. He was needy.

One night Norman turned and whispered to Rosa, "I can't hold my head up the way that I would like. I can't look after you and the children the way that I should. Always short of something. I can't make a decent living on this reserve and I hate being in debt. You know, if it weren't for that pension, we'd be worse off. I don't want to be worse off." Norman paused. "I'm going to have to go away, to Parry Island, to look for work. Men working there make good money."

Rosa said nothing. She couldn't quite grasp this pride. There were many other men on the reserve who could live with and be comfortable with "putting it on the bill."

"What will we do? How'll we get our food? Our wood! water! Why can't you stay home like the other men? How come you can't manage?"

"I'll make arrangements with Whicher to deliver what you need and you can hire someone to cut wood for you."

In the fall of 1921 Norman left the Cape, bound for Parry Island.

From the door Rosa watched Norman walk down the road with his little black satchel, turn the corner and, before he disappeared from sight, stop and wave. Rosa waved back, then took David's hand and waved it.

Part of Rosa wanted Norman to return; part of her, a small part, wanted him to leave, and not return. She wanted to hold him and tell him that being in need didn't matter, but her pride wouldn't let her. She resented the ease with which he could come and go in the name of getting ahead, staying ahead, while she had to stay at home; the furthest that she could go was to Mary Jane's or down to the corner.

Norman didn't take her worries and anxieties about David seriously, telling her that she worried too much. "He'll be alright. He'll outgrow his clumsiness."

At two years of age David still had not cried. His eyes didn't light up, nor did he reach for any object that Rosa held in front of him.

Ever since David had begun standing upright and waddling, she constantly had to keep her eye on him. He was always on the move, sideways. He toddled, got his feet tangled up, pitched sideways, forward, backward. He picked himself up and resumed his trek. "No! Stay away from the stove, you'll get burned, boo! boo! ... Don't touch the wood, you'll get a sliver in your finger, boo! boo! Stanley! Watch your brother while I make some bannock." Watching David was nerve-wracking.

The first time she spoke sharply to David, "Don't!" and slapped his hand to keep him from touching the stove, he sat down, his feet apart, and like a baby Buddha, fixed his gaze on some nail on the floor and chewed his tongue as if in meditation. And he sat in a snit, in a trance for an hour. David's reaction wasn't lost upon Stanley.

When Rosa later asked Stanley to "Watch David while I hang the clothes out to dry!" Stanley hissed at David, "Don't!"

David immediately froze in a Buddha-like pose.

"Stanley! Why did you do that?" Rosa demanded sternly.

"To keep him quiet! You told me to watch him!"

Rosa set her clothes basket aside. She gathered David in her arms and cradled him close to her and stroked his head. "My poor little David," she crooned, and she murmured other words to convey her feelings that would lift David out of his doldrums. "Stanley! Don't do that again."

She set David back down, thinking that she had cheered him up, to return to her housework. Except that David wasn't consoled. He sat brooding far longer than was natural.

Even without provocation from Stanley, David went into these trancelike states at least once a day, sometimes two or even three times a day. Nothing that Stanley did, making faces, snapping his fingers, talking, drew any reaction from his brother. For Stanley it was amusing, but for Rosa it was disturbing.

"Stanley! Would you ask the priest to call the doctor to come and see David the next time he comes to the reserve?" Rosa asked Stanley, just before he set out for school.

"What for? What's wrong with him?"

"Nothing really."

A month and a half later the doctor came to the reserve by horse and buggy. Rosa kept Stanley home to serve as her interpreter.

The doctor sat David on the table where he conducted the examination, poking and probing with his fingers and instruments. "Nothing wrong with his eyes, ears, heart, lungs, a strong, healthy baby," the doctor pronounced. Stanley translated. "But I'm sorry to have to tell you … your son is a Mongoloid. He has a condition known in the medical profession as Mongolism."

"What did he say?" Rosa asked Stanley.

"He says that David's Mongol-eyed."

"What's that?"

Stanley asked the doctor what Mongol-eyed was. "For starters," the doctor explained, "David has limited intelligence, he'll never be able to understand as much as a normal person. Just how retarded he is I can't say. I haven't dealt with many cases like this. For another, his tongue is tied and he may never be able to talk. The best place, if such a place existed, for David would be in an institution … when he gets older, of course."

"What did he say?" Rosa wanted to know.

As best he could, Stanley interpreted.

With a stifled moan, Rosa sank down on a chair and cried. Her poor, poor baby. She cried for him, and for herself. "To one He gave ten talents, to another, five talents, and to still another, one. To David, nothing."

"I'm sorry, Mrs. McLeod, but these things happen," the doctor said as he slipped out. But Rosa didn't understand the words. As she moaned and keened, David came to her, put his head on her lap. It was first time that he'd ever shown any sign of affection, and it made her cry even more.

Soon after the doctor was gone Mary Jane came over. She wanted to know what the doctor was doing at Rosa's house. Seeing Rosa hunched over and wailing, Mary Jane asked, "What's wrong? Are you sick? What can I do to help you?" and she put an arm around Rosa.

"No!" Rosa hesitated, then stammered. "It's David." Between sobs she gasped, "The doctor said … David … is backward … will never learn … will always be like a child …. My poor David."

"Eeeeyoooh," Mary Jane gasped. "Is he sure? Are you sure? How can he tell? David's still only a baby!"

"Mary Jane! … I'm sure … I know. What am I going to do? What's going to happen to him? Who's going to look after him if something happens to me?" And Rosa looked into Mary Jane's eyes.

"Maybe somebody's done something that can be undone," Mary Jane hazarded a guess, referring to a widespread belief that people who have been slighted or aggrieved exacted revenge by using the services of a sorcerer known as the Bear-walker.

"No! I've never done anything to anyone. You know that!"

"Not you; but maybe someone wants to get back at Norman," Mary Jane suggested.

"What for?"

"I don't know, but you never know." And Mary Jane didn't say any more; she'd already said too much.

What did it matter how David was afflicted? Revenge wouldn't make him better. And Rosa cried anew.

David. Her David. Her flesh, whose name betokened great deeds. Now destined for helplessness, never to amount to anything.

Mary Jane slipped out of the house.

Rosa held David. She looked at him. "I'm sorry, David, but I didn't mean that you should be born this way." At other times she looked away from David's accusatory gaze that projected the question "What did you do to me?"

"Kizhae Manitou! Zhawaenim! Zhawaeni-mishin." ("Oh Great Mystery! Have compassion on him! Have compassion on me!")

What next? How many setbacks can one suffer in one's short lifetime without breaking down, losing faith? Rosa reeled, bent; she wilted but did not break. She hung on to the thread, not so much for her own sake, but for David's.

For months she bore pain. Shame, guilt, anger, helplessness, self-pity scorched her soul until she could cry no more and her element became their element, and she became inured to the pain.

During this period of depression and doubt, Rosa's sole friend and comforter was Mary Jane. Only after she had reconciled herself to living with her cross did Rosa ask Mary Jane to explain what she meant by her remark that "someone may have got even with Norman."

Mary Jane hummed and aahed as she groped for the right words to explain her theory. "You know that Norman had many girlfriends before you married him. Many of these women were jealous of you;

they felt that Norman jilted them. Maybe one of them, you never know, got a Bear-walker to get even with Norman."

"Girlfriends!" The word, the idea, fanned the flames of jealousy that Rosa had not felt in years. The letters in Norman's trunk ... the photographs. In her mind she heard Norman recite poems to other women.

"You shouldn't have allowed Norman to go," Mary Jane had said. "You've got to keep an eye on them men, to keep them in line. Because you never know what they are up to; married men are just as bad. Like that Lawrence Keeshig got a couple of girls in trouble in Honey Harbour. Never bothered to marry them."

Mary Jane's remarks whipped the little flames of jealousy as a wind fans a forest fire. Rosa's Norman was easy on the eyes, a charming man. He didn't have to pursue or woo women; women pursued him. Trouble was, Norman was too willing to wait, to welcome women's attentions. The more Rosa thought about it, the more certain she was that Norman was fooling around. He didn't belong in her life.

"Where's Dad? When's he coming home? Why'd he have to leave? Why doesn't he stay home?" Stanley asked.

Norman came home a few days before Christmas with a bag full of groceries, fruit, and toys. "I missed you," he declared as he gathered Rosa in his arms and kissed her. In the next instant and motion he took David, squeezed him to his chest, and patted Stanley's head before fishing oranges out of his bag and giving them to the boys. He was buoyant, like the Norman of old. "I paid Whicher $175. I think I'll be able to pay off my entire bill come spring," he said, and at the same time handed Rosa $25. Stingy, Norman was not.

In those first few minutes Rosa's animosity and jealousy evaporated. Instead of dressing him down and showing him the door as she had intended, she asked, "Would you like some tea?" and in addition, fixed him lunch.

After the boys were put to bed, Rosa broke the bad news. "Norman, there is something wrong with David. I tried to tell you but you wouldn't listen." And she told him what the doctor had said.

It was as if an invisible hand had lashed Norman across the face. The smile, the gleam in his eyes dimmed. Words that came easily stuck in his throat.

"What are we going to do? How could this happen?" he asked after a long silence.

Norman went through the same agony that Rosa had gone through. Guilt. Shame. Anger. Depression. Christmas with a little tree had no meaning. "Merry Christmas, Norman," Father Cadot and neighbors wished him, but the wishes only mocked him. His suffering and that of Rosa was a trial sent by God to test them, as once God had tried Job. Why did it have to be so hard? Why did the test abide in David? It was not a test that came and went and could be overcome; it was one enduring assault.

Every night Norman and Rosa discussed David's condition and future and what they would have to do. For Norman it was clear that he would have to go out to work. He had no choice but to work for someone who was born under a luckier star. There were jobs out there, not in Depot Harbour but in the lumber camps around Gravenhurst and Huntsville in the Muskokas. The work was hard, but not as hard as that in Depot Harbour ... and steady. There was no other way but to go. If only he could find a job nearby.

Gone were Rosa's misgivings about Norman. She cried with and for him.

After New Year's Norman was gone, walking all the way to Wiarton, fifteen miles away, in the snow, to catch the train.

L ife was hard for Stanley, as it was for everybody on the reserve. Stanley figured he was worse off, that every other boy and girl was so much better off than he was.

It began in the morning as he left for school. His mother carped, "Don't forget. Come straight home from school." Carp. Carp. "You have work to do." When he got home from school, it was, "Get some wood … get some water. Hurry up!" The words bounced back and forth in the house.

If David weren't such a big baby, still "dumping in his pants," Stanley wouldn't have to carry pail after pail of water. If it wasn't for his dad's absence, Stanley wouldn't have to wait around just in case he was needed. In Stanley's mind he was the most underprivileged boy in all of Cape Croker.

Most of Stanley's troubles were brought about by David. Because of David, Rosa needed and used more water than anyone else on the reserve, except maybe for some farmers, to wash pants, socks, underwear, and shirts in order to have changes of clothing ever ready. The washtub was always on the stand, the clothesline bent with drying clothes, Rosa leaning over the scrubbing board.

"Get some more water … and make sure that you go around by the front gate and shut it after you. It's Isaiah's gate and well, don't forget."

"Do this! Do that! Don't forget." Stanley felt like clapping his ears shut.

Once in a while Stanley would have liked to slip through the gate unseen, get the water, and slip back home unobserved, but as long as Tracy, Isaiah's new dog, was on duty, this wasn't possible. For every time Stanley lifted the latch of the gate, Tracy barked and came over to greet and escort him. An instant later, Mary Jane appeared at the door to remind him, "Don't forget to close the gate .... You forgot the last time ... and don't muddy up the waters." Stanley felt that Mary Jane's eyes were glued on him.

Mary Jane had no business keeping him under watch.

If Mary Jane and Isaiah would let him climb over the fence near the well, Stanley could save himself one hundred and fifty steps and escape Mary Jane's surveillance. The first time he tried taking the short cut, the wire strands of the fence squeaked under Stanley's weight, rousing Tracy. The dog at once started howling and barking. "Shut up! Get away!" Stanley snarled. At the same time he picked up a rock to throw at the dog. Too late. Mary Jane saw him.

"You little scalawag! I'm going to tell your mother. What kind of man are you going to turn out to be?" And Stanley received a sharp sermon on doing things right, respecting other people's property, that short-cutting was nothing but an act of laziness. Stanley would turn out to be another John Angus.

Stanley had an overpowering urge to talk back. He wanted to tell Mary Jane, "Go haunt some old house or graveyard," but instead he apologized without remorse. "I'm sorry, Mary Jane, but I have only a small pail and I have to make twice as many trips as would a man. I have to work twice as hard ... and the wire handle cuts into my hands."

The next day Isaiah constructed a stile near the well.

For Rosa the new timesaving device did not lighten her workload by an ounce. It was scrub, scrub; wash, wash; wring, wring; and hang the clothing to dry.

David was now four. By now he should have been toilet trained. Every day for the past year and a half Rosa had coaxed and wheedled, "Go to the pot when you feel that you want to make stink ... and when you want to leak." David nodded, as if he understood. Words did no good. She sat David on the pot until he whimpered that his legs were numb. Rosa sent him to the outhouse with Stanley to see how it was done. That, too, was futile.

"Mom, David's wet his pants again! Mom! David smells like a dead horse!" Rosa dreaded and hated the words. There were times when she screamed and smacked David's bottom. Moments later, realizing that she was blaming and punishing David for what he could not help, she cried, gathered him into her arms, and held him. But as the months passed without David having learned to go to the pot, Rosa gave in. It was useless. Better to live with and bear the cross that life had given her. It was not David's fault that he was born the way he was.

But Stanley did not have to put up with his brother's faults. Someday he was going to grow up and get away.

John, now sixteen, came home that June. As he withdrew from Rosa's welcoming embrace, he told his mother, "I'm going to be a priest, a Jesuit." Come fall, he was going to enter the seminary in Guelph. If he thought that his mother would be thrilled, John was mistaken. While not opposed to John's vocation, she wasn't as receptive as John thought she'd be. He would be a man of God, educated, influential. But she was afraid. "People will hate you; they'll make fun of you. Your life won't be your own. You'll always be poor, and you're too young to be thinking of that kind of life."

Stanley and David stood back and looked on, uneasy and distrustful of the stranger. But she couldn't tell John anything. He'd already given the vocation a great deal of thought and prayer, and was ready to pay the price, to sacrifice.

"So this is David," John said after he'd detached himself from his mother. "You must be Stanley. You were just a baby when I left." Turning his attention to David, he remarked, "My, but he's strong. What do you feed this boy, Mom? He's going to be as strong as Samson when he grows up."

"Yeah, and he still dumps in his pants," Stanley broke in bitterly, "and he's going on five."

As he and his mother talked that afternoon and evening, John frequently made faces at David, mimicked birds and animals and imitated priests, brothers, and boys that he had known at Spanish to make David laugh. He smiled and laughed to see David stare at him from behind Rosa. "Little Samson," he called David.

John's laughter and spirit were infectious. Rosa, Stanley, and David were also infected.

By the next day Stanley was thanking the stars for having a brother such as John. "What do you want me to do, Mom?" he heard his older brother ask their mother.

For once, Stanley had nothing to do. "Can I go out to play?"

"Go on!" and Stanley was off at once, before Rosa changed her mind. For the first time in his young life, Stanley spent the summer the way boys wished to spend it: sleeping in, fishing, catching frogs, hunting squirrels, eating berries, swimming, playing ball, smoking, and teasing girls.

Father Cadot was glad to see John home and at mass every Sunday. John attended every service, daily mass, Friday evening devotions, benediction, and vespers. John was a model Catholic boy in Father Cadot's eyes. The girls squealed and giggled when John cast a smile and a glance in their direction and winked at them. Few young men were as charming, witty, or handsome as he. What a good husband he would make—always a smile, never an angry word.

For all of them summer passed too quickly, as quickly as if it had been but two weeks. On the last Sunday in August, a week before John was to leave, Father Cadot preached about vocations, "Come and I will make you fishers of men," as a send-off for John. Later in the week the young people held a party in John's honor at Sweet Corner, after which he nearly changed his mind about entering Holy Orders.

As he said farewell, John assured his mother that, through God, he would be closer to her than he ever was or would be in a secular calling in the secular world.

Rosa was grateful that John would remember her. Yet it was not the same as having him in the house, seeing his face, hearing his laughter. On leaving her sons all made the same promise, an oath they meant to keep but soon forgot. She too promised that she would keep him in her mind, except that Rosa kept her promise, praying for her boys every night.

Stanley missed and envied John. Except for a couple of weeks at Christmas, when his father was home, Stanley had no respite from carrying water, cutting wood, watching David, day in, day out, all winter, all summer. Boys such as his brothers were lucky to have gone to Spanish, he surmised, where they didn't have to do such hard and dirty work as he had to do. If only he were sixteen; if only he had a normal brother.

Except that he didn't. Not only was his brother incontinent but he couldn't talk. Stanley couldn't even play games with him.

Another fall came; David, going on six, still dirtied his pants like a baby. In a moment of generosity and brotherly affection Stanley tried to teach David "hide and seek." The game ended almost as soon as it began. Although David nodded understanding as his brother explained the game, and closed his eyes as instructed, he screamed in terror, as if he had been struck, when Stanley yelled, "Yoo! Hoo!"

Stanley ran back to his brother's side. "Shut up! You big baby. What's the matter with you anyway?" And he clamped one hand over David's mouth to keep him quiet.

At that moment Rosa came out. "What are you doing to your little brother?" she demanded. And without waiting for an answer, she grabbed Stanley by the arm and gave him a backhander on the side of his head while reminding him that it was his duty as an older brother to help look after David, not to abuse him.

"But I didn't do anything," Stanley protested, except that it didn't do any good. His mother made him sit on a chair to repent, and she helped him repent with periodic comments about their lot in life.

Repentance was the furthest thing from Stanley's mind. He was a victim, blamed and punished for nothing. Run away was what he would do.

While Stanley sat serving his sentence, deaf to what his mother was saying, Rosa saw from the corner of her eye David edging closer and closer to his brother. As he made his way toward Stanley, David shook his head, which Rosa took to mean something akin to "I'm sorry, brother, sorry for the trouble I've caused you."

When Stanley looked up and saw David next to him, he cried, "Get away from here!"

"David! Leave Stanley alone," Rosa snapped.

If only David were not part of his life, Stanley wished, but the reality was that he was bound to David just as much as Rosa was. He couldn't escape.

Some weeks after the hide and seek incident Rosa asked Stanley, "Will you take David outside for a while? I'm going to bake some bread."

"Come on, David!" Stanley invited his brother.

No sooner did they get outside than Stanley sniffed. David reeked. David's eyes were wide with the look of guilt and shame. "Mom! David's dumped in his pants again," Stanley shouted through the doorway.

"Well, you know how it's done. You clean him up. I can't come out right now. I've got flour on my hands."

Stanley looked at his brother with disgust and loathing, as if David were covered with leprous sores and reeking with decay. As he removed David's boots, socks, pants, and underwear, Stanley gagged and choked. He tried to control his breathing but could not. He flung David's soiled clothing aside.

"Mom, David's undressed now."

"Will you wash him for me?"

"Do I have to?"

"Do as I say."

Standing next to David with a bucket of cold water, instead of the lukewarm water his mother used to clean up David whenever he dirtied himself, Stanley recoiled from the filth and the stench. He could not bear the thought of touching David. "Why can't you learn to go to the toilet?" Stanley snarled. He drew the pail back and dashed the cold water on David. David bellowed like a wounded bull. Stanley dropped the pail and ran.

Later that evening Bert Ashkewe brought Stanley back home. "Rosauh! Look what I found wandering around North Bay. I caught him before a bear did. He's a nice little boy, don't you think? Ida and I would keep him except that we've already got six of our own. We're looking for his owners. He sort of looks like a boy I've seen around your house. If you don't want him, I'll keep him."

"Why thank you, Bert. I could use a little help with wood and water."

Stanley squirmed.

"Now, Rosauh, be nice to this little foundling. He's just like every other newfound gift. When you first capture it, you have to be kind to it and it will stay around, otherwise it will run away. If a bear catches one of these runaways, they eat them."

But for Bert's intervention, Stanley might have received a thrashing with a switch. Instead, he was treated as if nothing had happened, leaving him on edge for several days, waiting for the guillotine to drop.

Stanley was still on edge the next Saturday when Rosa asked him to look after David again while she scrubbed the floor. "Don't you splash cold water on him again."

Nature, as they say, called Stanley. He took David along with him, not so much to show him what to do but to keep an eye on his brother as their mother wanted. He made David sit on one of the holes while he occupied the other. In no time Stanley delivered his cargo, wiped himself with a catalog, and, hoisting up his pants, went out.

David rose to follow. With "No! You have to dump," Stanley forced David back down on the seat. "You're not getting up until you've dumped. I'm not going to carry water all day for you. Now. Dump! Meezeen!"

Cold, Stanley stamped his feet to keep warm. David whimpered from the cold and the discomfort of the rough seat. Rosa called from the back porch at least every minute or so, "What are you boys up to?"

"Teaching David to go to the toilet," Stanley shouted back and, in lower tones, "Come on, David, hurry up! Any other time you would have dumped in your pants by now. Hurry up. I don't care how long it takes, but you're not getting up until you've dumped."

"Hurry up! I'm cold!" a hundred times.

Finally, David called, "Lee-lee," his name for Stanley.

Stanley suspended pitching stones, which he had taken up to keep warm. "What?" he growled.

David was standing, half-twisted, looking down behind him.

"Sit down! What do you want, anyway?" Stanley demanded.

Without turning around David continued to call out, "Lee-lee! Lee-lee! Choo-a! Choo-a! Fewah! Fewah!" and pointed into the hole behind him and held his nose to emphasize his meaning.

Most likely nothing, Stanley thought, but he'd better check just to make sure.

It was true. David had done it. "That's the way, David! That's exactly what you're supposed to do." And he clapped David's back. "Just like a grown-up. You're not a baby anymore."

David grinned as he accepted Stanley's good wishes, and he took several sheets of catalog to wipe himself with. It was good to have a brother like Stanley.

"Mom! Mom! He did it. He did it," the words tumbled out of Stanley's mouth. He, Stanley, had done something that his mother had failed to do. He had made David dump in the toilet. Stanley's excited announcement was also a cry of relief that the ordeal was over. "Mom! Can I go play now? The barrel and the pails are still full."

"Yes, go on."

Stanley didn't wait; he was off to the Ashkewes to play with Nelson.

"Did you really?" Rosa asked David, who stood at the doorway grinning and beaming. She wanted to believe, yet she was doubtful. Maybe Stanley was conning her so that he could avoid chores. She asked David once more, "Did you dump? Make stink?"

"Choo-a! Fewah!" David muttered.

Rosa sat down in relief. If David had really gone to the washroom it would be the first time since he was born, more than five years before, that she would do one less wash in the day. It was almost too good to be true; it was like a respite given a slave to keep him alive and working.

All day Rosa waited for an accident to happen, but it wasn't until late in the day that David wet his pants. Rosa had only one wash to do that day; it wasn't much, but it was something.

The next day, Sunday, Stanley took David to the outhouse again when he went to dump. He wasn't going to carry water again. Let the cold numb David's buns; let the plants pinch his ass. David dumped. Again Stanley didn't have to carry water.

In the week that followed, Stanley took David to the outhouse before he went to school. "Put him on the pot, make him sit. Don't let him get up until he's done his job, Mom! It's quite simple. ...Ask him if he wants to make 'Choo-a! Fewah!'"

By Stanley's calculations, David's improved toilet habits saved fifty trips to the well, an exaggeration of course, and at least one, maybe two, washings a day. The next step was to teach David to go alone.

As well as reducing the household work, David's better toilet habits produced improved relations between Stanley and him. That is, Stanley did not growl at David quite so often as he had in the past. David, of course, smelled better, and smelling better earned Stanley's tolerance. Stanley didn't send him away with "Get away from me! You stink!" To be tolerated encouraged David to cultivate a closer companionship with Stanley. He wanted not merely to watch but to help Stanley.

In the spring, Stanley was constructing a model village in the mud near the house. David was standing nearby watching. He stepped forward, tripped. He pitched headlong into Stanley's village.

"Waaah!" Stanley howled. "Get out of here, you clumsy ox. You've wrecked my village. Waaah! Go on!" David got to his feet. "Get out of here!" And to give meaning to his words, Stanley turned David about so that David faced the house, then shoved David with enough force to send him sprawling. Half blinded by tears, Stanley returned to his play, rebuilding his village.

On his way into the house, David passed by the water pail stand in the porch. He stopped, removed the dipper from its lodging place on the wall. He dipped the vessel into the water and drank. Bubbles rose to the surface and burst. The sight of the bubbles, the pail, the water, stirred memories within that floated to David's consciousness. David took the pail and, without any special precautions to muffle his steps, made straight for his brother, whose back, bent over, was turned from him.

David heaved the pail of water on the unsuspecting Stanley.

Stanley gasped, stiffened. He flung his arms outward as if he'd been lashed across the back. Then he screamed and bawled.

"What are you two fighting about?" Rosa demanded, her voice sharp with exasperation.

"David," Stanley wailed, "threw water on me ... for nothing. ... I didn't do anything to him. Waaah!"

Rosa seized David's hand, spun him around, and smacked his behind. "Get in the house," she hissed, and in the next breath asked Stanley, "What happened? What did you do? You must have done something."

"You always blame me for everything," Stanley wailed anew.

Accused of bias and favoritism, Rosa drew Stanley to her and held him close for a few moments, then led him inside.

As he watched his mother remove Stanley's wet shirt, David's eyes shone. He heard the echo of his brother's shriek and saw the replay of Stanley's outflung arms. He sat back and savored his sweet revenge.

Mary Jane was untouched by any of the troubles that beset other women, other couples. Perhaps that was the reason why others' rifts so absorbed her. Rosa envied her, her only complaint being about Isaiah's tobacco chewing habit.

When a trouble finally overtook her, Mary Jane was distraught, driven to her wits' end by their son Alvin. "Eeeeyoooh, Rosauh! It's that Alvin," Mary Jane grumbled. "We started that farm for him and built it up. Now he doesn't want it; says that he doesn't like horses, cows, pigs, he doesn't own them, they own him. All that work for nothing. Now he's taken up with that Suzanee woman ... don't even go to the same church. We try to tell him that he should go with a girl who goes to the same church, but he won't listen. Says that he's got more friends that're Catholic than Protestant. That Suzanee's pretty face scrambled Alvin's brains. And before he met up with that girl, our son never drank. It's all her fault. Do all that for him. Doesn't want it. It's like a slap in the face. I don't know what to do."

In November Walter came home, dispirited after five years of drifting from one job to another, of being denied work because of his disability. Nobody wanted a cripple. He would work for himself, make the best of his lameness. If he could not meet men's expectations, he would meet life's challenges.

Only God would accept Walter as he was. Farming and gardening he would do, put to good use what he had learned from the farmers he'd worked for in the Niagara Peninsula area. Until he found a wife, Walter would stay at home during the winters and work for farmers in the summer.

Not long after he came home Walter was nicknamed "Half-Chick." Half-Chick was further foreshortened to Chick, a name Walter bore for the rest of his life. It's very likely that the only person to call him Walter, by his baptismal name, was Rosa.

For several days David shrank from Walter and moaned each time his older brother looked at him or attempted to pick him up. "Don't you talk?" Walter asked.

"No! He can't talk properly. Just mumbles," Stanley said contemptuously.

"STANLEY! I've told you before. That's enough." Then, turning to Walter, Rosa explained that David had his own language ... baby talk, almost ... maybe he would eventually learn how to talk normally.

Later, when David finally allowed Walter to pick him up and lead him around by the hand, his language lessons began.

"Say 'n'gushih'" (mother).

"Woosh!" was the best that David could manage, even after many attempts. Nor did the pronunciation improve, no matter how many times David was asked to repeat it.

"Stanley."

"Lee-lee."

"Chick," Stanley blurted out.

"Kik."

Walter was unable to train David to say either Isaiah or Mary Jane. Whenever he mentioned their names, David pointed to the Isaiah homestead with his lips.

Out of mischievous inspiration, one day as they were passing in front of Isaiah's house, Walter abruptly stopped to show David what Isaiah looked like. Putting the back of his right hand against his mouth just underneath his nose, with his fingers curled inward to represent a mustache, Walter told David, "That's what Isaiah looks like. Now, show me what Isaiah looks like." David showed him.

With Walter's care and guidance, David's world and vocabulary grew. Until Walter came, David's world consisted of the house, the yard, the barn, the outhouse. After supper in the evening Walter took David down to the corner, and on Sundays to church.

"The corner" was the intersection of concession roads that were then little better than wagon trails. To the south and diagonally across from Rosa's lot was a large meadow serving as a pasture for Andrew Taylor's livestock. This wide-open meadow, seventy-five acres in extent, was known as Kitchi-kitgaun, "The Big Meadow."

On their first field trip to the corner there was a large herd of cows, goats, sheep, and horses pressing against the fence. The cows mooed, the horses snorted and whinnied, the sheep bleated, the goats looked for someone to assault.

"David! Say 'cow'!"

"Ming."

"No! Cow!" Walter pronounced the word slowly, and as often as he repeated it, "cow" came out as "ming" in David's mouth. At least David had a word for cow. Next was horse. "David! Say 'horse'!"

"Ming."

"No, David. 'Ming' is 'cow.' A horse is different. It has another name. What is it?"

"Ming."

A sheep and a goat were "ming." For David to be unable to distinguish the difference between horses, cows, goats, and sheep, Walter figured there must be something wrong with his perception. In the event that David couldn't tell the difference between these animals, Walter resorted to the name-call method. "David! A cow goes 'moo,' a horse whinnies 'whee-ee-ee-ee,' a sheep bleats 'baa-aa-aa-aa.'" Under questioning, David mooed, whinnied, and baa-aa-ed. There was nothing wrong with his perception.

Until Walter came home neither Rosa nor Stanley had attempted to coach David in language. Both assumed that David would never talk, as the doctor had predicted.

What led Walter to coach David? Test his intelligence? Ask him what people, animals were called? Was it to help David? Or to amuse David and himself? Likely both.

David's education went along. His father, Norman, whose nickname was Chippewaush, was "Tsibih." Rufus, the eldest brother, was "Ish-ish." John was "Back-a-haw." The Nadjiwon family that later bought and lived in the Isaiah–Mary Jane homestead was collectively "Beeyah," after Vera, the eldest daughter of Francis and Ethel Nadjiwon, a name easier for David to pronounce than Clifford, Dorothy, Ernest, or Annette.

When David talked about one of the Nadjiwons, as he often did, it was never clear to whom he was referring. Which one David was talking about was adduced by a process of elimination. "Is it Francis? Ethel? Clifford? Vera? Dorothy? Ernest?"

If David were in a mischievous mood he would say "kuh" (no) to all the names as they were submitted.

"Well! Which one? I don't know what you mean."

And David would grin slyly.

There were only two other names that David was able to manage. One was "Em," for Ambrose, whose name had been abbreviated to "Am" by everyone. Everybody in the Resime Akiwenzie family was "Em"—Florence, Marilyn, Beverley—except for Shirley, who was "Shidly-shidl."

For the names of people in the community that David couldn't pronounce, Walter taught him sign language and mimicry. David excelled in this practice; a slow learner he was not.

Every person in the community had at least one distinctive trait that set that man or woman apart from other people: voice, laugh, appearance, habit, gait. For these individuals, no name was necessary. Mime and mimicry were enough to identify anyone with an uncommon trait.

"David! This is how Tom Jones walks," and Walter lurched to show David. Walter was a mime. He went through the motions of playing the violin and piano, carrying a potato bag slung over a shoulder, walking with his hands clasped behind his back. He pursued his lips as if about to spit, twisted and twined his mouth as if trying to dislodge a sliver of meat stuck between his teeth. He whinnied, rasped, and coughed to teach David the identities of people on the reserve, even though David had not yet seen them.

Supper was reserved not only for eating but for conducting reviews. "Ahow, Daybid! Who's Johnny McLeod (David's uncle)? Andrew Taylor? Mike Lavalley? Frank Lavalley?" As Walter mentioned each name, David clasped his hands in devotion, coughed and hacked, lurched, spit, squinted, pouted, pulled an imaginary rope, or hee he h'h-hee-hee-hee'd. There was nothing wrong with David's memory.

"Maybe he's got a name for all these people in his own language that we don't understand," Walter suggested to Rosa one evening.

David took this charade more seriously than Walter or Rosa expected him to.

Each time Mary Jane came to visit, she never failed to greet David. "Ahneen, Daybid!" Unable to return her greeting, David could only look dumbly at her.

She was nonplussed one day when, after greeting David, he gestured by putting the back of his hand against his mouth and curling his fingers inward. Strange, she thought. Was David thumbing his nose at her? Mary Jane clapped the back of her own hand to her mouth. David stared at her, astonished that she was mocking him.

"Eeeeyoooh, Rosauh! Do you know what David did when I greeted him just as I came in?" And she described David's gesture. "And he kept doing it until I did the same thing. It's so cute."

"Oh my God!" Rosa gasped. "It's that Walter who put him up to that. Because David can't say Isaiah, Walter taught him to scrunch his fingers and put the back of his hand against his mouth. That's supposed to be Isaiah's mustache."

But Mary Jane wasn't offended by David's greeting of "Hello, Mustache." On the contrary, she was amused by it, taking part in the practice by returning David's salutation in the same manner.

That evening Rosa recounted how David had greeted Mary Jane and then cautioned Walter that he "shouldn't teach David such things; some people might misunderstand and hit him for insulting them." Then she turned to David and warned, "Don't do that."

Though David nodded understanding, Rosa couldn't be sure that he grasped her meaning. Walter, too, impressed on David, "Don't do that to people; that's just between us here at home." He and Rosa could only hope that David would not forget and make a face or mimic someone like Joe Jones or John Wesley, two of Cape Croker's more short-tempered WASPS.

Walter was worth listening to. He knew so much. He drew not only David's attention, but also Stanley's.

When Stanley couldn't fraction whole numbers, or tell the difference between a gerund and a participle, or recognize the appearance of a new moon and an old one, Walter sorted out these difficulties.

While Walter dispensed his grade-eight knowledge and experience helping Stanley to unravel grade-six mindbenders, David stood at his side. From these private lessons David picked up some English. "Mook" for moon, "noo mook" for new moon, "goot" for good, and "too goot" for no good. He became trilingual, speaking some Ojibway, some English, and blending these into his own language.

Weeks before Christmas Walter began to tell David and Stanley about the upcoming holiday, about Joseph taking Mary to Bethlehem where they had to sleep in a barn, like Isaiah's barn, with horses and cows. Joseph and Mary belonged to the House of David and everyone belonging to David's house had to go to Bethlehem to be counted. By the time Joseph and Mary got to Bethlehem, all the inns and hotels were full. So many people belonged to the House of David that there was no room for Joseph and Mary anywhere. They had to sleep in a barn with horses, cows, goats, and chickens. In this cold barn baby Jesus was born. David shook his head in pity for the poor "Babeesh Cwise." Some shepherds who were watching sheep in the fields were led by angels who sang in the heavens and invited them to come and see the newborn baby.

A few days later three wise men came to the barn, bringing gifts for Baby Jesus. Now, Santa Claus brings gifts to all the children in the world. Walter promised Stanley and David a Christmas tree with decorations, and asked Santa Claus to bring some presents, maybe toys.

Every night when Rosa announced "Time for bed," David asked, "Kik? Babeesh Cwise?"

After the stories, Walter led Stanley and David in prayer in preparation for the celebration of the birth of Christ, the happiest day of the year in Christendom.

For Rosa, the forthcoming season was not one of hope and joy, gifts and goodwill. She dreaded the day and the season, for it would be one of pain, a day that mocked her and her life. At times she didn't want to go through with what she had made up her mind to do, and then she remembered Mary Jane's words, "Many girlfriends," and recalled the pictures of women she had seen in Norman's trunk. Mary Jane's insinuations were insidious; they fueled Rosa's frustrations and anger with Norman's long absences. Even if she couldn't read, she would have appreciated a letter. Walter would have translated it for her. But no, not a word. Weaken, she would not.

Three days before Christmas Norman came home, happy and noisy as a lark on its return to its haunts in early spring. He greeted Stanley, put his arms around his back and patted his head. "My, you've grown. Before long you'll be old enough to go out to work." Then he took David up in his arms. "How's my boy?" he asked. "You home for Christmas?" he asked Walter. Then, without waiting for an answer, he held his hand out to Rosa to draw her to him. She resisted. "Come on, cheer up, love. I'm home. You don't have to be a widow ... at least for a few days," Norman teased.

Rosa bristled. Her Lamourandiere temper shot up. If Walter weren't in the house she would have exploded and screamed at Norman, "Get out!" Instead, she swallowed her anger and, as calmly as she could manage, said, "I want to tell you something ... alone." Without putting on a shawl or a coat, she led Norman outside.

"Yes, Norman! I may as well be a widow. As it is, I'm no better off than a widow. For you, it's easy, come and go as you want, stay away as long as you please, come back and visit me ... as if ... I were just your sleeping companion .... I don't want to live like that anymore. You're welcome to visit our boys anytime and stay, but you are not welcome in my bed .... I don't dislike you. I just don't care anymore."

"Rosauh!" Norman got no further to appeal or to argue. Rosa went back into the house, her arms folded in front of her. Norman came in a step behind, his face drawn.

Walter guessed something to be wrong but said nothing. Stanley noticed nothing unusual. David noticed nothing at all.

S E V E N

n January 2, 1927, Norman left home, and the blowing snow covered his footprints. David didn't look out the window to watch his father as he often watched Walter and Stanley. Stanley didn't interrupt his play to see his father turn the corner.

Rosa no longer wanted Norman in her life and could do without his companionship, but how she was to manage to feed, clothe, and look after David without him occupied almost all her thoughts. Suppose he, like many other men, withheld support just for spite? It was she who had asked him to leave. How could she expect him to continue to support her and their children?

Once before, when Ed had died, Rosa had gone through a similar wrenching experience of facing a future without means. The band council had come to her rescue then by granting her monthly relief. Charity was not what Rosa wanted, but beyond housework and medicine, she knew little else; she knew how to serve a husband, but herself, no.

In the old days she would have been trained to do what men did— snare rabbits and partridges, trap beaver and raccoons—to help feed herself. Except that even if she had been, such training would have done her little good now, at least not with David holding her to the house. With Walter starting to court Frances Nawash, how long could she look to him to provide for her, David, and Stanley?

As did every other mother everywhere in the world where snow fell, Rosa hated snow and winter. Each time Walter and Stanley came into the house they tracked in clods and clumps of snow; the hats and coats they took off dripped water and let loose a shower of snowflakes. Firewood brought in and piled behind the stove was covered with snow and ice that oozed and dripped water on the floor as it melted. "Stanley, wipe your boots off before you come in. Shake your coat off outside!" Even if he had been an obedient boy and followed his mother's instructions, snow still would have clung to the firewood.

Rosa spread old coats on the floor near the door to absorb the water; she wiped the floor and she scrubbed it. Snow and water created as much work for her now as David had when he was still untrained, not long before. Old coats served a purpose but they were unsightly and hazardous, tripping up David often and, on occasion, Walter and even Stanley.

While she was braiding her hair one morning, her head bent forward, Rosa saw little else but an old coat at her feet. The old coat faded and was replaced by a woven mat whose braids were wound round and round like a sweet-grass mat. The vision passed. In place of the braided mat was an ugly, old army greatcoat.

When Rosa finished braiding her hair, she took her scissors, gathered up the old coat and, after unstitching the seams, cut the garment into long strands that fell on the floor at her feet. Behind her, David watched. "I'm going to try to make a mat, David. Now don't you touch the scissors or the needle."

Afterward Rosa braided the strips from end to end, then wound them round and round and bound them with thread. What she made did not quite meet her expectations. Her mat was course, frayed, but at least it lay flat on the floor. Not good enough, it went onto the porch. What were needed were finer, prettier fabrics: dresses, slips, shirts, trousers, ties, women's stockings.

"Walter! Will you ask the priest for some old clothes?"

"Why?"

"They're for making mats."

Father Cadot always had boxes and crates of old clothing on hand donated by the good people of Toronto. Despite the need for clothing, there was little call for these garments. Father Cadot's parishioners were unwilling to wear discarded clothing; they didn't want to provide CFRB with grist for her tongue. For sure she would have something to say. "Did you see so-and-so walking around with a new hat?" Sniff! "Think's she pretty good, her, acting like a White Woman. She should know that hat's been worn for years." Sniff. Or she'd say, "Did you see so-and-so walking away from the priest's house with a box full of stuff ... doesn't need all that stuff, her. People like that take all the good stuff, and don't leave any for the people that really need it." Sniff.

Father Cadot was pleased to dispense charity—not only fabric, but sermons to the spirit as well. However, he was more than a little curious as to the quantity of old dresses that Walter was picking out, many of which were too large for Rosa. Walter told him of Rosa's plan.

"Let your mother know that I'd like some mats for the house and the church. I'll pay her." There was little that Father Cadot liked better than to talk, and for people to like him as much as he liked them. But as many people as there were in the parish, and despite his invitation that "my door is always open, don't be shy," none came to visit him. After mass and at "pie socials" he sought to draw conversation, but the most that he elicited from his attempts were "Yes, Fauder!" "No, Fauder!" "Maybe, Fauder!" "I don't know, Fauder!" laconic answers that fell far short of being conversation. Now frail and near the end of his missionary days, Father Cadot longed for some sign or word of affection from his parishioners, even a short visit. Within months he would be relieved of his duties and retired to an old-age home for priests in Guelph. To know that he was liked as well as respected would be a great comfort for him in the twilight of his life. Father Cadot asked Walter directly why people didn't talk to him or visit him. Didn't they like him?

"Quite the contrary, Father," Walter assured Father Cadot. Then, very deliberately, measuring his words, Walter explained, "You know so much more than any of us do, Father. We're afraid that what we say may sound stupid or unimportant."

"But I've never put down any man's opinion," Father protested.

"That may well be," Walter paused, looked the priest straight in the eye to search for any hint of hurt, then went on, "Father! We're conditioned to listen. You tell us to listen! Our teachers tell us to listen! Our parents tell us to listen! You don't have to listen! You know more than anyone else in this community ... and if you could only listen to yourself, see yourself ... you'd understand."

Never had Father Cadot looked on the priest–parishioner relationship in that way. The priest conducted mass on a raised platform. When he delivered a sermon, he talked down at his parishioners; people looked up at him. The altar railing separated the priest from the congregation. As a Jesuit, Father Cadot had thirteen years of formal training; some people in the congregation may have reached grade eight.

In his twelve years at Cape Croker, Father Cadot had not been able to cross the barrier he had erected from the time he first took up his duties as pastor of St. Mary's, replacing Father Artus, who had been reassigned. Father Cadot had numerous opportunities to win converts from the many Methodists and non-churchgoers without a minister of their own, who flocked to the Catholic Church services. With them in the congregation, Father Cadot didn't mince words but came right out and told them that the Catholic Church was the only true church and that all other churches were false. As Reverend Peter Jones, an Anishinaubae convert and Methodist missionary, had urged the Saugeen-Nawaush people seventy to eighty years earlier to cast aside their pagan beliefs and practices, so now Father Cadot railed against understandings, ceremonies, and celebrations as sinful: offering tobacco in thanksgiving to birds and animals killed; offering food to departed ancestors on their graves; smoking the pipe of peace to commence public and religious events, purification ceremonies, powwows, first kill and naming celebrations. By the time Father Cadot was appointed resident missionary at Cape Croker, none of the ceremonies or festivals were celebrated in public, not even on the sly. He saw to it that Indian beliefs, ceremonies, and festivals would not make a comeback in his parishioners' lives. And, while Father Cadot did not remonstrate against speaking the native language, he recommended the adoption of English for advancement. Even private visits from Methodists were taken as opportunities to proselytize, as Tom Jones, later a super Orangeman, discovered. Tom went to visit the priest. Father Cadot sat him down, gave him a lesson in catechism, and then presented him with a book, *On Faith*. But that's the way Father Cadot was, committed to the fulfillment of his mission to spread the good news to the whole world.

Walter took home a box of old dresses to his mother. Rosa wound and rewound the strips of cloth that she had cut, braided and rebraided the strands until she made mats that were round and oval and square and many-colored, and that satisfied her standards.

One morning in early spring David came downstairs and, without sitting down at the table as he usually did to await breakfast, he put his coat and hat on. "Choo-a," he said, then went out. Up to this time, he had only accompanied Stanley. It was the first time David had gone to the outhouse on his own, without being led.

A miracle, Rosa thought. If only it were to last, then there'd be reason for celebration and thanksgiving. Until the miracle was reenacted and repeated it could not be accepted as anything more than a one-shot affair.

When David came back five minutes later, his face was aglow with triumph as a boy who had scored a goal or a run to help his team win a game. "Choo-a! Choo-a!" he repeated. Walter and Stanley were both at the table. They made a big to-do about David's feat, and indeed it was. "That's the boy! You're a man now. You can do things by yourself." It had taken David nearly seven years to do what other children were able to do in half that time.

A month later Rosa was sure, sure enough to mention David's development to Mary Jane, adding, "I hope he's finally learned. Maybe now we can all have a little rest now and then during the day, and not have to look after him every minute."

Mary Jane agreed that it must have been taxing and trying washing clothes more often than any other woman on the reserve. Seeing the mats, Mary Jane asked, "So many mats, Rosauh! What are you going to do with all of them?"

"Priest wants them," Rosa answered.

"I'd like some myself. Our floor is so cold, and maybe mats can save the floor and muffle the infernal squeak of that rocking chair when Isaiah rocks. ... How much is that priest going to give you?" Learning that Rosa didn't have the faintest notion of what to charge the priest, Mary Jane encouraged her to charge him enough. "He's got money. Gets it free from his collections every Sunday."

Placing a value on her work had never entered Rosa's mind until Mary Jane mentioned it. Put on the spot, she looked at the mats. They were made out of old fabrics that had been discarded and had no value. How could she charge for them? Besides, anyone could make them.

"Tau! Hau! Rosauh!" Mary Jane persisted, "they're not useless old rags anymore. What would you pay for mats like these in Colpoy's or Wiarton? ... fifty cents at least. I wouldn't take any less than that."

To receive $2 for three mats from the priest was like a windfall, a godsend. Walter, who had delivered the mats, in addition to the money, brought word that the priest wanted more mats. Also, Father Cadot wanted to know if the amount he paid was enough.

Her mats were worth something but no one knew how much, not even a smart, educated man such as the priest. Word spread throughout the community that Rosa made mats. Orders came in. When asked how much she wanted for them, Rosa invariably put the onus for determining a fair price on the buyer. "It's up to you." This spared Rosa the embarrassment she would suffer if she set too high a price for her product and earned herself the reputation of being greedy; customers were equally reluctant to tender an amount that would reveal them to be cheapskates. Bargaining was a ticklish process: fairness to the vendor and fairness to the purchaser.

Of course, CFRB got wind of Rosa's mat-making. To the fact that Rosa was making mats, CFRB added, "Rosa must be making money." When the righteous of the reserve heard the rumor, they sniffed, "Rosa ought not be doing what she's doing. Someone could have worn those dresses that she cut up. Norman's working. She should have enough money." But if not for Walter's help and Norman's support payments, Rosa eventually would have had to go to band council for relief and look to neighbors for handouts. What Rosa made from the sale of her mats would today be regarded as "pin money," except that there were no knickknacks for her to buy. What little Rosa made—pennies, nickels, dimes, quarters—she stored in a little bag she kept tucked under her pillow. It would be there someday when she needed it.

It only had been a question of time before Stanley was old enough to leave home; he'd been talking about it for the past three years. Now nearly sixteen, the magic age, and having completed grade eight, he felt ready and prepared to take his place among men in the world. He was leaving the nest, not to get away from David but because it was the thing to do. He no longer resented his young brother. Ever since Walter had come home and taken over the chores he had reluctantly shouldered, Stanley's attitude toward David had mellowed. He now concentrated his hostility toward his father for having abandoned them. He often said within David's hearing that "Norman's no good!" David, of course, repeated Stanley's sentiments, but without the rancor, "Tsihib too goot!"

"David! Don't say that! It's not nice," Rosa forbade both David and Stanley.

At first Stanley talked about working in Depot Harbour with the other Cape Croker men, but Walter talked him out of going there. "Work's too hard. You'd never last!" he said, having Stanley's size in mind. "You'd be better off going to Brampton or Niagara Falls. There's lots of work there."

Walter's experience and advice carried enough weight to persuade Stanley to change his course from Parry Island to Brampton and points south. Brampton now became the city of opportunity and destiny. With $15 in his pocket, given to him by Rosa and Walter, Stanley set out with high hopes. He did not, as did Dick Whittington, come upon and take with him a stray cat to bring him fame and fortune.

Even before Stanley turned the corner, Rosa was already fretting. "He's so small. He doesn't look as if he's more than twelve years old. Nobody will give him a job. Maybe he'll spend all that money ... maybe somebody will pick on him and take his money away from him."

"Oh, Mother, you worry too much. Trust in the Lord." Walter reminded Rosa to set her mind at ease. Walter trusted wholeheartedly in the Lord, and he expected everyone else to as well. Except that Rosa wasn't as sure as Walter that the Lord exercised such control over life and human fortunes that He would care for and safeguard Stanley. She was more inclined to believe that the Lord provided all that humans needed, and that men and women created their own personal worlds and forged their own fortunes and misfortunes. Still, Rosa felt twinges of guilt for doubting the goodness and mercy of God.

Walter was solid, solid as the rock upon which Christ promised Peter that He would build His church. But when he looked at Frances Nawash and she returned his gaze, Walter's knees shook and buckled.

Frances Nawash, a direct descendent of one of the oldest families on the reserve, was born Catholic, baptized as such, and received instructions in the faith in preparation for her first communion. She and her mother, Kitchi-Low-C (Big Lucy), were devout Catholics until the mother fell in love with Edgar Jones, a Protestant, and son of C.K. Jones. The courtship and marriage performed in the Methodist church caused a scandal in both congregations and another rift in the Jones family. For her trespasses Kitchi-Low-C was denied the sacraments. Unwelcome in the fold, Kitchi-Low-C quit going to the services. Following her mother's example, Frances stayed away from church.

Within a few years most people forgot that Kitchi-Low-C and Frances were originally Catholics, assuming that they were and had always been Protestants who went to church only when they felt like it. For all practical purposes Frances was "a Protestant."

As a good Catholic boy Walter ought not to have given Frances a second look or a second thought, but one look was all that he took and he was smitten. He tried, but he couldn't put Frances out of his mind. He too assumed that Frances, who was born, baptized, and practicing her faith while he was at residential school in Spanish, was a Protestant.

Deeply troubled by his love for Frances and his love for the church, Walter sought some answer, some consolation from Rosa. As far as she knew, Frances had been born and raised Catholic. What her status was in the eyes of the church only a priest would know. Rosa told Walter that the Nawashes were Catholic and that he should check with the priest.

Walter and Frances went to the manse to find out what Frances's status was within the church. At the same time, the visit would give Walter a chance to meet the new parish priest, Father Oscar Labelle, S.J.

"I'm Walter Johnston, Father, one of your parishioners. Frances Nawash and I want to get married."

"Is the girl in a family way?" the young priest asked darkly.

"No, she isn't," Walter bristled.

"Is she a member of this congregation?"

"Yes, she is," Walter answered.

"Can't she answer for herself?" Father demanded.

"She's shy and she doesn't speak much English," Walter explained.

"Then how could she have received communion without knowing English?" Father pressed on.

"Because Father Cadot spoke our language."

"When were you thinking of getting married?"

"Next year, sometime."

"Very well! What's your name?" Father asked, his tone warmer.

"Frances Nawash."

"Parents?"

"Low-C and Edgar Jones." Father jotted the answers down in a little black notebook.

"Very well. Thank you for letting me know in ample time."

The following Sunday after mass Father Labelle called Walter into the manse; he wore a foreboding frown. "I don't know if you're trying to pull a fast one or not but I can find no record of Frances Nawash in the baptismal or First Communion journals. She wasn't at church today as far as I could see. And her mother is a Jones, is she not? ... and the Joneses are Protestants, are they not?"

Walter was taken aback by the new priest's attitude and sharp tone. Weren't priests supposed to be compassionate, like Christ? He didn't know what to say except, "The Nawashes had always been Catholic. Frances's mother is a Catholic, Frances's father, long deceased, was a Catholic. It should be in the records."

"Don't argue with me," Father said pointedly. "Who's in charge of this parish anyway?"

What to do? The new priest was not like Father Cadot. With Cadot he would have been able to talk about it.

Walter was both hurt and upset by Father Labelle's hard-line attitude. As a staunch Catholic he wanted to live the Mother Church's teachings and laws. Under no circumstances would he flout church laws. He didn't want to be an outcast in this community and in the congregation as Alvin and Suzanee were outcasts by their open defiance of their respective pastors and congregations.

"I don't know what to do, Mother," Walter told Rosa.

Rosa didn't know what comfort she could offer other than the proverbial, "I'm sure things will work out."

While Walter was going through this spiritual hell, Rufus wrote that he was married to Mary Lafreniere, a good Catholic girl, and that he was about to become a father. Rosa was to become a grandmother, Walter an uncle. Lucky man, Walter thought as he read the letter. Things were going well for Rufus.

Walter read the letter to his mother, first in English, and then translated it.

"What do you want me to tell him?" Walter asked.

There was so much to tell, so many events had taken place since Rufus had left twelve years before. Neither he nor Bobby had come home in all that time. Rosa didn't know where to begin. She asked Walter to tell Rufus that David was growing bigger and that Stanley was now gone from home to work, no one knew where. Lastly, Rosa instructed Walter to tell Rufus that she had him and Bobby in her mind every day.

Following this letter, the first that Rosa had received from Rufus, correspondence was fairly regular. Yet, despite her questions, Rufus offered no explanations as to why neither he nor Bobby had come home or written in all the time they had been away. In the spring Rufus wrote that there wasn't as much work in Depot Harbour as in previous years. Less work made it tough for everyone. Everybody suspected that the shipowners were diverting their freight elsewhere. Many people were laid off and were angry. The bosses explained that there was less work. There were strange goings-on on the reserve. A wolf was heard to be howling in the swamps of Parry Island, but the older people were sure that it was not a real wolf because its howl did not resemble that of a real wolf. More likely it was the Bear-walker, they said. Ever since, people have been staying close to their homes at night, guns loaded and leaning on a wall near the door, ready for instant use.

Eventually Frances Nawash's church status was straightened out. During one of Father Cadot's absences, Baby Frances, then less than a month old, had suffered an asthma attack so severe that she was not expected to survive. Her mother, Kitchi-Low-C, gave her a conditional baptism according to church instruction. However, she neglected to tell the priest what she had done, assuming that nothing further needed to be done.

Father Labelle was thorough. He baptized Frances, and prepared her to receive Holy Communion and confirmation. Walter and Frances had to postpone their wedding until Frances received communion and confirmation at the hands of the bishop, who came to the church once every four years to administer confirmation. By the grace of God, they only had to wait two years to get married, the bishop having visited the parish two years previously.

Later that spring George Keeshig, Christine's son, Rosa's nephew, arrived at the house with word that "Bobby's had an accident; he's dead. Louis and Rufus want you to go right away …. I'll take you."

"Eeeyoooh! My Bobby!" Rosa gasped, and her gasp turned into a cry. "My Bobby! My Bobby!" Images of Bobby, seven years old, tears in his eyes, getting on board the buggy to Wiarton where he was to take the train that would bring him to Spanish flashed in her mind; and another image of him coming into the house upon his return home from Spanish, a strapping youth of sixteen who filled the door frame. Then, an image of Bobby leaving again.

In all, she had known him as part of her life for only seven years; she should have been part of his life, he part of hers, for at least sixteen years, and maybe more. But the fates had intervened. Her husband had died; she had remarried. The Indian agent and the church decided that a residential school was better suited and equipped to raise and nurture her children than she could ever be. She was not as fit to look after Bobby as was the clergy or an institution.

From Cape Croker to Parry Island Rosa relived the pains of what was and what would never be. She held David and listened to Walter's words of comfort without much solace.

At the funeral Rosa met her daughter-in-law, me, and Rufus's in-laws, Joe and Philomene Lafreniere, but she scarcely took notice of them. Beside her, David looked on.

After the funeral, on the way home, Walter suggested to his mother, to lighten her grief, that maybe it was better that Bobby died quickly, crushed by a sling of flour that fell on him when the cable on a crane broke. He didn't tell her that it had been only a question of time before Bobby's temper, which matched his prodigious strength, would have gotten the better of him. According to Walter, who had worked with Rufus and Bobby in Depot Harbour earlier on, Bobby was the only man who could lift a rock that lay to one side of the Parry Island Council Hall, a rock estimated to weight over five hundred pounds. Frank Nadjiwon and Gregor Keeshig could bear this out.

For days afterward David had a great deal to talk about with his mother and Walter. He talked about the trip and the scene in the graveyard, and the strangers who shook his hand, gave him sandwiches, and patted him on the head.

But Rosa remembered little of the trip. From start to finish her mind was occupied by the images of Bobby. Once before he had been taken from her by men; now he had been taken by God.

While Walter was waiting for the bishop to make his next visit, and was constructing a log house, John came home, driven back by the Depression and the rigors of Jesuit life.

When John walked into the house wearing a suit, white shirt, and tie instead of black clerical garb, Walter and Rosa were overjoyed to see him, yet curious to know what had brought him home long before they'd expected to see him.

"Priests give you a holiday?" Walter asked John.

"No ... I quit ... a few years ago," John explained slowly. "Three years was long enough for me. I was asked to leave after I got caught imitating the Master of Novices. I was going to quit anyway," and he paused, looked at his mother and brother. "I hope you're not too disappointed. It's a hard life." He trailed off and then, encouraged by his mother's reaction, "I'm glad you're home," John went on. He explained that, instead of coming home as he had intended, he went from city to city in the northern United States and southern Ontario looking for work but finding little except temporary jobs. After wandering about like a hobo, he decided to come home, ready to face whatever people thought of his expulsion from the Jesuit Order. "I wasn't religious enough, Mom ... Walter. With my attitude, 'You're not worthy,' Father Superior said."

John's homecoming was like the return of the prodigal son. Rosa cooked what John asked for: fried salt pork, mashed potatoes, gravy, and fried bread. As they waited for the meal to be cooked, they exchanged stories of their lives. Walter and Rosa told John of

Bobby's death, Norman's long absences, Rufus's marriage, and all the events that had taken place on the reserve: who got married and who died, and the appointment of a new priest. In turn, John recounted his own life and travels. Following his expulsion from the novitiate in Guelph, Ontario, he went from there to Detroit and to Chicago, riding the freights, looking for work, and finding little. Several times he thought that he'd be hired for good jobs, but as soon as prospective employers in Toronto learned that he was a Catholic and had studied for the priesthood, they turned him down. Prejudice was then rife in Toronto the Good; good for White Anglo-Saxon Protestants. It was easier to lie about one's religious background. And by lying, John finally obtained a job in Toronto, one that would be permanent. But after two years, John and the entire staff were laid off. The company had gone bankrupt. For the next year and a half he rode the rails again, with hoboes who were also looking for work.

"You couldn't have come home at a better time. I don't know why there's no work outside," Walter wondered. "There's no unemployment here. Just about everybody that wants to work is working; fishing, gardening, cutting pulpwood, and a few are making a pretty good living by farming. Tom Jones is buying all the fish that he can get his hands on and reselling them outside. Gudoohn (Peter Akiwenzie) is looking for a man to help on his farm and with his fishing. You should go see him."

From the moment that John came into the house, David hid behind his mother, stealing looks at John, to him a stranger. Each time that John caught him looking, he made faces at David, saying, "I can see you" and "peekaboo." But his antics did little except frighten David.

When Rosa mentioned Walter's forthcoming marriage, their conversation gravitated toward the care of Rosa and David. Walter had intended to look after and care for their mother and David in their new homestead upon his marriage. John immediately volunteered to look after them. He was single, without responsibilities.

The very next day John went to Gudoohn and was hired immediately as a farmhand, working with cows and horses, cutting wood, fishing, and doing whatever chores his employer assigned him to do for $10 a week, with room and board included. John was a misfit, miscast. He should have been an actor to make use of his talents for mimicry and dialects; he should have been a professional musician with his ability to play the organ, piano, violin, clarinet, piccolo, flute; or an athlete, with his gift for sports. But there was no theater, no orchestra, no ball club to play for. There was little for John to do except fish and hew wood. Besides, earning a living by these pastimes wasn't on anybody's agenda.

After Walter got married, and he and Frances settled in their home, John came home to live with and care for his mother and brother. For a few evenings he stayed home, keeping his mother and David company, like a dutiful son. But soon his feet got itchy. He longed for action. John was too young to settle in a chair and watch the cattle graze in the Big Meadow, or talk all evening with his mother as she wove mats, while David sat, sometimes for hours, chewing his tongue and staring at the floor in front of him.

Following a few days of twiddling his thumbs, John went to Isaiah's place, asked the old man for some old horseshoes that were no longer serviceable for horses ... and two iron stakes.

"What do you want old horseshoes for?" the old man naturally asked.

John explained that he intended to play a game with them. "A game?" Isaiah was curious how one could play with horseshoes. John told the old man, and promised to show him how the game was played. They found six horseshoes in Isaiah's toolshed and forge, and borrowed two surveyor's stakes from the corners of the adjoining properties. John drove the stakes fifteen paces apart, beside and parallel to the road that ran by Rosa's house. Then he showed Isaiah how to pitch the shoes, while Rosa, Mary Jane, and David looked on.

During the match between John and Isaiah, David did not once take his eyes off the players or the shoes that arched through the air. He bent his body to influence the course of the shoes. And when a shoe struck a stake with a resounding clang, and sometimes with a flare of sparks, David straightened up, clapped his hands, and shouted "Chau-koo!"

Isaiah played until his wife decided that he might throw his arm out, suffer a hernia, or something worse. He could come back the next day, Mary Jane told him. The old man grumbled as he was led away, and stuffed a pinch of plug into the pouch of his lower lip.

It was too soon to call the game. John was just warming up. He turned to David. "Do you want to play?"

More than willing, David grinned, then nodded. It was the first time that he'd ever been asked to play a game.

Giving David three horseshoes, John explained the game and showed David how to pitch shoes. David watched intently. "Your turn." Just as he had seen his brother do, David took his place on one side of the stake and put his feet together, he brought the shoe near his face, lining it up with the other stake. David was the image of concentration, standing there poised, ready to uncoil. Then he stepped forward, swinging his arm. The horseshoe sailed a good fifty paces beyond the target stake.

"Tau! Hau!" John exclaimed in awe and amusement. He looked at David, who looked frightened, ready for a scolding.

"Hey!" John exclaimed, "you're not supposed to throw them away! Not too hard! You might kill some poor little snake."

John and David played until dark. No teacher ever had a more dedicated pupil than did John; and no student a more patient teacher than David.

The next day, after John had gone to work, David took the horseshoes and played. Rosa sat on the front doorstep watching. Back and forth between the two stakes David walked, pitching shoes, some that fell too short and some that fell wide, and still others that fell too long of the mark and stake. When David struck the stake quite by luck and made the stake ring, he shouted, "Chau-koo!" For David, striking the stake was the whole point of horseshoes: to make the shoe and the stake crash and bang.

There was a price that David had to pay for this game. In pitching horseshoes, David struck the back of his leg from time to time, whenever his left leg stepped slightly out of line. Then David would wince in pain.

"You'd better put those away ... too dangerous!" Rosa warned David while examined his bruise. But David didn't put the shoes down until his fingers were nearly raw and his arm was weary.

After supper, Isaiah and Alvin came over to play a match with

John and David. Rosa, Mary Jane, and Suzanee made up the spectators' gallery. Even before David tossed the first shoe, Isaiah and Alvin, told of David's wildness, stood well back to one side of the stake. "Watch out! Duck!" they called out, and covered their heads in mock fear whenever David pitched a shoe. John and David were well behind in the score, but it didn't faze them one bit.

By the fourth game David was frustrated. He had come nowhere near to hitting the stake. "Okay, David! Take your time!" John encouraged him. David aimed. He pitched the horseshoe hard and fast, almost parallel to the ground. The horseshoe struck the stake dead on with a resounding "clang," spun, and then flew off at an angle, striking Isaiah, who had been standing a dozen paces to one side, full in the chest. He grunted, "Ooph!" and fell back. Both Rosa and Mary Jane gasped. They rushed to Isaiah's side, expecting the worst, and knelt anxiously beside the stricken old man. John, Alvin, and Suzanee looked on, apprehensive. Isaiah bent forward, coughing and hacking, holding his chest at the same time. John ran into the house to fetch a dipper of water. When he came back moments later, the old man was still doubled over, coughing. Mary Jane, herself ashen in alarm, tilted her husband's head back and, putting the dipper to his mouth, poured the water until the old man sputtered and turned his head aside. Then she forced him to his back and unbuttoned his shirt to examine the extent of his injury.

The next instant Isaiah twisted, tossed his head to one side, and threw up. Mary Jane wailed, "My poor Isaiah!" But just as quickly Isaiah straightened up. He spat, he sputtered, he coughed, he cleared his throat.

"Are you alright?" they all wanted to know.

"Plug went down the wrong pipe," Isaiah wheezed. He dug into his back pocket for his Club chewing tobacco. He bit off another piece to replenish what he had swallowed.

"Aaaah!" Mary Jane growled, "serves you right! That tobacco's going to kill you someday."

David was hooked; he became a horseshoe addict. Over the next while he pitched horseshoes until he had acquired a modicum of control over his arms and feet, and was able to govern the strength of his arm so he could cast a shoe in the vicinity of the stake. And best, he could play with Back-a-haw, as he called John ... and he could play alone.

There was no need for Rosa to call for him to know where David was. She heard the clank of metal and his cries of triumph, "Chau-koo!"

For John, pitching horseshoes was a pleasant way to spend an hour once or twice a week, but not every night. There were better things to do, except that there was no recreation on the reserve. It was all work, prayer, and attending the meetings of council.

Once a week Catholics went to church to hear the word of God delivered by the new priest, Father Labelle, S.J. Worship should have been a happy occasion, but more often than not, it frightened and unsettled some of the parishioners. Rufus once observed to Walter that God must be perpetually offended. Cape Croker's trespasses alone would be enough to darken God's mood. Jim Proulx was unsettled by Labelle's sermon about Judgment Day. Johnny McLeod, whom Jim frequently accompanied to church, was not feeling well enough to go to mass on one particular Sunday. As a favor, he asked Jim to stop by after service to tell him what the priest had said. Because of his limited English, Jim had difficulty understanding the sermon in its entirety, but told Johnny as much as he grasped. "Johnny, the idea of standing in front of God, being judged, scares hell out of me. I don't understand English too good, me. I might give the wrong answer and end up in the wrong place. Johnny, do they have interpreters ... where'd you get judged anyway?"

For entertainment people attended the monthly council meetings, which were particularly enjoyable when Elastus Sky or Levi Chegahno took issue with council. But the give and take between the band membership and its council was changing. Years earlier, when the Indians still governed themselves, the chief exercised real leadership, in consultation with the council of elders, which consisted of the eldest members of each clan, men and women. The chief was "ogimauh," the person who counted many followers, or the one whom many followed. The chief led the way, took first risks and first responsibilities. But now the chief was just a figurehead, the council had no authority. Authority and power rested with the Indian agent.

Still, band members spoke to the council, soliciting and expecting favors. During one of these council meetings the band council secretary failed to attend. After waiting for an hour, the chief and Indian agent asked for a volunteer to take the minutes of the meeting. Walter finally volunteered, and was duly sworn in. At the next meeting the incumbent band secretary resigned.

As band secretary, Walter received a small stipend. It wasn't much, $2, but it was something. Better than nothing. Like many others who had come from the outside world, Walter scrambled and scratched, working for Andrew Taylor and for Resime Akiwenzie whenever these farmers needed help. For his labor Walter received a small roast at hog slaughtering, or a large basket of vegetables. The appointment as band secretary, along with its small stipend, came when Walter most needed it.

Another man to return to the reserve was Lennox Johnston, a cousin to Walter and John and all the Johnstons. He too was a victim of the lean times that had overtaken London, Ontario. He had gone to London as a musician after World War I, believing that he could make a living as a violinist arranger for that city's philharmonic orchestra. From his experience as a member of one of the prominent brass bands in England, no one could say for sure whether it was the Coldstream Guards or the Grenadier Guards, Lennox was confident that he could make a career of music in Canada. Someone told him that London, Ontario, was cultured; its citizens attended operas, plays, symphony concerts, and poetry readings, and visited art galleries where they discussed paintings and "objets d'art." Alas, the citizens of London were about as cultured as wild prunes, preferring the new sounds of the big band era that was just in its infancy, and worse still, they were stamping and swinging to "square-dance music." Reluctantly, Lennox learned to play country music, "jigs and reels," and to play fox-trots and Charlestons and polkas with his clarinet and saxophone. Nearly broke, Lennox came home to a store that his father had built.

Cape Croker, home, Lennox remembered, a lively place before the war, with its own band and orchestra, many musicians, note-reading players and play-by-ear fiddlers, banjo pluckers, and bass fiddlers.

There was the North Star Club, which sponsored hockey, soccer, and baseball teams. The Cape Croker that Lennox came home to was without life, like a graveyard or even a funeral parlor. There was no orchestra, no band, though there were musicians aplenty, trained by Miss Moffat. There were no ball teams, no sports, nothing; not like in the old days. The North Star Club was dormant, maybe even defunct. Lennox didn't know that the North Star Club was merely in limbo. Every once in a while half a dozen or so young men in their late teens and early twenties, inspired by boredom, would meet in someone's house to revive the club, elect officers, and redraft the constitution and the regulations. Later in the evening, when a steering committee was appointed to look into fund-raising, enthusiasm waned, and the North Star Club expired once more after a short but enthusiastic resurrection. Lennox needed Cape Croker just as much as Cape Croker needed Lennox. Cape Croker needed to be born again. Cape Croker needed new blood.

New blood flowed.

Besides Father Cadot's departure, C.K. Jones' term as chief, which began on the day of his birth in 1854, came to an end. Some people snorted when they heard that old C.K. claimed he was a chief from the day of his birth. They refused to recognize that if he was hereditary chief, as he claimed, then he must have been born as such. He was now seventy-nine years of age. Oliver Johnson, who described himself as a misshapen, gnarled old cedar tree but sound throughout, defeated C.K. in the elections. The former chief retired to his home at "The Point" to tend to his vegetable garden and his beloved watermelons.

The new chief was tall, thin, and angular. Like Lennox, he was a musician, a superb pianist whose calling was not much in demand. He practiced and composed at home for his own amusement. Oliver would have played all day for nothing except that his family would have had nothing to eat or wear. There was no money in music, only in cutting wood and fishing.

When Lennox came home to take over the family store, he wanted to continue playing music, not in private but in public. Before he did anything, Lennox called on Oliver to discuss assembling an orchestra. They recruited John Bucket (Akiwenzie), a trumpeter, to join them. Russel Elliott and Fred Lavalley alternated as drummer and, until a guitarist was trained, would have to get along without a rhythm section. In the meantime, they would conscript Alfred Jones whenever he had all eight strings for his guitar, which was not too often.

A five-piece orchestra, the minimum. It wasn't much, but it was a start. In time, as more musicians were trained and served a three- to four-year apprenticeship in the brass band, more players would be enlisted to the orchestra. It was possible that Lennox would have a ten- to twelve-piece orchestra, as he dreamed.

From the attic of Public School One, Lennox retrieved instruments that had lain unused and unpolished since Miss Moffat had retired. He polished them until they gleamed and shone. At nights Lennox taught music and conducted practices, while his bread remained unsold and got stale.

Within two years, Lennox's brass band played Sousa's marches. Keen-eared, Lennox could hear mistakes committed by his musicians while he was playing his saxophone. In the middle of a passage, he would remove his instrument from his lips and pause until every member of his band had stopped. Then, in his nasal tone, and knowing full well who had messed up the passage, he prefaced his explanation with, "See! Someone strayed from the passage. See! The beat isn't tum, de tum, tum; instead, it goes tum, de tum. Alright! Let's do that again. Ahow. One, two, t'ree!"

Religion soon intervened in Lennox's dreams of playing at dances and making enough money to earn a decent living from music. Father Labelle condemned dances as occasions of sin, when men and women drank, weakening their inhibitions and clawing at and clinging to one another in lust. Lennox listened to the sermons and disclaimed any guilt for what any of the dancers may have committed during a dance. He had to make a living.

Father Labelle and the Catholic Church weren't the only impediments for Lennox. Both Catholics and Protestants were becoming super-Catholic and super-Protestant. Several Catholics joined the Knights of Columbus. Not to be outdone, several Protestants joined the Masonic Lodge. Someone said something that offended the other's sensitivities—no one can remember who, whether it was a

Catholic or a Protestant—and the Protestant members formed their own brass band. Cape Croker had two brass bands divided along religious lines, but it had one orchestra with both Catholics and Protestants.

But come a rare dance to celebrate a wedding, Catholics and Protestants, forgetting their religious differences, danced with one another, young men and women clawed and clung to each other, with no room for the Holy Spirit between them.

In his own quiet, slow, methodical way, Lennox restored some life and spirit into the community that had long languished. The rest of the country outside the reserve had little to cheer it. But then the financial soothsayers promised an improved economy. Soon the country would be out of the Depression. They sang and played "Happy Days Are Here Again."

It was during the summer that the North Star Club, which had been in limbo for some years, was revived. The club was reconstituted with the help of Walter, who drafted a new constitution with high-sounding, fancy legal jargon that proclaimed noble and lofty ideals, with numerous whereases and whereuntos and wheretofores to give the document respectability.

The club membership was inspired to sponsor a dance, with music provided by the Lennox Johnston Orchestra. From the proceeds of the dance the club bought a soccer ball. In another burst of enthusiasm the membership named their soccer club the Cape Croker North Stars, and made plans to form a soccer league in Bruce County. The club elected John a captain of the team, and entrusted him with custody of the ball.

As custodian, John took the ball home and delivered it every evening to the ball park for practice. At home, full of energy, John cut down two poplar saplings and erected them as goalposts on the south side of the barn, which served as a backstop. With the goalposts in place, John practiced in earnest. On the sidelines, David watched with equal earnestness. To dribble and kick the ball as Back-a-haw did looked easy.

"Come on, David! You want to try?" The invitation was welcome beyond words.

But that ball was not as easy to kick as it appeared, even when it rested on the ground. The field was uneven. David stepped back a few paces, as he had seen his brother do, lining up the ball in free-kick fashion. He ran forward. He kicked the ball, tripped. On picking himself up, David pointed at his feet, muttering "bitches" (his word for feet derived from "beetcheen," meaning "put your socks, shoes on"). He tried again with less recklessness, but as he swung his leg forward, David kicked the ground, sending clumps of grass and clods of soil upward and himself pitching headlong to the ground.

"David!" John called out. "You're going to wear out your shoes!" And he made all sorts of comments to keep David in good humor. "You'll hurt the flowers. Don't get mad at the weeds; they didn't do anything. You broke this poor cricket's house. Try again. Not too hard. Here, I'll show you again."

When John went to work, David spent his days pitching horseshoes and kicking the soccer ball. It took some days, but David tripped less often and could drive the ball against the wall of the barn with a "whumph." And he frequently kicked the ball over the roof of the barn. Within a few days David acted as if the ball belonged to him. Until then, John had taken the ball with him after the evening meal to practice. It was routine, almost a ritual, for John to wash, comb his hair, splash cologne on his face, and put on a shirt and tie before going out evenings. At his side David watched. He too received a splash of cologne.

One evening, as John took the ball from its resting place, David ran forward, put his hands around the ball, and pulled. "Kuh! Kuh!" (No! No!).

"Don't, David. It's not yours. It's not mine. It belongs to the ball club, do you understand?" John asked. "I'll bring it back."

Rosa added, "You've had the ball all day; you'll have it again tomorrow. You've had it long enough."

Deep within David's throat came sounds of whimpering, "Kuh! Kuh!" Then he made motions with his hands to indicate that he wanted to go with John.

"No, you can't go!" his mother said.

"One of these days I'll take you with me," John promised to pacify David, without knowing if his brother would understand.

After John left, David sat on his chair chewing on his tongue and staring at the floor in grief.

In the morning his beloved ball was back where it belonged. David took the ball and hung on to it, as if afraid that John would take it with him once more.

David practiced. In his memory he heard John say, "Attaboy, David. Bet you can kick that ball harder than anybody else. Someday you'll play with the men."

In one of his practices, David kicked the ball against the wall of the barn, just under the eaves. The ball didn't come back down. It stuck up there. Magic. It was fixed to the side of the barn, like the moon is suspended in the sky. David's face and eyes were as bright as those of a child who had just seen a magician pull a rabbit out of a hat.

Laughing and giggling, David ran back to the house. "Woosh! Woosh!" he cried, at the same time tugging at Rosa's sleeve to draw her along with him. Rosa got up and followed David, who raced ahead to the barn. David waited beside the barn, pointing upward, and grinning broadly.

"How did you get that ball up there?" Rosa asked.

David pointed to his foot.

"You kicked that ball up there?"

David nodded.

With a slender sapling that David fetched for her, Rosa pried the ball loose from the nail upon which it had been impaled. The ball fell to the ground, limp, without bounce. David picked up the flaccid ball. As he held it, David looked as if he were about to cry.

Rosa put her arm around David's shoulder. "Don't feel too bad. The ball can be fixed. Maybe John can get you another one."

Together they walked back to the house. Rosa returned to her mat-making. David sat on the doorstep with the limp ball on his lap, not knowing what to make of its lifelessness. He patted and caressed the ball, as if patting and caressing it would resurrect it to fullness.

"I wonder what John's going to say when he gets home tonight," Rosa wondered aloud. "I hope he doesn't get too angry."

David looked up in alarm. Vague memories of Stanley growling at him and shaking him stirred in his mind. When his mother wasn't looking, David edged away.

But Rosa heard the scuffle of feet and rose from her chair. From the front doorway she saw David go into the cedar grove in the next lot. A little later David came back and went to his chair to brood.

As soon as John came home, Rosa gave him the bad news, and described what David did after the accident. David listened. Instead of getting worked up, John shrugged his shoulders. "So you hurt the ball. You must have kicked it too hard. I hope you didn't hurt it too badly. I'll ask George (Keeshig) to see if he can bring it back to life. Where did you hide the ball?

David shrugged his shoulders. He ran a finger around his shirt collar.

"He hid it somewhere in the cedar grove," Rosa let John know.

"Where did you hide the ball?" John demanded.

David looked dumb, as if he didn't know what John was talking about.

John took David by the scruff of his neck in mock anger and pushed him outside. "Now, you show me where you hid the ball," he said sharply, "or else I'm going to take the horseshoes away from you."

David, trembling, pointed to the cedar grove.

"Take me there. Show me where you put the ball."

David whimpered and cowered, fully expecting a blow every moment along the way into the cedar grove, where he pointed to a log next to which he had buried the ball under a loose blanket of sticks and leaves.

As he withdrew the deflated ball from its grave, John warned David not to hide things or to lie. David nodded.

"Don't hide things, otherwise they'll get lost and not be found again. Somebody might come along and find them and take them away." He patted David's head and asked, "Do you understand?"

David looked as if he wanted to smile but couldn't, unsure whether John had forgiven him, whether his brother's warm tone was genuine.

The next morning the ball was in its usual place, round, full. It had come back to life, repaired by George with cement and a patch.

Though David often looked longingly at the ball, and wanted to carry it outside and kick it, he didn't dare touch it for the longest while, afraid that he might injure it one more time.

Shortly after John had returned home to the reserve, he became the church choir organist. To practice new Gregorian music, John went down to the church. Though Father Labelle never refused to unlock the church doors, he always looked crabby and complained. "Why can't you come early in the morning when the church doors are open?"

After mass on the first Sunday that he had served as organist, Miss Moffat, the schoolteacher, asked John where he'd learned to play. "At the seminary," he replied.

So began John's friendship with Miss Moffat, then near retirement. She had taught at Cape Croker Catholic School for over twenty-five years, and had introduced profound changes in that time.

Miss Moffat. Who knows where she came from? What did it matter? She was hired to teach reading, writing, and arithmetic. She had one other qualification that was not regarded as essential: She had studied the piano.

But so many musicians, so much love for music on the reserve only whetted Miss Moffat's own passion for music. How much more range and variety in their performances would the musicians have were they to read music? How many other boys and girls in the community would take up musical instruments other than fiddles, banjos, and guitars if they were available, and play selections other than jigs and reels? Miss Moffat envisioned a brass band, an orchestra, giving concerts, playing at festivals.

In her very first year of teaching, Miss Moffat asked C.K. Jones if the council would grant monies for the purchase of musical instruments. The chief and council turned down Miss Moffat's request on the ground that if they gave a grant to one school, they'd have to give a similar grant to the other schools. It wouldn't be fair. However, they were not against a music program.

Turned down by the council and the agent, Miss Moffat sought Father Cadot's support and help. Instead of seeing music and bands as Miss Moffat saw them, Cadot saw visions of hugging and kissing, and heard sounds of heavy breathing, preliminaries to the main event. "Miss Moffat! I'm surprised that you cannot foresee what music and dancing lead to."

"Father! With all due respect, I'm aggrieved that you should suggest such a thing. Can you not imagine a uniformed brass band playing 'Regina Coeli' on the feast of Corpus Christi, with the bishop present, or 'Adeste Fideles' at the Christmas concert? Can you not see that? Or do you see only sin?"

Instruments arrived: trumpets, trombones, baritones, basses, altos, clarinets, saxophones, drums, and cymbals were donated by wealthy patrons in Toronto. Lessons began in earnest.

Just as Miss Moffat suspected, there were many youngsters such as John Bucket (Akiwenzie), Lennox Johnston, Oliver Johnson, and Levi Chegahno who had no interest in stringed instruments. Lennox, Oliver, and Bucket, dull in reading, writing, and sums, now excelled in reading and playing music.

Within two years, Miss Moffat's band played at concerts and feasts. Music created a far longer lasting impression in the community than did reading, writing, arithmetic, or catechism.

John confided to Miss Moffat one day not long after they'd met that he hated to bother Father Labelle. "Crabby! I hate asking him to practice in church. Mind if I practice on the school organ?"

"Why, Johnny, you can have that organ if you want. Nobody plays it here anyway. Take it away."

"How much do you want for it?" John asked.

"I don't want anything. I'll be happy enough if someone just takes it and makes use of it."

"How can I thank you?" John answered.

To deliver the organ home John hired C.K. Jones, Jr., a farmer who earned extra money cleaning the public cisterns, serving as undertaker, and delivering furniture. For the smell of cisterns that clung to him following a cleaning, he was known as Oomb-auzimaugooss (Stinker). He was also known as Shawnee (Southerner). Stinker minded his own business. Never was he heard to utter a bad word about anyone.

Yet woodsmen and other teamsters were upset with Stinker for wrecking the sleigh trails they had painstakingly formed in the snow. Oomb-auzimaugooss was the only farmer with a narrow gauge–runnered sleigh. Frank Nadjiwon complained that the good trails were ruined because Stinker couldn't see too well, "always squinting, even in his dreams."

The wind was mad at him as well. His barn began to lean. Some said it was the doing of the big bad wolf, others pointed the finger at the Bear-walker. Stinker himself noticed nothing, gossips said, until his wife, Liza, his white-haired White wife, pointed out the cant of the barn to him. Stinker shored up his barn with long poles. Pisa had its leaning tower; Cape Croker had its leaning barn. It was likely that Stinker's horses became seasick in that barn, which could explain why they weaved from side to side in their passage instead of bearing the true course like other horses.

Stinker's wife was never heard to speak to him, or to anyone for that matter, in a normal, quiet fashion, but always in an upraised voice bordering on yelling, as if he had done something wrong or was deaf. And indeed Liza was Cape Croker's Mammy Yokum in the flesh, fists ready to fly.

To get even with Stinker the other teamsters and woodsmen stuffed a woman's panties into his lunch pail. No one ever learned what, if anything, took place between Stinker and Liza as a result. Stinker didn't sport a shiner or bat an eye or say a word. He kept right on squinting and spoiling the teamsters' winter trails.

John, Stinker, and David unloaded the organ and carried it into the house.

Once the organ was in place, John drew the stool forward, sat on it, and got up again. He twirled the round seat, which grew taller by inches. Nearby stood Stinker, David, and Rosa. John sat down once more, then slid the organ cover back.

The moment that John pumped the pedals and ran his fingers over the keyboard, the organ whined, groaned, and keened; David's eyes bulged, he staggered away, tripped, picked himself up, and dashed out the door.

"What happened to him?" John asked, without stopping his playing.

"I think the noise scared him," Rosa explained. As she said so she went out. Already David was halfway to the barn. They yelled at David to "Come on back! Where are you going?" John had to go fetch David.

By the barn John put his arm around David's shoulder. "Come on back! There's nothing to be afraid of," John explained to calm David's trembling. "It's just an organ, the kind used in church. You've heard an organ before." And John offered David his hand to lead David back to the house and as a sign that he would protect and look after David.

But David refused to take his hand. He shook his head vehemently, repeating, "Kuh! Kuh!" and he jabbered and gesticulated something unintelligible that John didn't understand.

Rosa interpreted and tried to settle David down. "David, there aren't any little people in that organ. You haven't seen any. There's nobody inside the organ. They're not crying to get out because ... they're not locked up inside. John will show you."

"I'll show you that there's nobody inside," John added. Still David refused, "Kuh! Kuh!" It was only after John promised to kick, slap, hit, whip, and drive the little people out of the organ that David returned reluctantly to the house. In the house John yelled at the little people to "get out; you're scaring David!" and "stay out" and "don't come back." For emphasis he struck the top of the organ with the flat of his hand. John exorcised the organ of evil spirits. In a loud voice he continued to bawl out the little people as if they were marching out the door, directing them to the woods on the other side of the road. Lastly, John opened the top of the organ to show David that it was now vacated.

As Stinker turned to go, John asked him to take the little people with him, as the Pied Piper of Hameln once led all the children of the town into a mountainside, never to return.

Still, David was wary, unsure that the little people had been driven out. From the opposite side of the room, he watched and listened to John play. No amount of coaxing could draw David to take a place beside his brother. Only after no little person came out of the organ following several days of surveillance did David venture to John's side during his brother's practice.

And there, after he overcame his fear, David stood at John's side reading the music sheets, turning the pages for his brother on cue, and tapping his feet to keep time.

"Your turn," is what David wanted to hear, and he heard it sooner than he expected.

Expecting to elicit music from the organ just like his brother, who made playing look like a breeze by running his fingers over the keys while keeping his eyes on the sheet in front of him, David sat down to attempt to do the same thing. His fingers stiffened. His feet balked. The right foot didn't lift up when his left pressed down, driving David to exasperation. For days David practiced his feet under John's guidance and encouragement, "Left down! Right up! Left up! Right down! Attaboy, David!" When he failed to induce his feet to alternate in rhythm, David stopped, pointed at them, and said, "Bitches." He said one word, but it spoke paragraphs: "I'm trying. I'd like to do more but my feet won't let me. They're no good." But after days of drilling, David managed to get his feet under control.

David practiced. When he tired of organ playing, he pitched horseshoes.

Previously, David would have gone into a snit, sat and chewed his tongue. Now, there was the organ to turn to.

There were times at first when Rosa would have taken that organ outside and burned it, if she had been strong enough to carry it. She hoped that David would get discouraged and lose interest in it. The organ groaned, whined, screeched, moaned. It was painful enough to listen to John practice passages over and over, but he at least played in harmony. It was not the same when David sat down. It was torture, comparable to the dripping-water torture. She wanted to put a stop to it except that the vision of David sitting in his chair, tongue hanging out of the side of his mouth, held her back.

She tried not to listen. It seemed like months, hours each day, but it was no more than two weeks after he began playing that David managed to control his feet so they now functioned in concert one with the other, and with his hands.

Like his brother, David took the music sheets and set them on the racks, adjusted the height of his seat. Then he sat down and opened a sheet that he had set on its bracket as John had the habit of doing. With as much solemnity as his brother had exercised, David studied the composition.

Only after he had studied the score did David play. Once in a while he'd stop during his recital to restudy the score as he had seen John do, and start over. Sometimes the chords he played harmonized for several bars; more frequently he blended sharps and flats into the major chords. And he'd play upwards of two hours, or until Rosa had had enough. "That's enough for now; you can play another time."

Except when it rained too hard, John went out every night, even after he had put in twelve hours of work.

As he put on his tie and jacket and took another look at God's handiwork in the mirror, his mother asked, "Where are you going?"

"To Chick's."

Cousin George Keeshig's place was respectable. George was a sensible young man. There John would never get into trouble. Rosa could go to bed without anxiety.

"Where are you going?"

"To band practice … to ball practice."

These were worthwhile pastimes that were healthy, virtuous, deserving of a mother's approval.

But "to the dance … a party" were answers that conjured up vague images of heads tilted back to ease the flow of moonshine down the gullet, of girls big in a family way … of fists cracking against bone. "How late are you going to be? You're going to have to work tomorrow. Don't drink now."

"Oh, Mother, you worry too much. What do you want me to do, stay in the house and get moldy? I'll have ample time to stay home in old age."

Rosa didn't want him going out too much. More recently, David didn't want John going out at all. While Rosa was asking him where he was going, David stood at John's side pleading, "Kuh! Kuh! Back-a-haw!": "No! No! Don't go. Don't leave me. I'm afraid. Take me with you. I need you. Please stay home with me," like a two-year-old afraid of being abandoned.

John patted David's head. "Don't worry. I'll be home. I'm just going out for a while."

His pleas not to be abandoned unheeded, David retreated to his chair.

"Come on, David, don't sulk. John will be back. Go pitch horse-shoes ... play the organ." But nothing that his mother could say could mitigate David's desolation and sense of rejection. He sat until he tired of sitting.

When the despondency left him, David sometimes stood by his mother's side at the window and looked at the Big Meadow and the world beyond.

Eventually David outgrew the stage of wanting to keep John at home. Instead of wanting John to stay at home, David wanted to go along with him. He pointed his forefinger at John, then at himself, down the road, last making his fingers perform a walking motion.

"No, you can't go. You're too young," Rosa objected sharply. "John doesn't want you along," a reference to John's predilection for female company and courtship. If John happened to meet Effie (Chegahno), he'd promptly send David home. Already Rosa imagined bullies roughing David up, David falling into a creek and drowning, a pack of dogs mauling him, Herman's horses trampling him. No. Better that David stay home.

"Not tonight, tough guy. Some other time, when you're older, big-ger," John promised.

"Not tonight! ... some other time ...." Rosa hadn't given thought to David venturing alone down to the village, or anywhere for that matter. Now, with John's implied promise, she had to come to terms with it. He was thirteen, big for his age. She couldn't hold him near or in the house; she couldn't prevent him from wandering down the road to expand his world on his own. Yet she was afraid.

John knew that David needed to go beyond the end of their prop-erty, down to the church, to the stores, to see a little more of life and the world than his immediate surroundings. Sooner or later, he'd strike out on his own.

"You want to go to church with me, David?" John asked his broth-er one Sunday morning. David had not gone to church since Walter had taken him, months earlier.

It was as if David had been asked if he wanted to go to a movie or to the zoo. He fetched his hat and coat at once.

"You shouldn't really take him," Rosa objected. "He won't under-stand." But what Rosa had in mind was that John taking David with him would open the floodgates, which would not again be dammed.

"He needs to stretch his legs, to get some of the lard off," and John patted David's little paunch. "Maybe God might like to see him in church."

Rosa sighed in resignation. To make David presentable, John put one of his shirts as well as a tie on David. A splash of cologne and David was ready.

Together David and John set out hand in hand across the Big Meadow. Behind, Rosa watched, apprehensive that John might not bring David back home immediately after church.

At the south end of the Big Meadow they came to the concession road, not more than a wagon trail that led east toward the church. To the right was Antoine Akiwenzie's homestead and barn, surrounded by lilac and apple trees, themselves dwarfed by immense elms. "That's Autwaen's (the Anishinaubae pronunciation for Antoine) house." Further on John pointed to the houses and who lived therein. "Susan ... Kitchi-Susan ... don't ever sass her. She'll set dogs on you and maybe little people. This is Chick's place. We'll stop here after church. Aesop and Annie live here. This is a hospital. This is where sick people are kept. This is a school; children come here to learn. This is a hall." John pointed to a building on his right. "It used to be a church."

John had to pull David along and tell him, "Come on, hurry up! Otherwise we'll be late for church." So absorbed was David in the sights of this other world that he had forgotten; he was like a child of three or four, seeing a gorilla, a ferris wheel, or an alien for the first time. He wanted to linger to take in the scenes and be taken in by them.

Outside the church, the parishioners milled about, some having walked from Sidney Bay, five miles away, others from Little Port Elgin, about the same distance. A few came by wagon.

"Ahnee, Aesop! This is David! David, this is Aesop!"

"Where'd you drift in from?" Andrew boomed out in his bass foghorn voice. David shrank under the supersonic boom.

In succession John introduced many others: "Rezeem (Racine Akiwenzie). This is Andrew (Taylor). Say Ahnee to Herman (Taylor). Kitchi-Peyae (Big Peter Desjardins). Frank (Lavalley). Muggs (Morgan Johnston). Rugs (Lucius Johnston). Chittum (Fred Lavalley). Jim Proulx. Hey, Jim, is it going to rain?"

Jim checked aloft and predicted "P'raps! P'raps!"

"Nixon (Alex Johnston), Joe Firpo (Joe Akiwenzie). Quaewaehn (Henry Johnston). Beedee (Peter Nadjiwon). Pont (Gregor Keeshig)." So many names, so many faces, David's eyes and head swam, seeing blurred images as one sees blurred forms under water, and his ears buzzed as if a gong had been struck next to his head. David stared at these people as if he were seeing them for the first time.

"Father! This is my brother David."

"And why haven't I seen you at church before?"

John explained to Father Labelle.

"Aha! An instrument of God, sent to remind the rest of us of our good fortunes."

"Father! Mind if I take David to the choir loft with me?"

"No! I'm afraid not. It would set a precedent for non-singers and women to ask for seating in the loft. Choir members only. Sit him in the back someplace where he won't bother or distract anyone."

Before going upstairs to the choir loft and the organ, John explained to David why he was turning him over to Will-ee (William Akiwenzie) for a little while, instructing him to do everything that Will-ee did. David tensed, "Kuh! Kuh!"

"Be quiet or I'll never take you anywhere again. I'm not leaving you. I'll come down once in a while to see you."

David looked at Will-ee. The man smiled at him and patted his head. On his way into church and to the choir loft Walter stopped by to welcome and greet David. "See you after church. Be a good boy. Listen to Will-ee." David still looked frightened.

All during mass David kept his eyes on Will-ee, doing everything that his guardian did, standing, kneeling, genuflecting, bowing, moving his lips in silent prayer, striking his breast in sincere penitence much as Will-ee did. At communion David followed Will-ee to the front of the church, without Will-ee knowing or being aware of David's presence at his heels. David too knelt down, followed Will-ee's example, opened his mouth to receive Holy Communion, but the priest passed him by. Will-ee led David back to the pew.

After mass Father reminded John that David was welcome in church but, as David had not received the Holy Eucharist and would never have enough understanding to receive it, was not to approach the altar railing.

John bristled and was about to say something but held his tongue in check. It showed.

"Better that you keep your tongue where it belongs," the priest remarked with a snide smile.

Within a few Sundays, David was one of the more devoted and devout Catholics in the community, attending mass, vespers, benediction, forty hours of devotions, the Way of the Cross, sitting at the back of the church like the publican in the parable, striking his breast as an expression of his unworthiness.

David was an outcast, even in church, unworthy to approach the altar of God.

After church on summer Sundays the congregation gathered outside to exchange news and gossip, to visit and to put the long walk home off by a few extra minutes. The men talked about the council, the weather and its bearing upon fishing and the crops; the women spoke about babies, grandchildren, berries, gardens, recipes, canning, Lennox's moldy bread, Nellie's sly way of resting one of her breasts on the weigh scale to add extra weight to a slab of salt pork. "You watch that woman; crooked as a stove pipe."

As the men and women walked and laughed, and the children fidgeted to get out of their Sunday clothing and to get home to play, David pressed himself to John's side. He heard about other people, about places: Twin Dumps, the Black Bush, Sweet Corner, Half-way, Clay Hills, Coaver Cork (Cove of Cork), Pine Tree Point, Partridge Point, the Big Prairie, the Little Prairie, the Point, Meedjlau, the Little Scarp, "the other side." People were saying that old C.K. was acting as if and telling everybody that he owned "the Point" and that people going upon it were trespassing. The other people sniffed and harrumphed, "Don't belong to him. He's starting to talk and think like a White Man."

On their way home John took David another way, by the main road, by Christine Keeshig's, Stinker's, Joe Jones's, Norman Jones's, and Edgar Jones's, and on the side of the hill in different lots, Peter Nadjiwon's and Will-ee's fine homes.

David took in everything and looked around. The world was larger. He saw the Harbour and "the Point," places he'd never been.

Hewing wood was something that John would have avoided if he had been able to, for it interfered with and cut into his social life. Whenever possible he cut corners to save time so that, instead of going to the commons to cut wood two miles away, he went into the adjoining lot where there was a generous stand of hardwood. He saved hours of walking and paying teamsters' wages.

While John cut wood at the back, David watched. He kept his eyes on John as John drove the ax into the trees and made the chips fly and spin, like sparks from a fire. David's eyes grew round as little moons when the tree began to lean and to creak before toppling to the ground. "Timber!" John bellowed. David yelped and grinned.

Before too many days David called, "Back-a-haw," pointing to the ax and then to himself as a way of letting his brother know that he wanted to have a turn.

"Not right now," John shook his head and explained. "You're too young. When you get bigger, after many sleeps, I'll get you your own ax ... but you can help me." David was more than willing; he piled limbs and branches into a heap, shouldered the poles, and carried them to the house.

"Attaboy, David. You're strong," rang in David's ears like a sweet tune. Still, David wasn't satisfied. His eyes were locked on the ax and, like John, he longed to drive it into a tree until the tree toppled with a crash.

Knowing what David had on his mind, John held his ax. There were other chores David could perform, less dangerous ones, such as sawing wood. There was nothing to that. Push, pull, arms back and forth; the saw sang as it bit into the wood, spitting out sawdust.

"Let me do it," David motioned.

John handed David the saw. The saw rebelled, refusing to do David's bidding. Sawing wood looked easier that it was. The blade refused to move forward, it refused to move backward. David looked at the saw. "Too goot," he declared, straightening up.

"David! You're pressing too hard. Here, take the other end of the saw and we'll saw together." David took the other end of the saw. "Now, easy ... not too hard," John reminded David repeatedly day after day, until he could feel and sense David's coordination and rhythm coincide with his own motion.

The first time John let his end of the saw go to allow David to go solo, David stopped his own motion. "Come on, David. Don't stop. You're going to saw alone. You wanted to saw. Now, saw!"

David sawed. "That's the way." The wood broke off. "Attaboy," and John shook David's hand in congratulation.

Next, John helped David set a groove so that the saw was in place on the wood. David was on his own. Harder to teach David was to draw a groove in the wood with the blade of the saw. Under his pressure, often too hard, and sometimes too light, the saw blade wouldn't bite, or it would bounce. Step one and step two, slow and painstaking, but David went forward.

It was one thing to teach David to saw wood, quite another to train him to saw the wood to the proper length. Until David learned how to measure, his services as a sawyer didn't save any labor at all.

When David failed to saw wood to the proper length using the sawyer's method that John had taught him, John made him a measuring stick. Then John hammered a nail into the sawhorse and hung the measuring rod from the nail.

At the end of each evening, John praised David for his work, felt David's biceps with admiration. He flexed his own muscles and invited David to feel them, small and soft compared to David's. With a wag of his head John gushed, "You're powerful."

At supper, John let his mother know that "You can't imagine how strong David is ... as strong as a man ... and work ... if only he could talk and understand."

But Rosa had ideas in mind other than strength and work. "If he gets hurt, it will be your fault. What will you do then? … It's me that's going to have to look after him, not you … making him work is too hard. You're just taking advantage of him."

On days when he and Gudoohn were finished early, John came home, picked up his ax and, accompanied by David, went into the woods to cut trees. David watched, piled the brush to one side, carried the poles back to the house, and sawed wood.

"Brother! I'd like to try cutting down a tree, like you," David asked by means of signs.

Every time David asked to have a turn in cutting down a tree, John put him off with, "Not today. Another time. Just watch what I do." At first John meant "No," but he didn't want to hurt David's feelings. So he said, "Not today. Another time," which implied that he would let David take the ax and chop a tree down tomorrow, the next day, soon, maybe later. But he would let David handle the ax by and by.

Except that David wasn't put off. He persisted in asking. He wanted to get his hands on the ax. One didn't have to be a genius to foresee what would happen if David were to do that. Mary Jane's tongue would flap and flutter like a flag in the wind in making David's accident as big an event as the drowning of six men in the reserve's waters in 1906. On the other hand, John mused, if David were trained to handle an ax and to take the extra care that woodsmen take not to injure themselves, Rosa wouldn't have to cut wood or have someone to do it for her. And John would save himself all sorts of extra work. And David would be able to do one more chore that came easily to others.

If he could train David to cut trees down and then to split wood, it would be easier for John to move out of the house and away from Rosa's prying questions: "Where are you going now? When are you coming home? Why don't you stay home? Why do you have to go out all the time, every night? Why don't you stay home with me? I have so many things to tell you. Aren't you tired? There's talk about … married women … and I heard that a couple of men are out looking for you!"

"You've been listening to Mary Jane again. Don't you know that that woman can't get anything straight in her head? You should know that by now, Mom!" And then, turning to David, John invited him, "Let's go. Time for work."

In the woods John handed David an ax that had not been sharpened for years, an ax he had got from Isaiah. "This is your ax. Look after it and don't you tell mother that you have an ax or else I'll give it back to Isaiah. Is that clear?"

David nodded.

"Now I want you to listen carefully and do everything that I tell you. I don't want you getting hurt. Clear everything about you, the overhanging limbs, the brush at your feet. Measure the distance between you and the trunk of the tree with the length of your arms and the handle of your ax. Plant your feet firmly. Keep your eye on the target and then swing," John explained as he went through the steps.

The demonstration was as somber as a golf clinic, and as verbose. A dozen times John went over the steps, reminding David that "this ax could be your friend, or your enemy that could hurt you."

For a good two hours John led David through the motions until David went through the steps without forgetting one in the sequence.

John chose a poplar for David to fell, a softer wood than maple, oak, or birch. David cleared the overhang, the underbrush, measured the distance, planted his feet firmly. With the first swing David tried to fell the tree. "Not so hard. Easy. Attaboy." David hacked at and gashed the poplar, wham! bam! whock! scarring the tree below and above the target line, unable to drive the blade into the same mark twice in succession. David frowned in exasperation at his failure. He grunted, he sweated. John didn't keep count of the strokes. One hundred and fifty? More? But at last the poplar toppled over. "Timber!"

David beamed, a smile that meant, "I did it, Brother. It was tough, but I did it," and then wiped his brow.

"Good man!" John praised. "I knew you could do it." And he clapped David's back. "Time for a smoke."

After John rolled a cigarette, he fished a match out of his pocket, worked it in his right hand, David observing every motion, and with a flick of his thumbnail snapped it into flame. He lit his cigarette, shook the flame out, then cast the spent match to one side.

The smoke came out of John's nose and mouth and curled around his head before vanishing into thin air. Magic. David touched John, who had been contemplating the end of the cigarette. "What?" John asked. David pointed to John's cigarette and to his own mouth, forming a V with his fingers as if he were holding a cigarette.

John extracted his tobacco from his shirt pocket, rolled a cigarette, lit it, and handed it to David.

Just like his brother, David looked at the cigarette and placed it between his forefinger and middle finger. David drew deeply; the smoke burned his tongue and, instead of rising and disappearing into the air above his head, swirled around his nose and eyes and sought to reenter his mouth. David gasped, coughed, hacked. Blindly, he handed the cigarette to John.

"No! You asked for it. You finish it. You mustn't waste tobacco."

David finished the cigarette amid bouts of coughing. When he threw the butt to the ground and ground it out with the heel of his shoe, David stuck his tongue out and spat several times in disgust.

For the rest of the day and in the weeks that followed, John and David cut trees, without David asking for another smoke. David's coordination in the handling of an ax improved, enabling him to hew poplar trees down with fewer and fewer strokes.

David was triumphant. He wanted to tell the world what he could do; he itched to tell his mother, to surprise her, please her, but didn't betray his brother for fear of losing his beloved ax and his brother's friendship. John, too, was triumphant. He too wanted to tell their mother, but only after he was absolutely certain that David knew how to handle an ax; that is, two weeks after David had been felling trees without accident.

"I knew," Rosa answered resignedly. "I could tell from his hands and the way he used to go through some odd motions after you were gone .... But I wish you hadn't ... it's just an added weight for me to carry ... but you never listen, do you?"

"I got a dull ax for him, Mom. And some day you'll be glad I taught him. If you had your way, David would never do anything. Mother, you can't baby him all his life."

After a month of Lenten abstention, David's craving for tobacco returned. He was willing to put up with burning his tongue, stinging his eyes, and other discomforts. And cough he did, but he stayed with the cigarettes.

John soon tired of rolling cigarettes for David. "If you want to smoke you must roll your own cigarettes," he said as he handed the package of tobacco and the packet of cigarette papers to David.

In David's hands the tobacco and papers would not lie flat and still as they did in John's hands. Tobacco spilled, the cigarette paper tore. David looked at John in frustration and guilt.

It was clear that having taught David to smoke, David's habit was going to cost him money. "No more cigarettes until you learn how to roll your own properly." For practice John tore a few sheets from a catalog and provided David with dried leaves. He explained, "Put some tobacco, not too much, in the palm of your hand. Place the cigarette paper over the tobacco. Now turn your hand over ... bring the edge over and on top. Last, lick the gummed edge and seal it. It's easy."

To roll a cigarette, so simple to do and to describe, but in David's hands and fingers, intricate and complicated.

Even after David learned how to control his fingers well enough to roll "a makings," his cigarettes seldom turned out like well-crafted cylinders; some were pudgy, like fat caterpillars, others were thin and limp. What did it matter? At least David was rolling his own.

But John shouldn't have taught David; his tobacco and papers were being used up at an alarming rate.

"Mom! Did you see my tobacco ... papers?"

"No!"

"David! Did you see my tobacco ... papers?"

A look of fright and guilt appeared on David's face as he shrugged his shoulders.

"What's in your pocket?" John demanded, fixing his eye on David's bulging pant's pocket. He went to David, dug into his brother's pocket, and brought out a package of tobacco and papers.

"You don't have to steal," John admonished David. "You must ask. You are not to steal." John looked David squarely in the eye, and asked, "Do you know what happens to thieves?" John paused a moment to allow the question to sink in. "The little people will find you out. A policeman will come ... put you in jail ... lock you up .... Don't take my tobacco and papers again. Understand?"

A nod.

"Attaboy, don't do that again."

But the craving for tobacco was stronger than the fear of little people or policemen. David was so hooked that he took risks to get his hands on tobacco.

One evening after John went out without leaving him a couple of cigarettes, David fidgeted, then rummaged around, going through the pockets of John's coats.

"What in the world are you looking for?" Rosa asked him.

David made a V with his fingers, put them to his lips, and blew out imaginary smoke.

"Aaaah!" Rosa exclaimed in her throat. "Stop digging around. You can do without."

Rosa tried to talk David into going outside to play horseshoes or even … the organ. While she was talking to David, Mary Jane came to visit. Rosa promptly forgot David. Only later, after Mary Jane had gone home, did Rosa find the house unusually quiet. "David!" she called out. Thinking he might have gone upstairs, she went up to check. No David. Out she went. "David!" she called. There was no answer. She looked on the ground, lightly powdered with snow. There were David's footprints leading in the direction of the barn. "David!" No answer. Rosa followed the footprints that led into the barn. Through the doorway she saw David sitting on the floor, moaning; he smelled of vomit.

"Oh, David! What happened?" And she offered her hand to David to help him rise, then led him back to the house and to bed. She gave him some of her own Indian medicine. David was soon snoring.

Later, when Rosa reached under her pillow for her shag tobacco and clay pipe for her nightly smoke, they were not there. In the morning she found them on the floor of the barn.

That evening John again asked David, "Where're my tobacco and papers?" He elicited only a shrug of the shoulders and a guilty look. Frisking David produced nothing. "Where did you hide them?"

The tobacco and papers were under his pillow. The next time these articles were under his mattress. Even Rosa's shag tobacco disappeared.

Rosa spanked David, not only for taking her tobacco but for going into her private hiding place where she kept her purse of money and other personal articles. At least David had not touched her purse.

Scolding David didn't do John any good. To put a stop to David's pilfering, John began buying David his own tobacco and papers.

"Don't complain about how much it's costing you. You taught him. If it weren't for you, he wouldn't be sneaking and thieving and digging around; you'd better watch your money. And there are ashes on the floor, burn marks on the tablecloth …. I have to watch that he doesn't burn the house down. And it smells up the house."

Every day, Rosa admonished, "Go smoke outside! If you want to smoke, go smoke outside! Never, never upstairs!"

John brought home a puppy one day.

"What did you bring that dog home for? Who's going to look after it? What's it going to eat? Lord knows we have little enough for ourselves."

"I got him for David," John explained. "He needs a dog to play with. He can look after it … and Badger can eat leftovers like other dogs."

John had promptly named the dog in keeping with the trend on the reserve of giving pets and domestic animals anglicized names. It was hip, civilized. The name was apt for the dog, harassing and badgering the local skunks, porcupines, groundhogs, squirrels, snakes … and David.

David couldn't say Badger; the best he could manage was "Bushuh."

Rosa was right. Poor Badger was born under a double whammy. The first occurred in the very beginning when all dogs were condemned to perpetual neglect and abuse at the hands of human beings whom they had befriended. The second occurred when Badger was adopted by a family that ate its own leftovers. Rosa made a little extra oatmeal and bannock. To survive, Badger resorted to his primeval instincts, killing groundhogs and grouse, poaching someone's chickens.

Right from the first "Bushuh" became David's dog and companion. Wherever David went, to the outhouse, to the woods at the back, "Bushuh" was at his heels.

Since getting the dog, David had become talkative, even garrulous. At times, when he was in the woods, David talked as if he were talking to several people, like a preacher preaching to a congregation. Rosa was drawn to the back door on a few occasions to see whom David was talking to.

But she could catch only the odd name and word, "Kik, Back-a-haw, Woosh, Bushuh," in the course of David's speech, which was interspersed with laughter and anger. As David talked, words tumbled out, words that she'd never heard before. Someone, Bushuh, was getting an earful.

For more amusement and conversation Rosa asked David, "Who were you talking to?"

"Little people with beards," David answered in his own language and through gestures.

Amused, Rosa asked David all sorts of questions in normal everyday language: where the Little People came from, what they did. But all she could deduce from David's motions and sounds was that the Little People came from the woods and sat near him. No, Bushuh didn't bother them.

"It must be that John or that Walter who planted those ideas in David's head," Rosa told Mary Jane the next time that she came to visit. "They tell him all kinds of fairy tales that they read at school when they were young, about cows jumping over moons and frogs turning into princes. No wonder David tells all sorts of tales .... White People have strange notions if they believe all that stuff."

"Oooohn," Mary Jane exclaimed.

"Now that John taught David to fell trees, saw and split wood, I have a hard time keeping my mind on my work while he's out in the back ... every moment expecting him to cut himself. Sometimes ... I'm glad he can do that ... other times I shiver, thinking about how awkward he is."

"Tau, Rosauh! You worry too much. You'd have other worries if David were like other boys. You'd have worries like mine about my son, Alvin. Suzanee left him the other day. Took the two kids, Gertrude and Huey; blamed me for everything. That hurt. So much we did for them ... and now Alvin's going to leave." From the corner of Mary Jane's eyes tears rolled down. "You know that girl's parents didn't teach her anything about cooking, housekeeping. I always had to watch her to make sure she did her work right. So selfish! She wants her own house; doesn't want Isaiah or me. You know Isaiah and I always expected Alvin to look after us when we got old, as in the old days .... Now they're going to leave each other and us ...."

Neither said another word, but drank their tea and looked beyond the Big Meadow and the bluffs. It was as far as they could see, no farther.

Just before going home Mary Jane asked Rosa, "If you can spare David, I'd like him to saw and split some wood for us. Isaiah can't do that anymore; some days he can't hold anything ... that art-right-us.

And that Alvin don't hardly do anything. Need someone tomorrow. I'm running out of stove wood."

"I'll ask him."

David agreed. Right after his breakfast David, followed by Bushuh, saw and ax in hand, went to Isaiah's. From the time that he started in the morning to noon, David stopped twice to smoke; otherwise he worked, sweat pouring down his temples. At noon Mary Jane served David three big bowls of soup and a plateful of sandwiches. After lunch David sawed and split wood until Mary Jane told him that he had done a good day's work, at around 5 p.m. Into his hand she pressed two shiny dimes.

David looked at them, just like the pieces of metal that John kept in his pockets. "Put them in your pocket," Mary Jane prompted David, "otherwise you might lose them." David put the coins in his pocket.

On the way home David set his ax and saw down three times to fish the dimes out of his pocket to admire them. What good were they? Why did John keep them in his pocket?

"Woosh!" David drew his mother's attention to the dimes he held in the palm of his hand.

"Twenty cents! Did Mary Jane give you that?"

A nod.

"This is 10 cents," Rosa took the coins from David, holding up one coin, and said, "and this is 10 cents. I'll keep them for you. You might lose them."

"Eeeeeh! Eeeeeh!" David whined, reaching for the coins. "Mmmmm! Mmm," he cried.

Rosa handed the coins back to David.

When John came home for supper David dug into his pockets and showed the coins to his brother.

"Where'd you get those?" John asked suspiciously, with an edge to his voice.

"From Mary Jane," Rosa answered for David. "He sawed wood for her."

"You made money. Here!" John said, extending his hand to David for the coins. "Let me see!"

"Ten cents! This is 10 cents!" John said slowly. "Say 10 cents!"

"Tet tsets!"

Winter was coming on. For the elderly and the women it was a time of confinement and enforced labor. From mid-November to mid-April they were imprisoned in their homes, venturing outdoors only to go to the outhouse and to go to church once a week.

Only the never-ending labor kept them from going mad with cabin fever.

For women, the day began sometime before dawn to stoke the coals that huddled deep in ash to keep themselves warm and lit. Only after the kitchen was warm did the husband get up, eat hurriedly, and then grab his lunch and make for the woods to cut wood until nightfall; if he was a farmer he'd get up with his wife and go out immediately to the barn to tend to the animals. Children got up last.

Before going to school, children grumbled; they quarreled, they didn't want to wear this or that. They suddenly remembered that they still had homework to do. After an hour of bedlam they trooped out of the house. Peace at last. Now the women could do the work that was still ahead of them. They drew water from icebound wells or collected snow that they melted in pails, tubs, boilers, reservoirs; they washed clothing on washboards in washtubs, hung it out to dry, then brought it, stiffened by the cold, back in later. Between these tasks women who had babies fed, washed, and attended to them; they darned socks, mended mittens, baked bread, sewed dresses, swept and scrubbed the floors, and kept the stove stuffed with wood. By the time these chores were completed it was time to begin supper: salt pork, potatoes, onions made into a soup, and a pan of bannock. Less lucky women fried leftover oatmeal and served bannock buttered with grease or lard.

When children arrived home from school to resume their feuds, the women's work doubled. Women hated winter with a passion.

Children were the only ones who looked forward to winter. They saw it as a season for snow fights, skating, hockey, sleigh-riding, and making igloos, forts, and snow houses. Best of all, Christmas came in the winter, bringing with it hopes that Santa would bring presents and toys such as those pictured in catalogs. All fall, children prayed and tried to be good to obtain Santa's goodwill. Despite the volumes of prayer and the exercise of goodness, all Santa left in the stockings in some households were potatoes; other households he bypassed altogether.

Fortunately, the clergymen had rich friends in the outside world who donated toys, books, crayons, and candies. Instead of delivering the gifts to homes, Santa dropped them at the priest's house.

Rosa dreaded winter. She had to listen to that accursed organ several hours every day for the entire winter.

In October Will-ee came to the house to ask Rosa if David would cut wood for him. He'd heard from Isaiah that David was available for hire. He and Flossie would provide David with a lunch and pay him whatever Isaiah paid him.

Told that Isaiah and Mary Jane had given David 20 cents, Will-ee promised that he and Flossie would match that sum.

David was willing. He knew where Will-ee lived. David returned home the next evening with two shiny dimes in his pocket. One he surrendered to his mother for safekeeping, the other he kept in his pocket. David was lucky to work for Will-ee and Flossie, well-off people, the only Indians on the reserve with a radio.

For the next three days David set out for Will-ee's right after breakfast, only to return an hour later in high dudgeon, swearing and shaking his fist. What happened Rosa could not tell. On Thursday Will-ee came over to explain that he and Flossie didn't need David every day, just once a week. Will-ee and Rosa arranged for David to go to Will-ee's every Friday.

Word spread that David, Crazy Dave, cut wood. Resime heard about it. With a growing farm and livestock, and with a son, Ambrose, still too young to work, Resime had little time to cut wood. Florence was in a family way again. Until now, Resime had hired various men to saw and split wood for him, paying them with produce from his surplus stock in the root house, baskets of carrots, onions, potatoes, cabbages, turnips. Some of the sawyers grumbled, "Cheap! Stingy!"

One evening on his way back from his property where he'd been cutting poles, Resime stopped by Rosa's house to ask if David would work for him, sawing and splitting wood, and how much he would charge. Resime told Rosa that he and Florence usually paid for services in produce.

"We could certainly use vegetables, but David wouldn't accept a basket of carrots for a day's work. You'll have to give him money ... he's spoiled," Rosa told Resime.

"Send him down tomorrow. I need a man right away."

Right after breakfast the next day Rosa sent David to Resime's.

Around 5 p.m., Florence called David. "It's time for you to go home, David. You've done quite enough for one day. Here," and she handed David a shiny quarter. "You come back tomorrow."

David looked at the coin and handed it back to Florence. "Tet tsets! Tet tsets!" he said over and over.

"What's wrong with that, David?" Florence asked, puzzled and hurt by David's rejection of the money that she'd offered him. "It's 25 cents. It's more than what other people give you! What more do you want? What's the matter with you? ... Here!" Florence pressed the quarter into David's hand but David let it fall to the ground.

"Cheewis Cwise! Goddab, sud-la-bitch ... Tet tsets."

Florence was shocked. The Catholic of Catholics, she murmured, "Jesus, Mary, Joseph, forgive him for he knows not what he says."

David had been shortchanged, he had no doubt. He blustered. By Kitchi-Peeyae's house he turned, shook a fist, and hurled a few more "sud-la-bitches" at Florence. At the church corner he shook his fist at the manse and pitched extra "sud-la-bitches" in remembrance of his expulsion. He blustered into Walter's house.

He told Walter, as best he could, what Mrs. Resime had done to him.

"She cheated you?" Walter deduced. It was incredulous. "There must be some mistake. But if she did, don't work for her anymore."

When David left Walter's place, he was much better disposed to the world.

From David's explanation, Rosa wasn't sure what happened at Resime's, but something had taken place that upset David.

The next morning Resime dropped in again. Handing Rosa a 25-cent piece he explained that he couldn't understand why David wouldn't accept the quarter that Florence had offered. "He carried on as if he'd been fleeced ... he swore just like John Bucket," Resime reported.

Holding up the quarter, Rosa spoke sharply to David. "Why didn't you take this? What's wrong with 25 cents? Don't you know that it's worth more than 10 cents? And why did you swear at Florence?"

David hung his head.

"He's a good worker. We'd still like to have him," Resime said as he turned to go.

"I'll send him down as soon as he's finished his breakfast," Rosa promised.

When David was done eating Rosa told him to go to Resime's to cut wood. "No!" David refused. Rosa argued with David, telling him that Mrs. Resime had given him more money than either Isaiah or Will-ee. Not knowing quite what to do, Rosa went upstairs and withdrew her purse from under her pillow. Back downstairs she poured the contents on the table—bills, coins of every denomination. David's eyes popped open. "Alright then, if it will make you feel better, here!" and she gave David two dimes and a nickel. David promptly gave her back a nickel. "Now, get down to Resime's."

While David was putting on his boots, Rosa nattered at him. "If you don't work, you won't have any money; you won't have any for tobacco and I'm not going to give you any." She paused to let this sink in and then continued, "People will say that David McLeod's lazy; he doesn't want to do anything. Poor Mrs. Resime has to cut all that wood by herself."

David didn't like being scolded and nagged. He dressed more quickly than usual. Then he was out the door. On the way across the Big Meadow visions of his mother's purse, the bills and the coins on the table, flashed on his mind's screen. Tobacco. But he also heard her voice, "Get down to Resime's," in an angry tone. His mother was sending him to get shortchanged once more. How was he to get back at Mrs. Resime for cheating him?

That evening David flung two quarters on the table when he walked into the house. "Too goot!" he growled. "Cheewis Cwise," and he broke into a flood of speech that Rosa didn't know how to interpret.

"I don't know why you're so upset! You've got 50 cents; five dimes' worth. Five packages of tobacco and cigarette papers."

"Tet tsets! Tet tsets!" David repeated.

Halfway through his breakfast the next morning David scrambled upstairs. Rosa heard him crawl into bed. Thinking that he might be sick, Rosa went upstairs to check on him. David lay covered from head to toe under a pile of blankets.

Rosa pulled the blankets back and asked, "What's wrong? Are you sick?" David looked frightened.

Someone was knocking at the door.

On the way downstairs Rosa called out, "Come in!"

Resime came in.

"Rosauh! I hate to tell you this, but David sawed all the firewood too long. That isn't any good. I'm going to have to get another man to saw it to size. And it isn't that he can't measure; he cut the wood the day before the way it's supposed to be cut. And Florence gave him 50 cents for working so hard."

"Eeeeyoooh!" Rosa was shocked. "Ahow! David'll go back down and do it right."

As soon as the door closed, Rosa stormed back upstairs. She stripped the blankets off of David. "Get up!" she snapped. "You get back down to Resime's and saw that wood properly."

David put one boot on and then took his tobacco out to make a cigarette.

"Hurry up! Quit stalling!" Rosa snatched the tobacco out of David's hands.

David whimpered; he held out his hand for the return of his tobacco. Until then Rosa hadn't known how much David depended on tobacco.

"Hurry up. Put your other boot on. I'm not giving you back your tobacco until you've cut Resime's wood to its proper length. Take your measuring stick to be sure. If Resime tells me that you've done what you should have done before, I'll give you back your tobacco."

David went down to Resime's and trimmed a few inches off each stick of wood he had cut too long the previous day. It was hard work, harder without tobacco. Each time he looked up he saw Florence looking at him. Revenge wasn't quite as sweet as he had imagined it would be.

Since David had got it into his head to go with John after supper, wherever it was that his brother went, he badgered John to take him along by whimpering and crying in his own way, "Don't leave me! I want to go! I'll behave!"

The same scene was reenacted every evening: the whines, the tugs at John's shirtsleeves, the pointing down the road, the putting on of coat and tam, John telling his brother, "Not tonight. I have a date."

"Not any night!" Rosa would break in. "Now stop your whining. You're staying home. Can't you understand that?"

The scenario seldom varied or changed until Walter and Frances were at Rosa's one evening for supper. After the little drama was reenacted, Walter suggested, "I think that you should let him go out, Mom. He needs to get to know people, just as people need to get to know him. I think that David's got more sense than he's been given credit for."

Rosa didn't say anything to Walter's remarks; she never questioned his judgment.

Not until Rugs (Lucius Johnston) and Victoria (Proulx) married did John offer to take David with him.

"Oh! Go on! Take him!" Rosa muttered in a tone that was not a willing grant of permission but an unwilling submission of "you're going to do it anyway, no matter what I say."

John made some signs with his fingers, then twirled around to show David that they were going to a dance. John pointed to David and then to himself, "You're coming with me. Bring your 10 cents. I'll show you how to buy tobacco and papers."

John groomed David, washing and combing his hair, and patting his cheeks with shaving lotion. John lent him a shirt and tie, and in the latest of styles, folded down the tops of his rubber boots so that an inch and a half of white was showing.

Before going into the council hall, John led David to Lennox's store to buy tobacco. "David! Tell Harriet what you want."

David put his fingers to his lips, which looked as if he were blowing Harriet a kiss. Harriet pointed to the different brands of tobacco until David nodded that Ogden's was his preferred brand. For cigarette papers, Harriet and David went through the same routine.

"Tell him how much, Harriet."

"Ten cents."

David dug into his pocket and handed over two dimes. "Tet tsets," he said.

"No, just one! One dime will be enough."

"Thanks, Harriet. You know, David made that money himself by cutting wood .... Lennox gone over yet?"

"Yes, he just went across the road. It's a wonder that you didn't meet him."

True to form, Lennox had gone over to the hall to be on time. He would be late for any other occasion or event, even church, but never for a dance.

On either side of the entrance to the council hall were shy, dateless young men, looking silently on or casting inane remarks in hopes of catching the attention of one of the Indian princesses going into the dance hall. The Indian princesses walked coyly by.

"Why don't you come in; all the girls are inside. If you don't go in, the older men will take all the girls," John teased.

"Wait till the dance starts; the old guys won't have a chance," the young ones wisecracked, but it was just an empty boast. They'd stand by the entrance for most of the evening, too shy to ask a girl for a dance, and look on in envy at the older boys, young men. About the only satisfaction they derived was in watching the dancers go to the back of the council hall, ostensibly to piss, but in reality to steal a drink from a homemade jug of mash they had brought along and hidden in woodpiles that leaned against the livery stables.

It seemed as if the entire population of the reserve was present to celebrate Rugs' and Victoria's marriage. Men and women sat on benches set against the wall. From the ceiling hung hissing Coleman lamps. The crowd waited for Lennox and his band and for the traditional "Haste to the Wedding" tune to kick off the evening's celebration.

John led David to the front of the hall and sat him down just to the left of the elevated platform and bandstand, directly in front of the orchestra. "Ahnee, John," John was greeted many times.

Tuning their instruments and setting up their music stands was the orchestra. With them was Ross Johnston, guitarist, the newest, smallest, and youngest member of the orchestra, seven years old. As the newest member of the band, Ross had to watch how he plucked the chords for if he plucked the wrong one, he was apt to be poked with the sharp end of the bow or rapped behind the ears. Under such tutelage Ross soon became a professional like his colleagues.

"Ahow! One, two, t'ree," Lennox gave the starter's count in his nasal voice, to break into "Haste to the Wedding."

The newlyweds, who'd been waiting just outside the door, made their grand entrance into the hall, and the dance was on. The people and the hall came to life; men and women rose from their seats to take their places in the dance; the caller, Aesop (Andrew Akiwenzie), boomed, "Four more, four more!" There was clapping and hooting and whistling, squeals, giggles, and guffaws.

David watched the dancers, listened to the music and to Aesop. "Y aan me left and corners all, a' firs' couple to the right ...." Dancers stomped and twirled, the floor rumbled and shook. Aesop's voice thundered, "Second couple to the right ...." David gulped and laughed to see young women airborne horizontally during "all swing."

After the opening number the newlyweds slipped out, leaving the dancers to continue the celebrations on their behalf.

Lennox changed the pace to give the dancers a chance to catch their breath after the feverish tempo of the reel and breakdown, and to give others a chance to dance. Waltzes, fox-trots, schottisches, two-steps, polkas, a song by Victor Lavalley, who had a voice like Bing Crosby's. Young men and women drew each other closer and danced as one, gazing into each other's eyes, or heads locked together, clinging to one another, just as the priest and minister feared.

Between dances there were no long intervals to give the dancers time to grow restless. Lennox had already preselected the music. It was now a simple case of turning over the music sheet. "Ahow! John, you come in on the fourth bar. One, two, t'ree." On cue, John came in, did a solo standing up, blowing notes skyward and to the four directions, just as Harry James was to do later. Oliver's fingers caressed and petted the keys, his hands gliding and waltzing over them.

Dancers who had lone-wolfed it to the dance now prowled along the benches asking girls to dance, or simply took a girl's hand and drew her to the dance floor. Nothing to it. And as far as anyone could see, no girl turned down a request for a dance. Even David noticed this.

At last David gave in to the urge. He rose to his feet to prowl the benches along with the other lone wolves. There was no scarcity of young women waiting for a young warrior to ask them for a dance. As gallantly as he had seen it done, and with as much polish as he could muster, David extended his hand to the first young woman. She turned her body and looked away. David, not expecting to be turned down, hesitated for some moments, then went on to the next young woman. She shook her head. The third woman rose from her seat and walked away. A fourth and a fifth turned from him. Finally, David returned to his seat, where he stretched out his legs. He chewed his tongue in dejection.

John had seen David being turned down. He came over and whispered in David's ear, "Don't feel too bad. You'll get to dance soon."

David pulled his tongue back into his mouth and, heartened, rolled "a makings."

Led by John, who indicated the call, the dancers and wallflowers chanted, "Step dance! Step dance!" When he and the band finished playing "Ramona," Lennox hung his saxophone on his music stand, took his violin from its case, and resined his bow.

"'Soldier's Joy!' 'Soldier's Joy!'" the crowd shouted. "'Turkey in the Straw!' 'Chicken Reel!' 'Golden Slippers!'" others yelled.

"D." Lennox turned to Oliver and ripped into "Soldier's Joy."

One after another the reserve's step dancers tripped to the middle of the floor: Joe Akiwenzie followed by his brother Ernest, Nelson Ashkewe, Orville Johnston, Howard Chegahno, Fred Lavalley, Malcolm McLeod, Elias Chegahno. The jigs were soon muffled by the hoots and clappings and the staccato beat of oxfords on the wooden floor as the step dancers leaped, spun, and whirled like dervishes, stopping only when sweat dripped down their faces and their chests heaved.

"John! John! Your turn! 'Golden Slippers,' Lennox!" John: clown, actor, dancer. He spun, skipped, slapped his thighs and the sides of his shoes. He drifted toward David, his feet drumming upon the floor.

He shot his hand out and closed it around David's, then pulled David to the middle of the floor without breaking his stride or rhythm. "Come on, tough guy ... dance," he yelled.

David, who had never danced in his life, moved his feet as fast as he could, jumping up from time to time, stiff-backed, stiff-legged, stiff-armed. He danced without a smile, looking straight ahead. "Smile, dammit, smile," John laughed. All around them were laughter, hoots, and shrill whistles of approval, as if the crowd was watching Bojangles, the renowned tap dancer. It got louder. Little bubbles of sweat formed on David's forehead and temples, coursed down his face. He started to gasp. John took David's hand and led him back to his place, to thunderous applause.

"You're a good dancer, tough guy!"

David blew, "Phew." He sat down, he beamed. He could dance alone. He didn't need anyone.

Periodically Aesop boomed out, "A donation for the orchestra," and someone would pass a hat around, then the method of payment for an orchestra. The bigger the collection, the happier and more inspired the band. As the evening moved on, the law of diminishing returns set in; the amount of ready, liquid cash dwindled.

Once, when the band played in Mar, the hat yielded but nine pennies. Lennox looked at the nine pennies ruefully. "See?" he said to John Bucket, "not even worth one dance." Then the orchestra broke into "Home Sweet Home," Lennox's traditional last dance, which was followed by "God Save the King." It was only 11:30 p.m. "Goddamn Indians just want to get rich," the crowd muttered. Never again did the Marsians come to the dance short of change.

The Cape dancers watched anxiously as the hat was turned over to Lennox. They were relived to see Lennox nod his head in approval after counting the proceeds.

On the other side of the dance floor, opposite David, two young men, bloated by too much or maybe too little moonshine, were eying each other like bantam roosters, their hackles raised by the mere sight of each other, Indian brotherhood and goodwill forgotten. At one time they hadn't needed an excuse to spring at each other. Now they did. They drew closer together, eyeball to eyeball, almost chest to chest, their voices louder, their breath hotter.

"You don't belong on this reserve. You get your orders from Rome."

"You're damned right I belong here, you syncopated Orangeman."

"What did you call me?"

Biff! Bam! Boom! Pow!

Women and girls screamed. The men nearby yelled at and scuffled with the combatants. There were shouts. "Enough! Get out! Go on home!"

But the scuffle was over as quickly as it had started. Two young brothers in their twenties picked themselves up, their noses bloodied, their lips cut. Three other young men, hooting and whistling in triumph, strutted across the floor and out of the hall, the victors. The orchestra played on while the dancers, who had paused to watch the fracas, resumed.

"What brought that on? Who started it?" the guessing began. But no one could say for sure. Most likely one young man danced one dance too many with the girl that the other man coveted. He didn't want to say what really provoked him, but resorted to the traditional "think you're pretty damned good" bit. Deeper down was the age-old inborn trait of the Anishinaubae to beat the hell out of one another.

As the defeated young men got to their feet they muttered, "We'll get back ... hit us when we weren't ready." They left the hall.

The dance went on, the dancers complaining that "those two families are always feuding about religion or some other stupid thing ... and they always fight at a dance. They never fight other times. Always want to spoil it for everybody else. Should stay home if they don't know how to behave."

David looked around the dance floor for John, but his brother was nowhere to be seen. Worried that he was left behind, David went home.

In bed upstairs Rosa first heard Badger "yip" and then heard David talking. About halfway across the Big Meadow, she guessed. Words tumbled out of his mouth and echoed across the field. Whatever David had in his mind had to be broadcast.

He came in, shuffled around in the dark downstairs to find his chair, where he took off his boots. He whispered something harshly to "Bushuh," something that might have meant, "Lie down!" Under his weight the stairs creaked and he crawled to his mattress on the floor. Soon he was fast asleep, breathing as heavily as a workhorse.

Shortly afterward John came home. He came upstairs, checked David's bed, then went back downstairs to his own bed.

In the morning the clash began.

"I thought you were going to bring David home. He had to come home by himself. The only reason I let him go was that you promised to look after him and bring him home. So much for your promise. I should have known better."

"But, Mom!" John protested. "I was going to bring him home but he left without me. I went outside the dance hall for a couple of minutes and when I went back in, he was gone. I left as soon as I found he wasn't in the hall." Turning to David he asked, "Why didn't you wait for me?"

David shrugged his shoulders. He looked troubled and guilty. He knew that he had done something wrong to get his brother in hot water with his mother.

"Mom! Nothing happened. You're always expecting the worst!" John protested. "David came home. That's what's important. He knows his way home."

"Yes! That's what's important to you." And Rosa went on about David being assaulted by bullies, bitten by dogs, and falling into ditches where he could break a leg, prompting John to hurry his meal and go off to work.

After John left, Rosa asked David about the dance. One question was all that David needed as encouragement. As he talked and gestured, his mother repeated for clarification. "You danced? With whom? John? There was a fight? Who? Who? Who? Resime? No? Jack Jones? Can't be! Blood? You ate lunch? You went to the store? Which one? Lennox's? You bought tobacco?" From David's descriptions and her questions and his answers, Rosa derived a picture of what had transpired at the dance.

From that night on, Rosa could not keep David home in the evenings. She tried pleading and scolding for a week, then gave up. Only thunderstorms and blizzards kept David at home.

As soon as supper was done, David groomed himself and was gone, bound for "the other side" where all, or most, of the action on the reserve took place or was expected to take place, and where the community's activities occurred: dances, elections, council meetings, ball games, band practices, fall fairs, distribution of annuity monies, and pool matches at Lennox's.

For David and those living on the north and west sides of McGregor Harbour, "the other side" meant the Indian agency, the stores, the Protestant church, the council hall, the wharf, and that entire neighborhood. For those living to the south and east of McGregor Harbour, "the other side" referred to the Catholic church neighborhood and beyond. It was an enigmatic term that only the locals understood.

Lennox Johnston explained it about as succinctly as anyone ever has when he helped a carload of tourists who had asked him where they were. "See!" he said, emphasizing the term "see," which he always uttered to introduce an explanation. "This is the other side. When you're on the other side, this is the other side. Now you're on this side ... see! ... so the other side is the other side. See!"

But the tourists, though they nodded understanding, went away scratching their heads, trying to figure out which side they were on.

On their way they met Ching (Victor Johnson), a fifteen-year-old lad who'd overheard Lennox's explanation. "Can you tell us where we are? That man in there doesn't know what he's talking about." Ching told them.

"See!" Lennox told Ching, "them tourists are dumb. Can't understand simple directions."

The term "the other side" originated in the early days when the community's residents used to portage their canoes from the east shore of the narrow neck of land to McGregor Harbour on the west shore. One side or the other was always "the other side," depending on which side one was on.

Because they are unseen and unheard, events are always expected to be more interesting on "the other side."

David was drawn to the center of the action, Lennox's store, which, since the installation of a pool table, had become a local hangout. Here anyone with a few nickels in his pocket came to play pool. Here, too, thirteen-, fourteen-, and fifteen-year-olds came to listen to experienced seventeen-, eighteen-, and nineteen-year-olds dispense useful advice regarding what girls wanted, needed, and liked; who was easy; and how to heat up girls. As well as useful advice about romance and sex, there was gossip to be heeded. Lennox's was the place where the locals matched wits and showed off their command of the language.

Elias Chegahno was a wit in his own mind and a boaster as well. He took pride in his endowment, and to demonstrate its dimensions he once took a long cucumber and extended it from his crotch, then proclaimed to the audience, "Just like mine."

"Auyauh," scoffed a woman from the doorway. "Like hell," it meant. The audience roared and hooted.

Poor Elias had to live with this put-down for the rest of his life. "Ahnee, Ely. How big is it? You want to show us?" Elias could only grin.

There in Lennox's store came homegrown Bob Hopes, Jack Bennys, Charlie Chaplins, clowns, mimics, raconteurs, and put-down artists, turning the store into a makeshift impromptu theater.

David came to listen and to watch "shoo-vooh" (pool).

At Lennox's he heard a dialect of English, spoken most fluently by John Bucket, the district's Harry James. John Bucket had recently discovered the alcoholic properties of Nerviline, Aqua Velva, and other products that lubricated his tongue and waxed his English syntax.

"Cheewis Cwise! Linnik! I got a goddamn son of a bitch of a cold. Dry. My goddamn t'roat feel like a goddamn gravel pit. Cheewis Cwise! If I don't do something about this goddamn cold, I don't t'ink I won't be able to play on Friday. Cheewis Cwise! You got some of that Nerviline stuff, Linnik? Bes' goddamn stuff for colds. My wife got a goddamn cold too. I got mine from her. Couldn't sleep a goddamn wink last night. Son of a bitch, Linnik. Feel like a goddamn bastard right now."

These were powerful words, forceful language. They stuck in David's memory.

ne of the people David took special notice of at church on Sundays was Kitchi-Peeyae, Big Peter Desjardins, a man of considerable bulk. David took special notice of the sexton because when he and John passed through the vestibule of the church, the man was pulling a rope up and down; at the same time the church bell was ringing. David couldn't take his eyes off that man as he was drawn past by John.

Kitchi-Peeyae also took notice of David soon after David began to attend church regularly. One Sunday Kitchi-Peeyae asked, "You want to help me ring the bell?" John allowed David to remain with the sexton.

Nothing pleased David more than to be asked to help ring the bell. He grasped the end of the rope.

"Just wait! Just wait!" Kitchi-Peeyae held David back. "I'll tell you when. We'll pull together." Kitchi-Peeyae studied his pocket watch and greeted people as they came in; winked or scowled at children.

"Ahow! Now!" Together they drew on the rope and, once David was pulling rhythmically, Kitchi-Peeyae let David pull the rope by himself. David was ringing the bell by himself. Little boys looked at him with envy, wishing that they too could ring the bell.

Every day at noon the church bell rang to toll the Angelus and the midday. When David happened to be in the vicinity at noon, a time that coincided with his hunger, Kitchi-Peeyae invited him to help ring the bell. Now, the tolling of the Angelus was not as regular as the pre-mass tollings. The ringing of the Angelus was measured and interrupted to correspond to the length of the invocations and the recitation of "Hail Mary" between the invocations.

Kitchi-Peeyae rang the bell exactly at 12:00.

It was a signal for the faithful to suspend their work, doff their hats, and recite the prayer; for children in school to close their books, stand, and pray.

At the tolling of the bell, Father Labelle closed his breviary, took off his biretta, and began: "The Angel of the Lord declared unto Mary."

Father Labelle represented new blood in the reserve's religious and spiritual life. He was a small, slight man with a black mustache and a black, pointed beard to go along with his pointed nose. Under his thick, black eyebrows were set coal-black eyes. On Sundays he spewed out "the good news" with the fury of a volcano. Labelle was a pugnacious bantam cock who'd won a featherweight title at university with his fists. He was fast with his fists, and with his feet. Behind the wheel of his car he drove as if he were competing in a Grand Prix race. Labelle was a little dynamo.

One day in the spring of 1935, David went by the church, just as his stomach began to rumble and cry out for salt pork and bannock. For him, it was a time to go home to eat, and for Kitchi-Peeyae to ring the bell. David waited at the church door for the sexton. His stomach churned and grumbled. Kitchi-Peeyae was late. Thinking that the sexton might already be in the vestibule, David went in. Seeing no one, he took the rope in hand.

Clang! ... C'clang! ... Clangety-clang!

In the garden adjacent to the church property, Mrs. Resime Akiwenzie doffed her straw hat and rested her chin upon her chest. In her pose she represented Evangeline, immortalized in painting.

Father Labelle had gone no further than "... the Lord is with thee ..." before he paused. Something was wrong. He glanced at the clock on the wall, 11:45 a.m. Maybe Kitchi-Peeyae had a touch of intoxicitis.

Labelle slammed his biretta back on his head. He gathered the ends of his cassock around his waist and raced from the manse and up the slope. In one bound he leaped from the walkway up to the top step that led into the church and yanked open the door.

David beamed from ear to ear. He pulled the rope down.

Father Labelle snatched the rope from David's hand. "Get out! Get out!" he spat. David looked hurt. He started walking out slowly, but not fast enough for Father Labelle. The priest pushed and shoved David out the church door, down the steps, and along the cement walkway. "Out! Out! Don't you touch that bell again! Stay out!" And on the road Labelle spun David about and kicked him in the seat of his pants. "Go on home!"

Father Labelle stood on the road with his hands on his hips, ready to run after David. "Go on! Get!" he repeated, stamping his foot for emphasis.

In the garden Mrs. Akiwenzie stood perplexed, not knowing whether to continue her prayers.

Miss Burke and the children in school, with prayers petering out, waited for the next cue. While they were saying their prayers, some of the older children had been looking out the window. They had seen part of the drama. The teacher glanced at the clock. "Please be seated. There's been some mistake."

Opposite his Aunt Christine's house, David looked back. Father Labelle was still on the road. Kitchi-Peeyae stood beside him. David went on a little farther, near Stinker's place. Here he turned completely about. He was fuming. Inspired by the vision of the Jones–Akiwenzie brawl, he shook his fist at the priest. John Bucket's vocabulary echoed in the caverns of his mind.

"God-dab, sud-la-bitch, Cheewis Cwise, Fung eye," were interpolated into David's tirade, cursing and heaping on Father Labelle's head uncatholic sentiments that would have been seconded and passed by the Orange community.

For Father Labelle it was humiliating to be publicly defied and denounced. "That boy needs to be thrashed and to have his mouth soaped," the priest snorted, darting a sharp look at Kitchi-Peeyae. Liza, Stinker's wife, who lived up the hill, would have liked nothing better than to see a priest assault someone. She'd have a field day with it. Father Labelle clenched his fists; he stewed in helpless rage.

"What happened, Fauder?" Kitchi-Peeyae asked. It was still five minutes before 12:00.

"It's all your fault for letting that David, that half-wit, ring the

169

bell," the priest turned on Kitchi-Peeyae. "Now he's taken to doing it on his own. I don't want you to let David touch that rope again ... ever. Do you understand?"

"Yes, Fauder!" Kitchi-Peeyae's countenance was contrite; inside he was smiling.

Up the road David was telling Liza what the priest had done to him, but Liza understood not a word, except for the swear words.

Scandalized by the language, she yelled at David in a voice that was said could blister the bark on trees, "Go on home! Your mother should wash your mouth with soap .... You're crazy!"

It was from this incident and from the mouth of Liza that the name Crazy Dave originated.

Farther up the road, by Edgar Jones' corner, David stopped, doubly incensed. He shook his fist at Father Labelle and at Liza, cursed both.

Rosa had never seen or heard David more outraged. Such language. It must have been John who taught David how to swear. She met David at the door. Rosa fairly yelled at David, "Stop it. I won't put up with that language in the house. Don't swear." And in a quieter tone she asked David what had happened.

David told her.

It was hard to believe. What David told her couldn't be true. Surely David was mistaken; a priest wouldn't have treated him that way. David had to be confused. Yet it was unsettling. What she had feared all these years had taken place; someone had set upon her David.

She'd have to ask John and Walter to find out what had happened.

That Sunday David refused to attend mass with John, nor did he go to church for several weeks, and each time John mentioned the priest's name David erupted like a volcano, spewing out colorful language.

But gradually David's enmity for the priest faded from his memory. Late in the summer he went to a box social bazaar sponsored by the Catholic Women's League. David loved festivals too much to stay away from them and from church. For him, there were always free lunches.

Father Labelle was in grand form and spirits. He greeted David like a long-lost prodigal son, shaking his hand and inquiring in

Ojibway, the language the priest was learning, why he hadn't come to church and urging him to return to the fold.

On the first Sunday in Advent, Labelle reminded the congregation that the forthcoming period was a time to prepare for the coming of the Messiah. That everyone should always be prepared to meet the Redeemer, for no man knoweth the day or the hour. Every person must be in a state of grace obtained by confession and repentance. No person was exempt from this moral law except infants who had died baptized, and people such as David who would go directly to paradise, unlike the rest who would spend some time in a halfway institution such as purgatory. Those that died in a state of mortal sin, unreconciled to God, would go to hell.

David lifted his head from his meditation to hear his name mentioned, probably wondering if heaven was on "the other side."

ne day Badger didn't come home, and after two weeks' absence, Rosa gave him up for dead. Either wolves had ganged up on him or one of the farmers had shot him for killing his chickens or one of his other livestock.

John, who had been working for and was now living at Peter Akiwenzie's, acquired another dog, whom he named Chocolate, "Choc" for short, a collie. He brought this new pet to Rosa.

Choc and David immediately became fast friends. The new "Bushuh" was more playful than his predecessor, running off with David's socks and boots, and more affectionate, sleeping by David's mattress and remaining with David in the woods while his master cut wood.

Since David had begun going out in the evenings to "the other side," he seldom played horseshoes. One afternoon, after he quit playing "chase the stick" with Choc because the dog refused to follow the rules, David took the "shoes" from their resting place on the wall and went to the horseshoe pits. He pitched a horseshoe. The next instant Choc was there gathering the horseshoe in his mouth and then running off with it, out of range, into the field to the south of the homestead. There Choc stood, tail wagging, daring David to retrieve it.

"God-dab, sud-la-bitch! You bring that shoe back here, you desiccated sheep-head ... Cheewi Cwise!"

Rosa went to the door to see what was upsetting David. She saw David shaking his fist in helpless rage at Choc, who was standing in the field with a horseshoe in his jaws. David could only hurl imprecations at Choc.

That night, David, still angry, refused to let his friend into the house for spoiling his game. Choc, outcast, promptly dug a hole under the house.

Rosa liked Choc. She didn't want him wandering the roads and the woods, raiding chicken coops or sheep pens. She wanted Choc to stay in the yard and go no farther than the corner.

Once Choc understood his limits, he seldom ventured beyond those bounds to anyone's knowledge. He accompanied David as far as the corner and no farther, sitting there until his friend was out of sight. When Choc heard David, while his master was still a long way off, he'd run to the corner and wait. At night, Choc sometimes ran halfway across the Big Meadow to meet David, but otherwise he abided by the boundaries that Rosa set on his freedom.

The Big Meadow served as a pasture for Herman Taylor, who kept his horses, cows, sheep, and goats in it. Sometimes they were huddled in the near corner where David and other travelers climbed over the fence.

On an evening not long after Choc had come to live with Rosa and David, the cattle were pressed against the corner, blocking David's way.

"Shah! Shah!" (Out of my way! Move!) David commanded the cows, who swished their tails, mooed and delivered extra cargoes of fertilizer, with stirring effect. When the cows refused to give way, David let his temper loose. "Shah! Move! Sud-la-bitch! Cheewis Cwise!" he shouted and clapped his hands to imitate the crack of a stick.

For Choc, clapping was a signal to attack in defense of his friend who was in need of help. Boundaries were forgotten. Choc barked, sprang forward, squeezed between the rails of the fence, and burst into the enemy's midst. Choc was outnumbered twenty to one, but he didn't give two sniffs of care. He barked and snapped at the heels of the foe. The enemy panicked and gave way in every direction. David, sitting on the fence, cheered Choc on to even greater efforts. "Sib-ae! Sib-ae!" (Sic 'em!). The herd thundered off to various parts of the Big Meadow. Choc went home. David continued on his way.

All the way across the field David chuckled as he replayed the scene of the stampede in his mind. Later that night, on his way back home, he recounted the retreat of the cows from one little dog to the Manitous and the Little People.

The drama was worth seeing again. David invited Choc to accompany him the next night. It was fun. On the third evening of "stampede the cows," Herman Taylor, cattle baron and owner of the meadow, was lying in wait. He caught David and Choc in the act, dead to rights.

"Alright! I never want to see you or your dog chasing my cows. I'll shoot your dog! If you can't behave, I won't let you cross my field." Herman marched David home.

"Your boy and his dog have been running my cattle, Rosauh," Herman complained apologetically. "Caught him and that dog red-handed. A couple of my cows are ... in a family way. I don't want to lose no calves. Milk's going to curdle in the milk bag. I'd appreciate it if you'd speak to David, otherwise I'll have to report him to the chief and the police."

"Eeeeyoooh!" Rosa exclaimed. "I had no idea. I'm sorry, Herman. It won't happen again."

"I wouldn't have known except that Stinker's wife told me. She saw them," Herman explained.

"David!" Rosa wheeled on David, her voice sharp. Herman, thinking that she was going to spank David, slipped out of the house. But she didn't; she merely blistered his ears for a good ten minutes non-stop. "Don't ever do that again!"

As an added precaution to protect his cows, Herman set a bull and a goat in the Big Meadow. To David, the bull was "ming," the goat "ming."

David was going to take a short cut regardless of Rosa's warnings not to cut across the Big Meadow.

Rosa watched David and Choc go down the road. Choc went no farther than he was allowed to go. David descended into and went up the other side of the ditch. He was going to cross the Big Meadow, despite her warnings. Bull-headed. Maybe he just didn't understand. Directly on the wagon trail was a herd of cows under the guardianship of a bull. Rosa gasped.

She ran outside, screaming, "Don't go across. David!" Too late. Already he was on the other side of the fence. Rosa ran down the road. "David! Come back!" But David didn't hear her. She could only watch in horror.

David waded into the midst of the herd. "Shah! Shah! Sud-la-bitch, Cheewi Cwise. Move." And he pushed the bull, whose disposition was as sour as that of John Wesley (Keeshig), it was said. Rosa ran on, screaming and expecting the bull to charge; her heart thumped. The next moment David was pushing and slapping the bull's rump and shouting at it to get out of the way. The bull swished its tail and scored the ground in annoyance, then gave way. The cows drifted off to one side of the wagon trail to give David the right of way.

David kept going. Rosa went back to the house, her heart beating. Every time David went out to go to the village or to "the other side," Rosa pleaded with him not to cross the Big Meadow. It was useless. She could only pray. But that bull paid no attention to David. Walter speculated later that the bull's control over its temper must have come from some inner sense that David was to be pitied for his condition.

Some mornings Rosa was mending garments. From time to time she looked up to relieve her eyes from the strain. It was just before noon that David hove into sight, coming along the main road. There was something peculiar about the way he was walking.

Rosa stopped sewing. David was weaving from one side of the road to the other, like Budeese when that man was tanked, lurching forward, then drawing up short to catch his balance. David drunk! No, he was walking more like a boy learning to propel a hoop with a stick. In his hand David held a stick. He was driving something.

Rosa put her work aside and went out. She stood on the front doorstep to get a better look at what David was driving home. Because of the tall grasses and plants, Rosa couldn't see what it was.

Finally, after ten minutes, a mother skunk and her three kits came into view on the road. David ran forward to head the mother skunk off from continuing on toward Isaiah's. He gave her a couple of taps on the side of her head with his stick to change course and go left. For emphasis, he cussed the skunk.

"Don't you bring those skunks into the yard. Let them go!" Rosa screamed. Already she foresaw David's condition for the next few days, reeking of skunk gas.

Rosa's scream woke up Choc, who had been snoozing under the house. He emerged. Choc saw and smelled the enemy, already halfway across the two-plank bridge. With a good growl deep in his throat, Choc lowered his head and charged. Horatius to the bridge. In a flash the enemy turned and fired. Choc caught the blast full in his face. He yelped. He reeled. Half-blinded and half-choked by the gas, the gallant defender tumbled off the bridge into the ditch. There Choc whined and writhed in agony.

The victorious skunks calmly marched across the road with their tails held high in haughty triumph. They entered the undergrowth on the opposite side of the road and vanished.

David coughed and wheezed. He sputtered swear words at Choc. David brought his stick down on Choc's writhing form. Upon the first blow Choc ran off under the house to escape further punishment and to nurse his wounds.

Within minutes, the house smelled like a skunk's den. Unless she coaxed Choc from her sanctuary, Rosa wouldn't be able to sleep in the house that night, let alone stay in it for Lord knows for how long. "David! Stay outside; get your clothes off." Rosa went into action. In the porch she took a soup bone out of its storage. With this bone that she'd intended to make soup with, Rosa lured Choc out of hiding. She threw the bone away from the house. Before Choc could take the bone under the house, Rosa grabbed a shovel and sealed the dog's entrance. This done, she went indoors and opened the windows and the doors to air out the house. To prevent Choc from digging his way back under the house, Rosa got a heavy skidder's chain and tied Choc to the clothesline pole at the back of the house.

Back to David. "You haven't taken your clothes off as I told you. You want to go around smelling like a skunk?" And she stripped him.

"Mmmmm!" David whined, like the wind moaning through the eaves of a house. He covered his genitals with his hands and pointed down the road and into the woods with his lips. Nor would he stand still, high-stepping as if he were walking on fiery coals.

"Oh, cut the whining!" Rosa fumed in exasperation. "Nobody's going to see you." She went back inside to fetch a tub, into which she poured two pails of lukewarm water. Throughout the sponge bath David moaned. Nothing that Rosa said could shame him into stopping his moaning.

Later, as she hung up David's clothing to give them a thorough airing, Rosa could not detect any skunk odor. David and his clothing should have been rank, but they were not.

By late afternoon the house was deodorized.

For days, David was inconsolable over the loss of his pets. Each time he glanced at Choc he swore at the dog and threw sticks at him for good measure. When Choc obtained his release from the chain, he had enough sense to stay out of range.

But the skunks weren't gone; they'd merely absented themselves for a few days, exploring John Bucket's field across the road. A week later they emerged from the culvert at the corner as David was passing overhead from an excursion to "the other side."

At once David broke a dried branch from an apple tree that stood at the side of the road. As before, he drove the skunks toward home. While David drove them forward and kept them on the road, he talked to and laughed at the kits' play and tumble on the road.

Since the battle with the skunks, Choc had been trying to do something to win back David's friendship, without success. Every day, whenever he heard David's voice, Choc roused himself and ran to the road, wagging his tail to show that he was glad to see his friend and hoping to receive a pat on the head in return for his show of affection.

On this day Choc ran out to the road. But his delight and goodwill turned to rage and jealousy when he saw his friend in the company of the enemy. It was an insult. He bristled, growled. Then he remembered. Slowly, in helpless rage and spurned love, Choc turned and retreated to the far side of the house.

The mother skunk saw Choc. She squealed, then turned into the grasses at the side of the road, followed by her kits. David swore at the skunks, tapped them with his stick to keep them in line, but they ignored him.

David's association with the skunks continued well on into the summer, until the kits grew too big to allow themselves to be treated as common domestic animals and wearied of human companionship. David didn't appear to be too upset by the skunks' departure from his life; perhaps he too had wearied of their companionship and sensed that their relationship, while rewarding and satisfying, was not meant to last.

Not once did the skunks spray David, as they surely would have any other person.

Even before the skunks abandoned him, David and Choc made up.

Not long after the Choc-and-skunk skirmish, David left the house one morning right after breakfast and went up the road. As she watched him Rosa guessed that he was going to Mary Jane's to cut wood, except that David didn't have his ax and saw in hand. Rosa didn't give David another thought; she gathered the dishes and washed them.

At noon there was no sign of David. Probably having lunch at Mary Jane's, Rosa guessed. She returned to her mat-making.

Supper hour came. Still no David. He'd never missed an evening meal before; Rosa started to get edgy. She started to eat but stopped. She couldn't eat in peace with David's absence on her mind. She pushed her plate aside, wrapped a shawl around her shoulders, and went to Mary Jane's.

David wasn't at Mary Jane's. The last time Mary Jane had seen David was that morning. At that time he was heading toward Bert Ashkewe's, a direction that David seldom took. Mary Jane hadn't seen him since.

Mary Jane and Isaiah accompanied Rosa to Bert Ashkewe's place to see if David was there. Along the way they stopped and called, "Daybit! Daybit!" But there was no answer.

At Bert's place, Benjamin, Bert and Ida's second son, told them that he had seen David earlier in the day with their goats in the field just south and adjacent to Norman McLeod's property. "I'm not sure what he was doing, but he looked as if he were trying to catch one of the kids."

Bert and his entire family came back with Rosa, Mary Jane, and Isaiah to the field where Benjamin had seen David that morning. They called from the road, knowing that David would not return their call; he didn't answer. They went to the verge of the woods, called out, kept still and listened. There was no answer.

By now evening shadows were setting in and growing darker. Even if they were to hear an answer, they would not get to David. "May as well go home," Isaiah suggested. "Getting too dark in the bush. … Maybe David took Bert's short cut to Will-ee's and the main road. Might even be at home now."

"Yes!" Bert agreed. "Best that you go on home, Rosauh! Isaiah may be right in thinking that your David may be home now, waiting for you. Me and the boys will stay up and keep watch and listen. You can hear better at night."

Rosa didn't know what to do. She wanted to stay with Bert and Ida to keep watch, but she felt drawn home in case David had returned. Mary Jane helped Rosa make up her mind by taking her elbow and leading her away. To put Rosa's mind at ease, Mary Jane told her, "David's alright. I know. I haven't had any premonitions for some time now. I always have those whenever something tragic is about to happen. David'll be alright. You just mark my words."

But David wasn't at home when Rosa and Mary Jane entered the house. Rosa started to cry.

"Don't, Rosauh! It's a bad thing. You'll only bring about what you're thinking ... make it come true."

"It's all that John's fault for starting David's habit of tramping the roads instead of staying at home like he used to. He said that nothing would happen. But a mother knows better ...." Rosa stopped. She didn't want to cause an accident by her expectation of the worst. She tried to put the pictures of the dangerous waters of Little North Bay out of her mind and follow Mary Jane's advice.

But as the hours slipped away the images of disaster came on faster and lingered longer.

Around 1 a.m. Rosa and Mary Jane heard voices and saw the glow of a lantern casting eerie shadows on the trees. The party turned into Rosa's laneway. Her heart did a skip and jump when she heard David's voice.

Rosa opened the door and drew David into her arms. "Where did you find him, Bert?" she asked.

"Just below the Little North Bay hill, about twenty steps off the road, with our goats. He was holding a baby goat so tightly that he made it bleat. That's what we heard. We just followed its cries and David was with them. It's a wonder that the billy goat didn't attack him," Bert explained.

Other than the smell of goat that clung to him for several days, David suffered no ill effects.

Across the road Mary Jane and Isaiah, too old to keep up such a large house, decided to move to "the other side," into their son's house. Alvin's wife, Suzanee, had left him and their two children, Gertrude and Huey, to live a life of her own elsewhere, outside the reserve.

In preparation for the move Mary Jane cleaned house. She gave tools, utensils, and household articles that she and Isaiah no longer needed to Rosa, and retained the furniture and the furnishings they wanted to take with them to their new house.

On the third day, Mary Jane cleaned out the cellar. There were jars of preserves. The preserves that were still good she put to one side; the "spoiled" preserves she set to another side for pitching out. She sent Isaiah to fetch David to give them a hand in opening the jars that had sealed too firmly for either Mary Jane or Isaiah to open. Isaiah and David were to dump the residue and the spoiled preserves somewhere in the woods across the road.

Isaiah and David toted the "spoiled" jars of strawberry, raspberry, plum, and blackberry jams across the road. It was a good thing that Isaiah and Mary Jane had conscripted David. For even David, despite his strength, grew red in the face in straining to twist open some of the lids. He grunted, "sud-la-bitch," and sweated.

The sweet-sour odor of fermented berries assailed Isaiah's keen nose, awakening a long-dormant appetite. He had not had a drink in years. Before spilling the contents out, the old man told David to "hold the bottle till I come back." The old man returned a short time later with a pail, a sheet, and a dipper. "The stuff's too good to be thrown out, David," Isaiah remarked. With David holding one end of the sheet over the pail, Isaiah the other, the old man poured the contents of the jar over the sheet. Then Isaiah took the other ends of the sheet from David, and twisted and twirled until the fermented juice seeped out of the ball and into the pail. The fragrance took the old man's breath away, and the sharpness brought tears to his eyes.

Isaiah dumped the residue on the ground. Both Tracy, Isaiah's dog, and Choc snarled and were at each other's throats like two bosom drinking buddies arguing over who had taken the extra drink without the other's knowledge. Choc, bigger, younger, and thirstier, bowled over the other dog, gulped down the residue, and licked the grass to avoid too much spillage. He wagged his tail for another round.

David held the pail as Isaiah told him to do. The old man dipped the dipper into the pail, then drank deeply. "Aaah!" He cleared his throat. "I'll give you a drink, but don't tell anybody! Is that clear?" David nodded.

Isaiah handed David the dipper to drink a toast to their friendship, to the memory of long-dead ancestors, and to prosperity. David downed the sweet, fiery liquid and cleared his throat as a way of saying "damned good stuff" and to clear the way for more.

"Wait! I'll go get some more sealers. Don't touch what's in the pail."

Five round trips later, Isaiah, with ten toasts drunk to various causes, sat down, carefree. He put an arm around David's shoulder. "You poor boy ... but maybe ... you're luckier than us ... don't have to worry 'bout n-nothing. H-h-have another drink. I don't give a crap if Mary Jane gets mad. C'come on, David, let's celebrate life. Let's sing."

Choc, too, had not held back. But after ten large helpings of residue he was beginning to reel. Like a sensible dog, he went home, leaving Tracy to polish off the rest.

Mary Jane called, "Isayauh!" but neither David nor Isaiah answered; both were beyond caring for anyone or anything.

Receiving no answer to her calls, and suspecting an accident may have befallen her mate, Mary Jane went across the road. She met Choc in the ditch as he was staggering out of the bush. "Go on home!" Mary Jane spat at Choc. A little further on she found her mate and David sprawled under a small apple tree, snoring. Tracy was slurping wine-colored liquid in a pail. The place reeked of liquor. Mary Jane took the pail and dumped the juice to the ground and then, taking the stained sheet, left the sleeping forms to their dreams and to the mosquitoes.

Rosa looked out the front door just as Choc was crossing the bridge ... like a tightrope walker.

"Poor Choc!" echoed in her mind. She hurried to his side. "What's wrong? Oh, my poor dog!" she murmured as she examined Choc's flanks for blood and bullet wounds, but there were none. There was only this sweet, pungent odor. Poison. She had smelled it before. When? Where? Choc went limp in her arms; a lump rose in Rosa's throat. Memories and pictures coursed disjointed through her mind. Choc running off with horseshoes; Choc spinning round and round in dance; Choc stalking and killing bees who had invaded the house; Choc leaping to his feet the instant that the alarm "White Man!" was raised and racing down the road to the corner, there to drive back the enemy; Choc smiling on cue, "Smile, Choc!"; Choc lying at her feet in the evenings, keeping her company. The thought of Choc passing out of her life drew mist into her eyes.

Choc was breathing heavily, unevenly. Rosa placed Choc's head on the ground and hurried to Mary Jane's for help, if help could save Choc. Along the way she dried her eyes to conceal her grief about a dog.

"There's something wrong with my dog, Mary Jane. …"

Mary Jane "pshawed" Rosa's worry. "There's nothing wrong with your dog. Your dog's drunk, just like my dog … and Isaiah and David."

"Eeeeyoooh!" Rosa broke in, uttering an exclamation she seldom used except when she was taken aback or upset. In this instant her tone resonated upset.

Mary Jane hastened to reassure Rosa. "You needn't worry; they'll revive. Come in and have some tea." And Mary Jane explained what Isaiah had done to extract the juice from the pulp. Then Mary Jane had other news. "Did you hear that we have a new agent … Tupp … Tuppner … yes, that's it, Tuppner. Everybody's hoping that he's better than the other man … didn't know anything … You know, Rosauh! I'm lonesome already … I don't want to move."

Rosa also felt lonesome. At nights she'd be alone, with only her dog, Choc, and her cat, "Weezoohn" (black as a shadow at night), to keep her company.

On her way back home Rosa followed Mary Jane into the thicket to check on the men. They were still asleep.

Just before dark David came staggering home, moaning and muttering, "Too goot! Too goot!" He pointed to his head and went directly upstairs to bed.

Whether it was the Depression that altered the eating habits of the country not even the soothsayers could say for certain, but there was a bigger demand for fish. The first person to take notice of the heavier demand was Budeese (Bob Nadjiwon), the man to profit most by it. He wore even fancier clothes than before, bought another new car, and squired even more girls. To discourage Budeese from romancing a certain young woman, an admirer of the same young lady told Budeese that the woman in question had "the dose." Thinking that "the dose" was an added attribute, Budeese thanked the young man for this information.

Budeese was the only man who didn't believe that his life would be transformed from rags to riches by taking up a trade or tilling the soil, as Indian Affairs and the church had promised. He continued to live as his ancestors had done, by fishing. Budeese smoked, dried, and salted fish. He ate fish for breakfast, dinner, and again at supper.

The lake, the trout, and the whitefish did not let Budeese down.

Tom Jones, ever the entrepreneur, bought Budeese's fish, then delivered and shipped them to buyers off the reserve. "I can sell all you can catch," he promised. Budeese bought more nets, more lines and hooks, and an inboard motored boat. He trolled. Tom bought all the fish.

Other Indians wanted part of the action. Tilling the soil, working off the reserve had let them down. Back to fishing they turned, and the waters yielded their abundance.

Fishing was a duty. It had always been regarded as such, as was hunting and harvesting; like hunting, harvesting, and keeping watch, it was a constituent of the word for "work," "anookeewin," something that had to be performed to survive. When the people of the Cape took up fishing, they were resuming a duty they had not exercised for some time. It saw them through the Depression and gave them back some freedom from want and debt, and some control over their lives. To pay their debts and go home exhausted after rowing ten to twelve hours a day gave the people a renewed sense of accomplishment and pride. "There were only two people on relief during those years," they boasted.

By performing their duty, the Cape people helped themselves and supplied what Wiarton and Owen Sound needed.

Other reserves envied the Cape and its people.

Norman had come home that spring, after having worked in the lumber camps around Gravenhurst and Huntsville for some years without getting as far ahead as he would have liked. Still, he had saved enough to enable him to make his house habitable. He'd be better off at home fishing like the other people on the reserve who were, he'd heard, making an average of $5 to $6 a day; Budeese was making at least twice that amount.

He commissioned Alan Sky to build a rowboat for him but, because he had four other boats to build, Alan wouldn't be able to complete Norman's order until late summer. Until his boat was ready, Norman had to rent one from Tom Jones, who had a fleet of rowboats that he'd acquired from debtors who had defaulted on their credit. Tom rented these boats for 25 cents per day. There'd be no difficulty in paying the rental charge.

Fishing looked easy, but it was hard work rowing a boat while dragging sixty to seventy fathoms of wire against the wind and the waves, or in 90 degree heat, for ten hours a day. Few but the very young and the very strong, such as Wilmer Nadjiwon, fished alone. Men fished in pairs, with another man, a wife, or a son, and spelled each other off from the long, grinding, grueling labor of pulling the oars.

Norman was neither young nor strong. He needed a partner. The only one he could think of was David. If he could train David to row as John had trained him to fell trees, saw and split wood, David would be an ideal partner. With his strength David could row all day. On the other hand, he could get seasick, panic, and upset the boat.

Best to drop it, Norman thought, but the idea was too appealing. Without help, Norman's fishing career would have to be dropped.

On his way home Norman stopped at Rosa's house. "How would you like to have a few days of rest? I could look after David, take him fishing with me; and if it works out, I can take him every day ... and if it doesn't work out, I won't take him out anymore."

Rosa's mind recoiled. David didn't know how to swim. Suppose he panicked and upset the boat. A vision of David thrashing about in the water and sinking out of sight flashed in her mind. "No!" She wouldn't think of it.

To Norman "no" didn't mean "no." It was a stall tactic that meant "not right now, I need to think about it." Nothing was ever accomplished by those who accepted "no" for an answer.

Norman argued. Rosa didn't want it to appear that she was too possessive of David and was holding him back; eventually, after a few days, she reluctantly gave in.

When told that Norman would take him fishing, David couldn't stop talking. The evening before he was to accompany his father, "Tsibih," he chattered all during supper, telling his mother and Bushuh that he was going far away. Beyond the bluffs. That evening he went to Walter's to spread the good news. Later that night David told the Manitous and the Little People that he was going somewhere to do something with Tsibih. "Aehn-Haehn! Mah-ka-kayauh!"

Five a.m. "Time to get up, David. Your father'll be here in half an hour. You'd better be dressed. You still have to eat. Remember, you're going with your father."

David groaned and rolled over. Rosa pulled the blankets off him. "Come on! Hurry up. Remember you're going fishing. You were all excited last night."

"Too goot! Too goot!" David muttered.

Rosa took David by the hand and drew him to a sitting position. She helped him dress.

David was ready in body but not in spirit when Norman came calling at 6:30 a.m. Norman was full of bounce and brimming with good cheer.

"Hurry up, David! Don't hold your father back, now," Rosa added her own encouragement.

Norman was like a racehorse champing at the bit, waiting only for the gate to open so that he could spring loose. Outside he immediately set a brisk pace, soon leaving David one hundred paces behind. David sauntered as he always sauntered. "Hurry up! We'll be late. The fish won't wait. The other fishermen will laugh at us." Norman would wait for David to catch up, then he'd be off again. Finally, in exasperation, Norman took David's hand to pull him along at his pace; at least drawing David along kept him from stopping. An hour and a quarter later Norman and David arrived at the dock, the last fishermen to do so, just in time to get the last herring from Mike Lavalley, the bait vendor.

After Norman baited his lure he slipped his rowboat into the water. "Alright, David, all aboard," the captain called out to his crew. David put a hand on the gunwale of the rowboat. The boat listed under David's pressure. "Come on, David, put your foot in. It won't tip over." And Norman took David's elbow and conducted him aboard to the aft end, where David settled into the back seat. Norman shoved the rowboat from its slip and away from shore, nimbly leaping onto the fore deck. The rowboat wobbled and pitched.

David's eyes rolled like those of a terrified horse. He gripped the gunwales and moaned.

The moaning was a bad omen. "Shut up!" Norman hissed. "You'll be alright. Don't lean to one side. Sit in the middle. Watch what I do, because you're going to row later on."

David moaned.

Norman rowed straight out from the dock until he saw the Little Port Elgin road, then changed course to follow the fishing lane that ran roughly parallel to the shore all the way to the lighthouse. He let his line down. There was a slight breeze from the west, offshore, a good wind. As far as he could see and estimate, there were sixty, maybe seventy, rowboats, twelve and fourteen footers; one or two launches powered by "one lungers"; and a lone sailboat owned by Enoch Taylor. Oars flashed rhythmically in the sun. Some boats were bound for Hay Island, a mile and a half from the mainland, mere specks in the distance; some were making for the lighthouse, Cove of

Cork, Benjamin's Point, and as far as the Little Scarp. Most would go back and forth between the lighthouse and the grove of birch a half mile north of the dock, until 6 or 7 p.m. Along the shore were landmarks—the birches, Twin Dumps, the Black Forest—that had meaning only for fishermen.

David moaned. He looked over the side of the rowboat; though he could have touched the water, he looked at it as if it were a thousand feet below and if he were to move he would fall headlong into the abyss.

"David! Look! See that man over there, standing up in his boat? He's caught a fish. There's another one over there." To see other fishermen stand was a good omen; the fish were biting; it also sparked a tinge of envy. "That's what I'll be doing, David."

At Twin Dumps they met Elias Chegahno, a lone wolf, already on his return from the lighthouse. "You got any yet?" Norman shouted.

"Two," came back the reply.

"Big?"

"Four pounders."

"Where?"

"Black Forest."

"How deep?"

"Bottom."

Fishermen's talk, a conversation that would be repeated that day and every day during the fishing season.

At noon the fishermen rowed ashore to one of the many landing places. Norman, yet without so much as a nibble, pulled in at the Black Forest. "Come on, David. Time to eat. You must be hungry." David would not budge. Seeing Norman's difficulty with his crew, Elias, Fred Lavalley, and Ephraim Ashkewe came to help Norman draw his rowboat farther up to give it more stability. They all helped David get out.

"Like an old man," they teased as David stretched his legs and massaged his rump to restore circulation and flexibility to his joints and system that had gone numb after sitting in one position for four and a quarter hours. More than anything else he wanted to go to the toilet. He went behind a chokecherry bush.

Here on shore, as on the water, they were all fishermen, struggling against the winds, currents, heat, and what luck nature may have bestowed upon them. They often felt like giving in but they went out again. No one gave in. There were no differences between them, in religion, politics, or status.

The lunch conversation started on the subject of fish and where the fish would likely be striking in the afternoon and what Budeese had to say about the weather. And they complained about the prices of fish.

They rested. They still had at least five hours of rowing, a numbing, repetitious, depressing task.

Over their sandwiches and tea they relived the comical moments, the misadventures of their fellow fishermen. They loved to laugh.

"I was rowing 'longside Rugs (Lucius Johnston) this morning when he caught a fish," Ephraim recalled with glee. "From the way he was struggling he looked as if he had latched on to a big one. I went on for another hundred yards or so, then came back just as he pulled in a big, flat combed rock. Well, you shoulda heard that Catholic swear, almost as good as the people from Syndenham township. Me and the missus covered our ears. Rugs heaved that rock back into the lake and glared at me. 'Don't you say a word; I know what you're thinking.' So I told him that he shouldna thrown that rock back into the lake; he'd only catch it again." And Ephraim sniggered through his nose, "Heee-h-hee, h-heee-heee-heee."

"I always get a big charge out of Oliver (Johnston). After he lost so many fish near the boat, he bought a gaff hook. First time he got a chance to use it, he flubbed it. Here he was, kneeling at the back of the boat, trying to catch that fish by the gills with his bare hands. Meanwhile, his wife, Iola, was yelling at him, 'The gaff! The gaff!' Oliver took the gaff, stood up. The fish dove under the boat. Oliver yelled at Iola, 'He's gone under.' Iola pulled hard on one oar. The boat jerked to one side. Oliver lost his balance, fell overboard. As he hit the water, he shot his arm out, catching the gunwale. He drew himself back into the boat and flung that gaff as far as he could."

"Tau! Hau!" Iola remarked. "First time I see anyone jump in after a fish.'

"From the way they were snapping at each other, with Oliver doing most of the snapping, I thought he was going to make his wife walk the plank. It's a wonder that they didn't get a divorce. That Oliver should stick to piano playing."

Fred (Lavalley) always had a twinkle in his eye. "Watched Levi (Chegahno) pull a fish up. He was bending ever lower and his arms were pumping faster as he drew the trout nearer the surface. The fish broke and churned the water alongside the boat. Levi lunged at the trout but he couldn't grasp it. He then yanked the line to jerk the trout into the boat. Instead of flying into the boat, the trout flew off, the lure whipped into the air. In the next motion, Levi was on his knees, dipping his arms into the water like a raccoon. The lure descended and caught in the lobe of Levi's ear. He kept right on plunging his arms into the water, trying to land that fish with his bare hands. With that lure dangling from his ear he reminded me of a Zulu. All he needed was a spear.

"He looked up at me, sad as can be," Fred recalled. "Lost my fish … that's my meal … but the bugger made off with my lure."

"When I told him that his lure was suspended from his ear, he let out a holler like a wounded bear. I had to go help him remove his ear-ring."

"Did you hear that story about Bondy, the Wikwemikong fisher-man? They say he was greedy. First one out on the lake, last one back; always had to make one more round trip. Never satisfied with what he had.

"Fished just like us. Ate lunch ashore just like we do.

"This one time the other fishermen told Bondy that it was time for lunch. No, he wouldn't come ashore with the rest; he had to make one more round trip to the point.

"He came in half an hour later but, instead of unpacking his lunch and making tea, he just sat down on a log as if he were sick.

"At first nobody said anything to him. Then when Bondy hadn't stirred, his friends asked him what was wrong. He didn't answer. So they asked him what had happened. 'Nothing,' he said. But the other fishermen knew that something was wrong. They could tell from the complexion of his skin, from the dilation of his eyes. His 'nothing' meant 'I don't want to talk about it,' and they didn't pursue the matter any further.

"Except for one, Trudeau. He remained by Bondy's side. He

wouldn't leave Bondy alone. 'There's something wrong, I can tell. I know. Tell me.' Finally, Bondy relented. 'I s-saw … a s-sea serpent, near the boat … a head like a horse's with humps on his back.' Bondy slurred and stammered as if he still saw the monster.

"'I'll get you some tea,' Trudeau promised him.

"At their campfire Trudeau told his companions that Bondy had seen 'a sea serpent.' Some moments passed without a word before one of the other fishermen quipped, 'He should have clubbed it. I heard that they're good to eat.'

"At any other time the other men would have roared, but this time they bit their tongues to keep from laughing aloud. Later, they'd laugh.

"Bondy went home that afternoon. Never went fishing again. Sold his boat and his equipment."

"I wouldn't go fishing again either if I saw one of them monsters," Fred added.

"Sounds like one of John Angus's stories," Norman remarked.

"Yeah! Old C.K. Jones would have said that he would have killed it," Fred put in.

"The guys at Wikwemikong like to make things up … just like the Irish."

"I don't know about that," Ephraim drawled as he gathered up his dishes and utensils for washing. "Heard that them Johnston kids at Sidney Bay saw one, not too long ago. Scared them to fits. For my part, I hope I never see one. I'd probably dump in my pants."

"Well, David, if we see one we'll club it and eat it," Norman quipped, and he gathered his utensils, washed them, and repacked them in his lunch basket.

"All aboard!" he barked cheerfully.

"You got your crew rowing yet?" Ephraim asked.

"No, not yet. It's just his first day. Once he gets over his fear of the water, I'll get him to row. Come on, David, let's go!"

David sat on the log unmoving. He shook his head and managed a feeble "no." To get to David to move, Norman took him by the hand and led him to the boat. It was like pulling a mule. To get David on board Norman half-lifted and half-pushed him.

Norman launched his rowboat into the swell that had been stirred by a shift in the direction of the wind. Now it blew straight out from the southwest, directly offshore. Before mid-afternoon, the waves would be white-capped choppers, not big but vicious, because of tightly packed formation sequences.

From the shore to the fishing lane, Norman's boat rolled from side to side. Each time the boat pitched one way and then the other, David's eyes rolled and he began to moan.

"Shut up! Am I going to have to listen to you all afternoon? I should've left you at home," Norman muttered.

In the fishing lane Norman changed course directly into the wind. The boat now behaved in a different manner, bucking like a bronco in a rodeo; the bow would rise to ride the wave's crest, then pitch down and forward into the trough, sending sprays of water up and aside. Norman, with his back to the bow, frequently had to glance over his shoulder to read the waves.

Before Norman let his line out, David turned pale. He swallowed, he coughed. He threw up on his shirt and pants. He put his head down between his legs, groaning as if he were in agony.

"Keep your head up and your stomach will clear up. You're just seasick. Everybody gets seasick the first time out. You'll never get sick again." But David kept his head down. He moaned. He rasped to keep his guts where they belonged.

Late in the afternoon Norman caught two fish, nice ones that, at ten pounds, would fetch around a dollar. He lost two others alongside the boat that he would have landed, he believed, had David been able to help him.

Around 5 p.m. Norman couldn't stand David's moaning anymore. "Shut up! I'll take you home. I hope that will make you happy." At Twin Dumps Norman turned and headed for the dock. Twenty minutes later, Norman turned into the harbor, with David still moaning.

Onshore there was a crowd of people, almost the entire village, wives and children of the fishermen, to greet and help their men with cleaning the fish, pulling the boat up, and putting the fishing equipment away. Standing near their trucks were Tom Jones, Bob Mercer, and an Eldridge, their scales, fish boxes, and ice ready. As competitors, they didn't speak, each one hoping that the others would keep to the 9 cents a pound rate.

Waiting too were the seagulls, watching the fishermen and each other. Overhead, they wheeled and banked, birds of great beauty and grace. But deep within, their souls and spirits were ugly and vicious. They were ever ready to gouge the eyes out of another seagull, their own offspring included. Their beaks were open, their voices shrill with anger and hate. Theirs is the look and sound of selfishness. Forever to eat what is vile and unwanted is their sentence. They filled the air with their flutterings and with their screechings and squealings.

Near shore Norman drew his oars into the boat and let the craft glide in. His arms were tired, his hands sore. When the boat touched bottom, he stepped over the gunwale and into the water. He pulled the boat up as far as he could. "Okay, David. You're ashore. You're safe. You made it," he chirped. Norman wouldn't have to put up with any more moaning.

David looked up. He remained seated, as if riveted to the end of the boat.

Norman walked alongside the rowboat to the aft end, which was still resting in six inches of water, to help David disembark. "Stand up, Son. You can hold onto the gunwales."

As soon as David stood up, the rowboat tilted to the starboard side. David lost his balance and fell sideways. Norman lost his footing on the slimy, slippery rocks. He fell backward, with David on top of him.

David yelled and then whined. Norman sputtered.

The fish buyers, women, and children who had seen the accident ran forward to lend a hand. Tom Jones pulled David to his feet and to land. "Are you alright?" he asked. David looked stunned. Only his sleeves and the bottoms of his pant legs were wet. The other men pulled Norman to his feet. Other than the back of his clothing being soaked, he wasn't hurt.

David now cried. He held his hand up. At the same time he was half dancing. Tom grabbed David's hand to examine it. Clinging to David's index finger was a crab of medium size. It had a firm lock on David's finger. Tom pulled the crab off.

While Norman cleaned his fish, the other fishermen began arriving.

The crowd came to life. Talk, which until then had been subdued, increased in volume and pitch. "Wonder if he got more today? I hope he's had better luck!" Boats scraped onshore. Fishermen hailed one another, "How many, Bert? How was your day, Adam? Sixteen? That's good. How many, Autwain? Fourteen! Where'd you get them? Hear that Little Dave (Solomon) got a fifteen pounder." The seagulls added to the hubbub. Overhead they lashed and whipped the air, they shrilled and shrieked at the fishermen to hurry, they screamed at each other to keep their distance. When the fishermen threw entrails to them, they fought. They grew bolder and more daring by the minute, standing just out of reach of the fishermen, ready to seize and carry off a fish in an instant. Fishermen and children yelled at them; they threw sticks and rocks to drive them off. Everyone was talking and shouting; the seagulls squawked even louder.

The shore smelled of fish: the good smell ever present. The rocks, the dock, the boats, the shrubs, the water all bore the smell of trout. Evenings, when the men came home, the smell was even stronger. It was the smell of the sea, the harvest, like the smell of a hay field, ripe, full of goodness.

Norman received a dollar for his fish. He now walked about in a pair of oilers to keep his modesty from being sullied while his clothing dried near a fire.

Seeing Norman dressed in a fisherman's outfit, Ephraim teased, "I see you're dressed for sea serpents!"

When Norman returned David home to Rosa later that evening, he told Rosa that their son was not cut out to be a fisherman; he was too afraid of water. "And he got seasick, puked."

Other than, "I tried to tell you, but you wouldn't listen," Rosa had no comment.

After Norman left, Rosa asked David how the day went.

David erupted. He swore, "Sud-la-bitch, Tsibih. Too goot! Aha."

From David's speech and gestures, Rosa gathered that the boat was drunk, wobbled from side to side, was sick and couldn't go to the toilet.

Then David's mood changed. His eyes twinkled and he grinned. "Aeh-haehn! Tsibih, choomp. Ha! Ha!"

"Norman fell in the water?"

"Aehn, haehn!"

"Where? How? Far out in the lake? Oh my goodness!" That

Norman had fallen into the water was all the information that Rosa was able to elicit from David.

Later in the week Rosa took her washing to Pine Tree Point, taking David with her to help carry the hamper and to give him his weekly bath.

First she laundered the clothing on the rocks, then hung them on the branches of shrubs to dry. It was now time to give David his bath. When she bade him to get undressed, he said no, something he didn't often do. She snatched his tobacco from his shirt pocket, catching him off guard. "Now, get undressed."

As he reluctantly took off each article of clothing, David whimpered, keeping an eye on the water.

"What's wrong with you, anyway?" Rosa wanted to know. Thinking that David might have been the victim of a sudden attack of modesty, Rosa uttered "aaaah" derisively. "Nobody's watching you, except the seagulls and the ravens ... and they're not going to tell anybody. Do you want to go around stinking like a skunk? Get a move on, so we can go home."

But David had not the slightest intention of hurrying up. Urged to hurry, he went even slower. He couldn't refuse; he could only stall.

Rosa stripped him, then pushed and shoved him into the water up to his kneecaps. David now cried. With one hand he covered his crotch, with the other he pointed to minnows darting here and there. David shivered; he pranced.

"What's got over you?" Rosa demanded, exasperated with her failure to understand this change. She thought that David's newfound aversion to water was due to his newly acquired sense of modesty.

On the way home David kicked and swore at Choc whenever the dog happened to drift within close range. "Chau-mauh! Sud-la-bitch!"

"Cut it out right now!" Rosa demanded. "Choc didn't do anything to you." Choc, too, must have been puzzled by his friend's kicks.

As soon as they got into the house, Rosa told David to change into fresh clothing while she folded the dried clothes and towels.

No sooner did David go upstairs than Mary Jane came over with some fresh news. There was talk that the Protestants were going to get a new minister. Rosa was caught up in her neighbor's latest tidings. David came downstairs and went out the back way of the house without returning Mary Jane's greeting.

"David looks upset," Mary Jane remarked.

"Oh, he's put out about something. I don't know what," Rosa explained. "He's been in a snit since I bathed him in the lake. He took a sudden fright of the minnows. I had to take his tobacco from him to get him into the water. I don't know what came over him all of a sudden …" and Rosa giggled as she recalled David's squeals and high steps in the water brought on by the sight of minnows and other darting, flashing creatures. Then, reaching into a pocket of her apron, Rosa drew out a package of tobacco. She sighed. "David was in such a huff that he forgot his tobacco …. Oh well! He'll be back as soon as he misses his smoke."

At Tom Jones' store, David, all smiles, leaned against the counter. He pointed at tobacco, cigarette papers, and matches. Nellie took these articles down and placed them on the counter in front of David. David plunged his right hand into his pocket and extracted rolls of bills bound by elastic bands, which he tossed on the counter.

Nellie's eyes popped. "Tom! Come here, right now!"

Tom lurched into the store from the living quarters.

"Look!" Nellie gasped, pointing to the rolls of bills on the counter. "David must have stolen that money from somebody."

"Where'd you get this money?" Tom asked. He came around to the front of the counter. David's grin expired. "Where'd you get this money?" Tom asked anew. David shook his head and said something that Tom didn't understand. Tom frisked David. There were more bills, fistfuls of coins. Tom took the money and handed it to Nellie. "Put it in a bag and wait for me," he said to his wife, and to David, "Stay here!" David looked thoroughly cowed. He now saw the images of Percy Pitwaniquot and handcuffs. He protested, "No! No!"

Tom went back into the store's living quarters. Less than two minutes later he was parked in front of the store. "I'm taking David home to Rosauh's. I'm guessing that this money belongs to her," he said, taking the paper bag from his wife. "Come on, David!" David got in the car.

From Tom's store to Rosa's place David said not a word in response to Tom's questions. In less than ten minutes they were at Rosa's house.

"Ahnee, Rosauh! Are you missing any money?" Tom asked when he sat down on the chair that Rosa offered him.

"I don't think so! Why?"

"Because David was carrying around bundles of money," Tom said.

"Eeeeyoooh!" Rosa exclaimed. "Wait, I'll go see," she bade Tom. She went upstairs. Just as quickly she came back down. "It's all gone," Rosa's voice quavered.

"How did you keep your money?" Tom asked.

"I had it rolled and bound with elastic bands," Rosa explained.

"I guess this is your money then. Here," Tom said as he handed Rosa a brown paper bag.

"Thank you ever so much. All my savings; not much, but it was everything," Rosa told Tom.

After Tom left, Rosa snapped at David and chewed him out as she had never done before, her voice sharp as a razor for raking through her personal possessions and stealing from her. The money that he took was for their food. It was a good thing Tom caught him, otherwise they would have had nothing to eat. She didn't raise him or look after him so that he'd be a common thief. He'd better not steal again, for if the agent and Percy found out, they'd arrest him and lock him up.

David nodded and shook his head in penitence and understanding during Rosa's harangue. But as an added precaution, Rosa made herself a money apron that she wore around her waist, between her slip and her dress. Only at night did she take it off.

Walter, John, and Tsibih learned not to leave any loose change lying about. David lifted whatever loose coins he saw. He was no angel.

.

Every evening during the summer fishing season, the center of action was at "the other side." When the fishermen had drawn their boats up and put their gear away for the night, they and their families streamed up to the store to buy "grub" and to make a payment to reduce their accounts. The till clanged, children clamored for ice cream, pop, candies. The fishermen discussed the formation and color of the clouds. For up to an hour Tom Jones' store was the hub of the reserve.

Even though the action began at the dock around 6 p.m., then shifted to the stores an hour later, David avoided the dock area after his one fishing expedition.

By the end of August the trawling season was over. The trout moved to even deeper waters. The offshore winds blew with greater force, making the lake even more dangerous. Like the trout, the people changed their routines and adjusted their lives according to the season. Until the fall fishing season began in late September, the men and women turned their attention to their gardens and the apple orchards to put away the harvest.

Children also adjusted. After a summer of play, staying up late, swimming, catching frogs, picking berries, hunting squirrels, playing "pig," Cowboys and Indians, and catching poison ivy or nursing bee stings, children now had to do homework and go to bed early. They now had to go to school, some for the first time, others for the last. Here they would be modified and molded for the adult, Westernized world. "Sit up straight! Listen! Obey! Don't talk back. Be on time.

Get your homework done. Line up, one behind the other. No laughing! Ask permission to talk. Ask permission to go to the toilet."

The teachers had absolute authority. In the desk rested a strap. At home, fathers wore belts, not only to keep their trousers from falling, but to keep their offspring in line for teachers. Behind parents was Father Labelle, who handed out penances freely. Behind him was the agent, who could declare wayward children "delinquent," and have them committed to a residential school or a reformatory.

Students toed the line. They did their seatwork; they did their homework. They spoke English and English only in class and in the school yard. The terms "piss" and "shit," inoffensive in the Anishinaubae language, were not to be uttered in English.

No one, so far as is known, quit school or suffered fits of depression; no one assaulted a teacher for having been strapped or made to stay after school. Children who broke a rule were caught and punished, had no right to complain. They deserved what they received. That was part of life. There may not have been affection for a teacher, but there was no burning resentment either. Under this strict system the Cape Croker people were, for the most part, God-fearing, law-abiding people.

The White Man's world was governed by "thou shalt nots." Thou shalt not smoke. Thou shalt not swear. Thou shalt not leave the yard. Thou shalt not speak Indian.

The teacher was humorless; the texts were humorless; the school was cheerless, except at noon.

Between the commencement of the school year and Christmas there was only one festival that children and teenagers looked forward to: Halloween. As the Cape Indians understood Halloween, the spirits of the dead left their graves that evening and went around the community as ghosts, doing mischief to annoy and inconvenience the living. In former times Indians remained indoors to avoid meeting ghosts and giving them offense, but in more recent years, the young people had lost respect and fear of their ancestors and took it on themselves to help ghosts in harassing living adults.

Pranksters were particularly fond of moving toilets from their foundations to another location, or simply pushing them over. They especially liked to remove Mike Lavalley's wagon from its parking place near the barn to the water just offshore, near the Indian agency. Adults kept watch later into the night to foil pranksters, or to turn the tables on them, as Mrs. Mike Lavalley once did. Tired of having to recover the wagon from the lake, Mrs. Lavalley coated the wagon's tongue, wheels, and back with a liberal mixture of horse, cow, and chicken manure, blended with axle grease.

Mike and his wife turned out the lamp and waited by the open window. They didn't have long to wait.

The raiders had hidden in a grove of plum trees, biding their time. They giggled in anticipation. "Shshshsh! Alright boys ... you, you, and you grab the tongue ... you and you grab the back wheels. You and you and me will get the back."

In the dark, feet scurried and scudded. The wagon tongue creaked, then dropped with a thud. "Oh shit! Shit! What a god-damned, mean, low-down trick." And the stinking, slimy ghosts slunk away into the night, muttering unghostly sentiments.

Other pranksters hid on the side of the road with one end of a rope in their hands. On the other end was a bundle made up to resemble an animal, perhaps a skunk, which was set on the other side of the road. These ghosts startled many a Cape resident to near heart failure by drawing the dummy directly in front of unsuspecting passersby.

The pranksters' brains were ever fertile, conceiving new schemes for creating mischief in keeping with the times. Some enterprising prankster evolved the scheme of putting fence rails on the road to inconvenience the growing number of motorists; there were then eight cars on the reserve.

The Sunday before All Saints' Day, Father Labelle, who'd been vic-timized several times, mentioned the practice in his sermon. If it wasn't stopped, someone was going to get killed or seriously injured. Father Labelle ran his eyes over the grade seven and eight boys in the congregation. "Such a thing should never cross the mind of a good Catholic boy. ... Besides, no schoolboy should be out tramping the roads at night."

At the back of the church David shook his head in disapproval.

On Halloween, a couple of days later, David went to "the other side" to watch "shoo voo" (pool). There were too few pool players with too few nickels to keep the store open. So Lennox closed early. Besides, he too had to keep watch for ghosts. David went home.

Just below the Indian agency corner he tripped on a log that was set on the road. This he dragged to one side. Above Harry Taylor's he came upon more cedar railings. He heaved them into the ditch. By Stinker's place he found Stinker's wooden gate on the road. David bent down to pick up the gate and drag it off the road. A car came up the road. David looked up, directly into the lights. He couldn't see. He put his arms up to shade his eyes.

The car braked, stopped. "So! It's you that's been putting the god-damned rails on the road," a sharp raspy voice bit into the night. "Caught you right in the act. Take that gate off the road right now, you damned idiot, before someone gets hurt. What in damnation is wrong with you anyway? Move it!"

David picked up the gate and carried it off the road.

"Now! Get back in front of the car where I can see you!" David shuffled into the glow of the headlights. "What's your name?" the voice paused for an answer. "Where do you live?" There was no answer. "Why in hell don't you people learn English?" Still no answer. "So! You won't talk. Play dumb. That's quite alright. I'll find out who you are!"

Liza, Stinker's wife, better known as Shaunae-quae, had the road under surveillance, as usual. She didn't want to miss anything.

Hearing a strange voice immediately set her want-to-know-it-all instinct on fire. She wafted out of the house and forward, as a faint breeze. The man's voice was unfamiliar. The stranger stood by the car looking at David, who was spotlighted by the car's headlights. Liza planted herself by the car's rear bumper.

"I'll find out who you are," she heard the stranger say.

Liza coughed to draw the stranger's attention.

"Who are you?" the stranger demanded.

Liza, a White Woman, stuck her jaw out and glared at the stranger in the dim light. In posture and in temperament Liza was the incar-nation of Mammy Yokum of L'il Abner fame, ready to stand up to any-one, White Man or Indian, jaw to jaw, eyeball to eyeball, her fists set to stiff the person giving too much lip. All she needed was a pipe clamped in her teeth.

"I'm Liza, Shaunae-quae. That's who I am. Now! Who are you? Some bootlegger peddling booze from up the Peninsula?"

"The name is Tuffnell ... Mr. Tuffnell." Then Fred Tuffnell honed his voice to cow this woman with the hillbilly name. "I'm the new agent on this reserve."

Liza snorted. "Hope you're better than that last good-for-nothing that was here," and she mouthed his name, TUFF NULL. "What kind of a name's that anyhows? And what are you doing in this neighborhood prowling around?"

"I'm tending to business," Fred Tuffnell bristled. "If I hadn't come along, this idiot," he said, pointing to David, "would have caused an accident."

"Oh, him! That's Crazy Dave. He can't talk right. Can't understand too much, but he's harmless. He don't bother nobodys."

"Harmless!" the agent fairly spat. "Harmless! How can you say he's harmless, putting rails on the road ... for cars to run over. You say he's crazy. Then he should be locked up. And where are his parents?"

"He don't bother nobodys!" Liza's voice went up one octave. "You hear me!" And she glared at Fred Tuffnell in the dark and moved one step closer to him. "Besides, he's not the one that dragged our gate on the road ... some other kids done it."

Tuffnell was seething. His authority was challenged. He was being defied by a woman, by a White Woman. He turned his attention back to David. "Go on home! Don't let me see you on the road again tonight. Move!"

"God-dab, sud-la-bitch ..." and David shook his fist and stomped off.

"See!" the agent smirked triumphantly. "See what he's doing? Do you hear what he's saying? ... And you say that he's harmless!"

"Can you blame him?" Liza boomed out in a voice that conveyed a wish that David would stiff the agent. "You started it. Picking on him just like some kids around here like to pick on him. It's you that should go home."

Fred Tuffnell's ears were burning and his hands were shaking with rage as he drove off. A backwoods woman yelling and arguing with him as if he were just ... anyone; an idiot swearing at him, showing him a fist. At Edgar's corner he turned right, drove up Peter Nadjiwon's hill, then on to Jack Jones' road, back to "the other side." It was pitch black, the wind was whistling, leaves were falling and flying.

By Muggs' (Morgan Johnston), there were cedar railings on the road. Fred Tuffnell got out of his car. Before he could put a hand on the first log to move it, a small black creature fell out of the sky just in front of him. Banshees screamed and moaned in the bushes. Fred Tuffnell nearly collapsed in fright. He staggered back into his car, his heart hammered in his chest. From the prune tree grove issued peals of ghostly laughter.

He had work to do. The people in Ottawa had instructed him to wean the Indians away from their Indianness and not to put up with any nonsense from any chief or councillor. Fred Tuffnell had the authority of the Department of Mines, the federal government, and the RCMP. It wasn't going to be an easy task to prepare the Indians for admission into civilization.

Until this evening Fred Tuffnell had not known where to start. Now he knew. He had to instill law and order, something that his predecessor, Mr. Norman Post, it was clear, had failed to do. The reserve constable should have been on duty. No wonder children and youth flouted the law. Where in hell was the policeman anyway?

And the chief? Band council? What kind of chief and band council would tolerate lawlessness and neglect of duty by their constable?

In the morning he drove to Oliver Johnston's home. Even before he finished knocking, someone inside shouted, "Peendigaen (Come in)," but Fred didn't understand. He knocked again. This time three boys, all under the age of twelve, opened the door. They looked at him as if he were an alien. "Mom! Dad! There's a White Man!" they shouted, and stared at Fred Tuffnell so that he felt uncomfortable.

"Come in," a male voice invited.

"I can't. I'm in a hurry," Fred Tuffnell explained. He wasn't about to fraternize with Indians or enter their homes. Indians were to come to his office ... on time.

The chief was slipping his braces on over his shoulders. "Sir! Anything wrong?" he asked.

"I want to see you in my office at 9 a.m. sharp." The agent was brusque.

Oliver Johnston didn't get to the agency until after 10 a.m.

"Mr. Johnston, I'm not accustomed to being kept waiting. You're going to have to learn to be on time for appointments."

Oliver scratched the back of his neck.

"I want you to call a meeting of council at once, for tomorrow, 9 a.m. sharp."

"Why? What's so important?" Oliver asked, trying to remember what was on the last month's agenda.

"You don't know?" the agent asked derisively. "You don't know! You're the chief; you're supposed to know. If you don't know, then I'll tell you." And Fred Tuffnell recounted the list of offenses. "I've never seen so much vandalism … kids out on the road after 8 p.m.; kids dismantling fences; putting fence rails on the road for cars to run over; a crazy man on the loose in the reserve; parental neglect …." And Fred Tuffnell paused to let this charge sink in.

"Anyone hurt?" Oliver asked.

"How am I supposed to know? I've had no reports as yet," the agent responded testily. "Now, about the meeting!"

"I don't think that's possible." Oliver scratched his head.

"And why not?"

"Because we had one a couple of weeks ago while you were away and the councillors can't come just anytime. A couple of the councillors are busy fishing, and the other ones are killing pigs or cutting wood. You just can't get them to drop whatever they're doing to attend meetings."

"I want you to see what you can do about calling an emergency meeting. We'll need to establish order on this reserve and find out why the constable wasn't on duty last evening."

"I'll see what I can do, Mr. Tuffnell, but I don't have a phone or a car," Oliver said as he got up to leave.

Fred scowled.

At lunch he complained to his wife that "the chief doesn't seem to know what's going on and doesn't realize the seriousness of hooliganism."

Promptly at 1 p.m. Fred Tuffnell returned to his office. Agency work was, for the most part, routine, at least up until now, consisting of distributing medication to people who came in looking for relief from sciatica, asthma, menstrual pains, hemorrhoids, headaches, acute intoxicitis, rheumatism, and arthritis. The office was more like a drugstore, with a huge cabinet that occupied the entire wall behind his desk filled with jars of pills, laxatives, liniments, lotions, salves, ointments, and tonics. It was a good thing his wife was a nurse, able to read the Latin names printed on the labels.

Fred Tuffnell had come a long way from the barrens of Oliphant by way of Markdale to Cape Croker. A farmer's son with only a grade four education, Fred Tuffnell had risen to a ranking position with status and responsibility, from obscurity to prominence.

His teacher had sentenced him to sit in the dunce's chair in the corner of the classroom. His own father had not regarded him highly enough to give him a share of the family's farmlands. Girls in Markdale turned their crooked noses up and sniffed at him, as they did to some of the other farmhands. Corporals and sergeants had barked at him in training camps in World War I: "Boy!" or "Little Boy!" If they could see him now.

Fred's life and fortunes turned for the better after he joined the United Church, the Masonic Lodge, and the Progressive Conservative party. People now called him "Sir." The Cape Croker Indians respectfully called him "Mr. Tuffnell."

Fred Tuffnell had also married well; he married Adeline Murdoch, a homely single mother with a daughter whose father came from Markdale; others thought she was from the Urbshott clan that farmed on the outskirts of the reserve. Adeline may have been homely, with a hawk's nose and a husky dog's eyes, but she was a registered nurse with more education than all of the supercilious girls who had spurned Fred.

Mr. Tuffnell was gratified that his wife had an education that enabled her to help him with the Latin names printed on the pharmaceutical bottles and jars. All the same, Tuffnell was embarrassed to have to call his wife into his office to decipher pharmaceutical terminology and to help him pronounce "acetylsalicylic acid," syllable by syllable as if he were a schoolchild just learning how to read. It made his wife look smart and him stupid. She was a good woman, but a touch too loving and friendly for Mr. Tuffnell's liking. She called him "Dear," and continued to do so even after he had growled at her a thousand times, "I've told you not to call me that." And whenever he called her into the office and women were present, she never failed to greet them with a smile.

"Hello! I'm Mrs. Tuffnell ... Adeline ... and what is your name? Mrs. Akiwenzie? Have I got the pronunciation right? I'm so pleased to meet you. Now, what is wrong? You can tell me. I'm a nurse."

In private, afterward, Fred rebuked his wife. "We're not here to make friends with these people. We have our own friends."

"But, Fred, dear ... we have to live here with them."

The people, mainly women, who came to the agency left with a good impression of Mrs. Tuffnell, "Such a nice person," and with a less favorable one of the agent, "Such an old grouch. Can't read. Has to get his wife to read for him."

When he wasn't dispensing medication from the medicine chest, Fred studied the Indian Act, trying to understand and master its sections, subsections, and sub-subsections. No one was going to trip him up. At the same time, he studied a manual entitled *How to Conduct a Meeting*.

Oliver came by several days later with word that the councillors could not meet any sooner than the next regularly scheduled meeting. No, he didn't have an agenda. "The other agent used to prepare it."

Fred Tuffnell was at the council hall at 8:45 a.m. for the regular monthly meeting. He was the only one there. He looked at his watch. With nothing to do but to wait, he drummed his fingers on the table in impatience and nervousness; it was his first meeting. He studied the hall. In the dim light it was difficult to tell whether the walls were painted yellow or were yellow from age. The Union Jack was faded and crookedly hung. Above the Coleman lamps were dark streaks. Dangerous. The hall needed a new paint job, new lights powered by a "Delco."

The agent took a black notebook from his briefcase and jotted down, "New paint, Dalko."

A few minutes before 9 a.m. a man with a journal tucked under his arm came in.

"Good morning. My name is Fred Tuffnell, the new Indian agent ... and what's your name?"

"Walter Johnston, Band Council Secretary. People around here call me 'Chick'."

"Where's everybody? The chief. The councillors?" the agent asked, annoyed. "The meeting is supposed to start at 9 a.m., isn't it?"

"Yes, but the councillors usually don't get here until 10 a.m. or after, once they get their chores done."

"They're just going to have to get up earlier. Where's their sense of responsibility?"

Shortly after, people began drifting in, taking their places on benches set against the wall. They made up the audience come to watch and listen to the proceedings. They glanced briefly at the new agent before turning their attention to each other. Soon they were talking in low voices and laughing boisterously.

Another hour went by before the fourth councillor arrived, constituting a quorum. The meeting began, with the chief calling the meeting to order. "Ahow! Mee suh tchi maudji-tau-ingobun ...."

Walter read the minutes of the previous meeting, first in Indian and then translated them into English, amid the scuffling of boots and the occasional cough.

"Chief!" the agent broke in immediately after the minutes were read. "The meetings are to be conducted in English only, the language of the country. There's no need for translation, and it's rude to speak another language in the presence of people who don't understand."

"But, Mr. Tuffnell, some of our old people don't understand English, or not enough to enable them to follow the discussions. The other agent allowed us this privilege."

"Forget what the other agent did. You're going to do things the way they're supposed to be done."

Oliver, normally a mild-mannered man, shot back, "Anyone who wants to speak English can; and anyone who wants to speak Anishinaubae can. Now, if anybody has any special request to make at this meeting, they may do so before we go to the agenda."

Before anyone could speak, Fred Tuffnell broke in once more. "Chief! You didn't ask for the acceptance of the minutes. According to parliamentary procedure, the meeting is supposed to follow the agenda ... petitions should be dealt with under other business."

"We do it that way so's people don't have to wait all day to address council; the other agent—"

"I don't know what the other agent did or didn't do. I'm going to do things the way they're supposed to be done. It's the only way that you're going to learn." The agent put his pencil down as a signal of finality.

The audience looked at the councillors; the councillors looked at their chief.

"The first item on the agenda, Chief, is hooliganism. It's the issue that you're going to deal with," and Fred Tuffnell described the acts of hooliganism that he had seen on Halloween night. He had actually come upon one delinquent in the act of putting a fence gate on the road. "Where was the constable? Why weren't the parents keeping their children?"

"Mr. Tuffnell," Oliver Johnston addressed the agent.

"Yes!" the reply was gruff.

"You're right about hool'ganism. I don't like it myself. Nobody likes that stuff, and I think that we should talk about it and fix it today. But I want your permission to listen to the people's special requests first, as we have always done. You see, sir, some of them came a long ways from here, like Ruben Ashkewe and Bryce Elliot. They live near the boundary, about four miles from here, and they walked all the way here to put something before this council. And they want to get back to work. There's others here who left their farms and put their work off for a few hours to come here to ask for a favor. They can't stay here all day and listen; they can't afford to do that."

"Well, in the future they can come in the afternoon to speak to the council."

"Thank you, sir. Anyone got any special requests?"

Hands went up.

"Elastus. What is it?"

Elastus Sky, a swarthy little man who wore a thick black cardigan even on the hottest of days in the summer, took his pipe out of his mouth, rose to his feet, and looked about mischievously. The chief, the council, and the audience looked on Elastus with anticipation; what was he going to say this time?

"N'ayee igoh nauh … I should have brought a laxative." Elastus paused. "The new agent looks like he's constipated. Only time I see a face as red as that is when a person is having a difficult time delivering in the outhouse." The council hall erupted in laughter. Elastus's expression remained unchanged, whimsical.

Fred Tuffnell was the only one in the council hall who wasn't laughing. There was nothing funny about the way the little man had turned the meeting into a farce, a vaudeville. How, the agent thought, were these people ever going to prepare to take their place in civilized society if they spoke only their language and showed so little respect for the democratic process?

"Is there something else?" the chief inquired, after he managed to suppress his laughter.

"Yes, there is. I want permission to cut twelve pine logs."

Walter whispered to the chief, then riffled the pages of the minute book. Finally he stopped, held the book no more than four or five inches from his eyes, and read the minutes from a previous meeting.

"Elastus! According to the minutes, we granted you permission to cut twelve pine logs in May. You've used up your quota for this year. You can apply next year."

"But that was for Peter Nadjiwon."

"It's in your name. If you gave or sold them to Peter Nadjiwon, it's your hard luck. You can't have any more this year."

"Alright then, I'm asking for permission in Peter Nadjiwon's name for me."

"You can't do that."

"Can I cut pine logs on my own property?"

"Yes."

"Then I want to claim twenty-five acres up in Little North Bay commons right now."

The audience roared once more. "Trust that old Elastus to keep the council hopping."

After Elastus, there were other petitioners asking for small loans for the repair of roofs and fences and the purchase of calves from the Urbshotts, requests they made in halting, long-winded speeches.

Boring! Fred Tuffnell doodled in his notebook. Periodically he looked at his watch. He shook it and held it to his ear. No, it hadn't stopped; it was still ticking. From the discussions, conducted partly in English and partly in Indian, the Indian agent couldn't tell if any progress was made. At last, it was noon.

"Time to adjourn for lunch, Chief."

"Time for lunch," the chief announced, and rose to his feet.

"You've got to have a motion first, before you can adjourn," the agent informed the chief.

"Just to have lunch?" Oliver asked incredulously, but he asked for the formality.

The chief and the councillors ate their lunches in the council hall. They talked about the new agent. "What do you think? I don't know. Wants to change everything. I don't like that. Looks like he's against us, instead of being for us like he's supposed to be. Let's not judge him too fast. He's just new. But suppose he really wants to change things? What can we do to stop him? Alfred! What can we do to stop the agent from changing the way that things are traditionally done?" Alfred Jones, son of old C.K., though young, was already well known for his growing mastery of the Indian Act, a copy of which he kept in his back pocket. Alfred read it as other people read the Bible, daily. Alfred could quote verbatim whole passages, then whip out his battered copy and point to the relevant passage to confirm his words.

Alfred, in a voice of authority and knowledge coming from the depths of his being, told the lunching councillors, "There's nothing you can do. He's got all the cards: the Indian Act, the Canadian government, and the RCMP. He's got all the power. He can dismiss chief and council, have a person arrested and held in prison. He can do anything that he wants that's in the Indian Act, and you … us … we can't do anything. We're nothings, made nothings, nonpersons by the Indian Act. All you can do is 'filibust,' that's what the White People do. Stall! At least, you can try. Stall, talk! Talk! Talk! Waste time. And we've got lots of good talkers on this reserve."

The council meeting resumed at 1 p.m. By 2:15 Fred Tuffnell had had enough of special petitions. At this rate he was afraid that the council wouldn't get to the agenda until the following day. The normal business day was from 9 a.m. till 5 p.m. These people would have to realize that.

"Chief! This nonsense has gone on long enough. It's time to get on with the purpose of this meeting, and to discuss hooliganism, lawlessness, and the lack of policing on this reserve. And there's a crazy man at large."

"Who's that?" Oliver asked, surprised.

"David McLeod ... Crazy Dave, you call him! He should be in an institution."

There were gasps; there were protests at once. "Now! Now! You can't do that. Leave David alone."

"That's my brother," Walter protested. "He doesn't bother anyone; he's never bothered anyone in his life. You don't even know him."

The murmurs subsided; the audience looked to the councillors, especially to Stephen Elliot. They wanted to hear him put the agent in his place, give the agent a piece of their collective minds, and make him back off, as only Stephen Elliot, Cape Croker's finest orator in years, could do. Elliot didn't look like an advocate; his clothing was rumpled, his face half-bemused, half-bewildered. But when he was worked up, he could breathe fire and brimstone. The audience now craved fire. At the moment he was conferring with Alex Johnston, nodding his head. Then he rose to his feet.

For a good twenty minutes Stephen Elliot blistered Fred Tuffnell's ears in Indian and in broken English, the gist of which was, "What you intend to do, Mr. Agent, is what cowards do. You pick on David McLeod because he can't defend himself, he can't even talk for himself. He does not belong in an institution. He belongs here, not in some asylum or reform school where he'll be abused. He belongs with his mother. He represents the only possession that she has. You mean to rob that woman of her son. You are no better than Herod, who ordered the slaughter of innocents." Stephen sat down, fuming.

Several members of the gallery muttered, "How! How!" (Hear! Hear!)

Fred Tuffnell's ears burned, his face reddened. From the way his mouth pursed and unpursed, he looked as if he wanted to speak but was unable to think of what he could say in retaliation.

After this tirade, as calmly as he could, Tuffnell returned to the subject he wanted the council to resolve. But his voice quavered as he recounted what he had seen with his own eyes, telling the councillors that the issue was now in their hands. "It's up to you to decide what you want to do. You're the council. But I must report to Ottawa whatever you decide. If you decide to send this David McLeod to a training school, you will be doing him and the community a favor. If not, you will bear the responsibility for whatever happens. It's not as if David McLeod would be sent off for good; he would return home once he'd learned to control himself. Gentlemen, it's up to you." And Tuffnell opened his black notebook and made notations in it; at least, he appeared to make notations.

The councillors mulled over the agent's words.

Alfred "Indian Act" Jones addressed the chief, "All-boohn! Can I say something?"

"Sure! What's on your mind?"

"I'm going to speak in our own language first, then in English. That man is trying to force you to make a decision today, to hurry up. But you don't have to make up your minds today or tomorrow. There's nothing in the Act that says you have to make a decision in one meeting." Alfred looked at the scowling agent, then continued, "You can talk about a subject for as long as you want. You just keep talking, fast or slow. That's what the White People do when they don't want to make a decision about something they don't like," and Alfred talked very slowly as an example, "they talk it out. I read in the *Owen Sound Sun Times* that White People always do that; it's very democratic. We should do the same thing. Nothing wrong with that."

"Is that why Keegitoohnse is called Keegotoohnse?" Elastus broke in, inciting a burst of laughter. This was a reference to C.K.'s Indian name. Keegotoohnse had been interpreted as "orator" by some, "talkative" by others.

In the peal of mirth and laughter, Alfred sat down, irked by the slight to his father's name, quite forgetting to interpret what he'd said for the agent's benefit. But the tension was broken.

Council turned its attention to "hool'ganism" with devotion. The people in the gallery addressed council in their own language, using the term liberally.

At 4 p.m. the gallery started to drift away; the councillors began to fidget and to sneak peeks at their pocket watches every few minutes. "Gotta feed my horses pretty soon," Alex Johnston whispered to Oliver. At 5 p.m. Oliver turned to the agent, with only the councillors in the council hall. "It's time we went home, Sir. We got some chores to do."

"But we haven't finished dealing with the first item on the agenda," the agent protested.

"I can take that up at the next meeting. We have to think about that."

"Then you'll have to make a motion deferring discussion of hooliganism until the next meeting."

Oliver asked for the said motion, which was seconded and unanimously passed.

"Now you'll need a motion to adjourn."

"We do? ... Never done that before."

"Yes, you do," the agent said tersely. "That's how meetings are closed. But before you do that, you must set a date for the next meeting."

"Well, do we have to do that? It's always been the first Monday of every month ... first Monday next month?"

A motion to adjourn was made and passed and recorded. It was all official.

Walter closed the minute book.

"Where do you keep the minute book, Mr. Johnston?" the agent asked gruffly.

"At home," Walter answered.

"From now on it will stay in the agency where it belongs. It's government property, I'll have you know." And Mr. Tuffnell took the book from Walter.

Outside, a councillor complained, "One of these days I wouldn't be surprised if we had to make a motion just to go for a dump."

ntil this council meeting, few on the reserve had given David much thought. When they did, it was to look on him as an object of pity; a pathetic figure; short, pudgy, slant-eyed, with bags under his eyes; thick-lipped, slack-jawed. He wore a black tam, a dark shirt, a coat, and blue trousers tucked into his rubber boots whose tops were pulled out and then down, showing a neat white trim, as whitewalled tires. He wasn't normal, for normal people didn't talk to themselves as David McLeod did as he walked along the road alone, or walk amid bulls and goats without being attacked, or shake their fists at the thunder for being too loud. Poor boy. To one God gave five talents, to another two, and to still another, one. To David, He gave none. David wasn't worth much thought.

But now they thought about him, this God-neglected human. They wished he were normal like themselves, but then he wouldn't be special, different. David gave them a chance to care about him, to exercise the care they should exercise toward all their neighbors. It took a half-wit to remind them what they should be like. He was the only one on the reserve who never gossiped, never fought anyone, never got jealous or stole another man's woman, never borrowed anything, always minded his own business, never complained about his condition, and got drunk only once. Poor human being. God didn't give him enough talent to enable him to look after himself.

Walter, too, was perturbed. As Alfred Jones had pointed out in council, the agent held all of the cards. He could call all the shots.

And from his performance in council, it looked as if he were going to do just that. He was going to run the meetings and the reserve according to the Indian Act. If he did what the Act allowed and authorized him to do, the agent would never have to worry about politicians or his superiors in Ottawa. Indians! They didn't count. For Fred Tuffnell to say that it was up to council to decide what was to be done with David McLeod was not entirely correct. Council had no authority; they were merely figureheads.

There was nothing that anyone could do to stop a person who did everything by the book. A reasonable man, perhaps; an obstinate man, no. Walter could already envision boys and young men in an institution, pushing, punching, kicking, teasing David for being stupid, as if stupidity were willful. He also foresaw the mental and spiritual anguish that Rosa would suffer. If David were taken from her, she would break. Of that he was sure. Walter was equally sure that, sooner or later, Fred Tuffnell would send David off to some institution, regardless of what council decided.

On his way home, Walter stopped at Father Labelle's to ask the priest to do what he could to persuade the agent to drop his plan to send David off to some institution. Father Labelle promised to speak to the agent; as well, he'd write to the bishop.

Women who came to Tom Jones' store to buy groceries often stayed a little longer to chat with Nellie. News came to Nellie, whether she wanted to hear it or not. Half an hour after council had adjourned on the day that David McLeod's name had been brought into the discussion, Nellie heard what had taken place in the meeting from the people who came into the store. She knew as well how the people felt.

At supper she mentioned what she'd heard to Tom. "That's too bad," Tom commented. "That's the worst thing they can do. I hope they use some common sense. They shouldn't even talk about the matter; the boy's never hurt anyone in his life."

Tom wasn't interested in reserve politics. He was much too engrossed in making a go of his business. There was the price of fish to think of, the collection of money from his debtors.

Tom had gone to Normal School. After obtaining his teacher's certificate, he had taught in Curve Lake and on Beausoleil Island, where he met Nellie Toby, a Roman Catholic girl, before returning to Cape Croker and then teaching at Little Port Elgin.

For getting carried away and marrying a Catholic, Tom incurred the wrath of his older brother, C.K. Jones.

Teaching was an unrewarding profession. The salary was poor and the children obstinate. There were better ways of making a living than by teaching children who weren't interested in doing their homework.

A store, a good general store, was what the reserve needed. People wouldn't have to go to Purple Valley, to Colpoy's Bay or even to Wiarton, spending all their money in town instead of spending and keeping it on the reserve. A store on the reserve would save the people long, cold trips in winter.

Tom constructed a store on the south corner of the main intersection, opposite the council hall, which stood on the west corner, and the Methodist church, which stood on the east corner. Tom sold everything from Kotex to bloomers to saw blades to rubber boots to ax heads to brilliantine.

In Nellie, Tom had an ideal wife and partner. She managed the store; he ran the fishing operations and maintained their farm and horses. Together they drew enough business away from Colpoy's Bay and Wiarton to enable them to live in style, better than the agent.

As a businessman doing business in Wiarton and Owen Sound, Tom did what other businessmen did: He joined some service clubs and the Masonic Lodge. He was busy, with little time for politics, but he was not indifferent to the well-being of the reserve. By being a merchant he was contributing in a direct way to the betterment of the reserve. He was doing what he had been counseled and what he counseled the young: "Do something for your people."

From the day of her husband's appointment as Indian agent, Adeline Tuffnell did her shopping at Jones' General Store. Nellie learned a great deal about the new agent from Mrs. Tuffnell. How he had risen from being a farmhand to a ranking civil servant through his own hard work. Adeline was proud of her husband and his accomplishments. Yes, he liked to bark and growl and glower, but deep down he was a pussycat; he'd do anything for her. Right now he was learning the Indian Act and how to write and spell, things he didn't learn because his father had taken him out of school before he went into grade five.

After Mrs. Tuffnell had come shopping several times, Nellie couldn't agree more with the other women's opinion that the agent's wife was "such a nice person," not like her husband at all, who was a miserable little grouch.

"Mrs. Tuffnell!" Nellie said to the agent's wife the next time she came in, a good month after David's name had been mentioned in council. "I heard that your husband wants to send our David McLeod away someplace. People are very disturbed."

"Who's David McLeod?" Mrs. Tuffnell asked.

Nellie told her.

"No, he hasn't mentioned it. Usually he tells me everything. I'll ask him about it."

At supper, as casually as she could, Mrs. Tuffnell brought the name of David McLeod into the conversation.

"And who told you this?" Fred broke in, interrupting his supper.

"Mrs. Jones! She told me about the poor boy, tongue-tied, muscle-bound, a two-, maybe four-year-old in a fifteen-year-old boy's body. Sounds as if he's a Mongoloid. There's no cure for that. From what Mrs. Jones tells me, that boy's never bothered anyone. He doesn't belong in an institution. There's nothing that can be done to correct his condition ...."

"I've got a job to do, you know. It's really none of your business, Adeline!" Fred spoke sharply. He went on about the hooliganism and vandalism committed by the young, not only by David McLeod. He complained about a council that wanted to run things its own way. "They haven't a clue about procedure or manners, no sense of urgency. They don't have a commitment to their duties. The idea of calling emergency meetings to deal with important matters as they come up is something that they don't seem to understand; they're so bound to doing things one way and one way only. *We meet only once a month!* There's no sense of duty; easy come, easy go. The matter of sending David McLeod away is in the council's hands. When I put it to them, they didn't know what to do with it, Adeline! I don't want you to listen to these people. They don't know what they're talking about; can't even talk English."

"I was just thinking of his poor mother."

"Mother! What kind of mother would let her child in that condition wander about the reserve? That should tell you something about the care that parents around here exercise, shouldn't it? ... It's just another thing that I have to change around here."

Next to the Indian agent there were two other people in the community with education and influence: the priest and the minister. They could speak to the agent, to bishops, lawyers, and government people in their own language. They could write letters to important people and get action, while an Indian could not. White People listened to other White People, especially those with education and influence.

Many people went to their priest or minister to ask him to write letters, to speak on their behalf. It was rare for a Catholic to speak to the minister, rare for a Protestant to ask the priest for a favor. Unthinkable, but it happened occasionally.

Father Labelle was reading in his study when a knock interrupted his spiritual exercise.

"Come in!"

In walked Oliver Johnston, chief, Protestant, one of the musicians who occasioned sin, maybe even an Orangeman to boot. He stood there at the doorway, half in, half out, his head cocked to one side like a rooster, waiting for an invitation. Oliver wasn't familiar with White People's customs, or clergymen's. He didn't know what he'd do if he were asked to kneel or cross himself.

Father Labelle was momentarily struck speechless by the apparition of a Protestant at his door, but he recovered quickly. "And to what do I owe the honor of this visit?" he demanded.

"What?"

"What brings you here?"

"Sir!" Chief Johnston, who did not know that Walter had already asked Father Labelle to speak on David's behalf, began, half turning his back and winding his fingers around as Catholics do in telling their rosaries, groping for words and confidence. "Sir! I come here as chief ... to ask you to do a favor for David McLeod. You see ... Sir! ... the agent wants to send him away, maybe to a reformatory. I would like you to speak to the agent ... ask him not to send David away. Can you do that, Sir?"

"Sir." The term burned in Father Labelle's ears. There was not a hint of reverence in it. It was discourteous.

"The correct title of address is 'Father' for a priest, Mr. Johnston, not 'Sir.' ... I'm sure the agent has good reasons for considering David McLeod's committal somewhere."

Oliver turned slowly away, but just before closing the door behind him, looked over his shoulder. "I was hoping that you weren't as hard as people say you are ... I guess I shouldn't have come."

Father Labelle was speechless; the nerve of that man! He returned his attention to his office, but he found it difficult to keep his mind on the text. "Hard." The word echoed in his mind. Is that what people thought of him; a person without compassion? He managed to finish his office. Then he thought about David McLeod and what was best for the boy. There was no doubt that David would receive better care in some kind of institution; better meals, changes of clothing, loving care. Where does David's mother get her income? And how much was it? Suppose something were to happen to her; who would look after David? Would the chief or any of the councillors ... or anybody else be willing to take David into their homes? Not likely. It was difficult to take up a cause that was based solely on emotion and sentiment.

That night Father Labelle prayed for guidance to his Master, Jesus Christ, whom he had chosen to serve and to emulate. Hard! His Master was hard on occasion, flogging the money changers for desecrating the temple. But those men were evil-doers. More often Christ was compassionate, curing the lepers, restoring the dead to life, healing the deaf, the lame, and the blind.

That afternoon Father Labelle called on the agent. Despite his advantage in education and his superior intellect, Labelle could not get through to Tuffnell. Tuffnell held the royal flush. When the priest delivered his peroration, Tuffnell didn't reply immediately. Labelle took the deliberation as a hopeful sign. But the agent said nothing of the issues that Labelle had raised. Instead, he said, "Reverend! I don't need you to tell me how to run the agency. I don't go telling you how to run your church. Good day."

Labelle was dismissed. He went out, seething and boiling with helpless rage at the humiliation. *That* man was *hard*, without an ounce of compassion. That man was hard. Was he hard, like that man, un-Christ like? No. People were not made of stone; he was not made of stone.

He'd fix that little wart. Labelle sat down and wrote his superior, the Father Provincial. The bishop and those higher up would put that supercilious publican in his place, where he belonged.

To Walter fell the most difficult and unpleasant of duties: telling his mother what the Indian agent had proposed be done to David. That the Indian agent had proposed it to the chief and council. It was Walter who had to twist the dagger that was already imbedded in her heart, all the way into her soul and spirit.

He agonized over it. How to phrase it so that it produced the least amount of anxiety and heartache. He prayed at night and offered a novena for guidance. He went to C.K. for counsel. "Tell her," C.K. rumbled, "that the new agent is a miserable wretch who has promised that he isn't going to put up with nonsense from anyone, old or young, and that she'd better tell David to be on his best behavior and keep him away from the agency area. I know the kind of person you're dealing with. Need a book to tell them when to go to the toilet and how to wipe their asses afterward; can't trust their own senses ... afraid, afraid to make mistakes. Best thing to do is to trip them up over their uncertainties. Polish them up. They want you to call them 'Sir!' and polish their boots. Call them 'Sir.' Be nice to them. Keep an eye and an ear on them. Sooner or later you'll find what they're hiding about themselves." As to how soon the agent could carry out his intention, C.K. wasn't too helpful. In his experience as chief, C.K. said that some of these matters took ten, fifteen, even twenty years to get acted on by Indian Affairs in Ottawa. "Maybe this new fella don't know the Act as well as people think he does."

Walter followed C.K.'s advice, choosing his words carefully, toning down the reality of the agent's intention as "barks of warning into the night." Rosa sucked in her breath and cried silently for a while before asking, "Why doesn't he keep an eye on the people who make trouble? David's never hurt anyone. What can I do?"

"Mother!" Walter said, choosing his words so as to avoid creating more alarm. "We won't let him send David away. Council and I will stand up for David. Father Labelle is going to get the bishop to speak up for David. Trust in our Lord. But we must tell David to be careful, stay out of sight, take the short cuts instead of walking on the main road." Then, turning to David, he said, "There's a man down there. If he sees you doing something wrong he'll tie your hands up and lock you up ... and take you away." For emphasis, to make David understand, Walter got some rope from the porch and tied his hands and locked him in the porch until David cried out. "See, that's what's going to happen to you."

"I hope he understands," they both prayed.

"Do you want to be locked up?"

"No! No!" David shook his head and looked scared.

"Alrighty, then don't go around by the agency."

To everyone on the reserve Mr. Tuffnell had the position of positions, one that only the educated could perform. The agent was in a class above everyone else, a government man.

In short, Fred Tuffnell was, as Indian agent, a man for all seasons, for all stations. Well, maybe not all, but quite a few. He was welfare officer, chief administrator, executor, chief electoral officer, official guardian, peace officer, social worker, financial officer, apothecary, registrar, statistician, archivist, notary public and, on occasion, a judge.

One spring day each year Tuffnell basked in the rays of sufferance. It was on that day that the annuity monies were distributed, known as Pay Day among the locals. Indian Affairs, the Great White Father, giving out money was conducted in pomp and formality. Tuffnell occupied a great armed chair behind a long table. On his right sat the chief to share in the thanksgiving of the Indians; on his left sat the band secretary, who checked off the names and numbers of band members as they came forward to receive their shares and handshakes from Tuffnell and the chief. At either end of the table stood two red-coated Mounties. Behind them, on the wall, was a picture of the king and queen, underneath which was draped the Union Jack. On this day Tuffnell was the benevolent benefactor, stacks of money at his elbow.

Tuffnell doled out money in public, but he doled out justice in his office. Big Doug (Johnson), a notorious tease, lodged a complaint with the agent, claiming that Vernon Jones had punched him, bloodying his nose and jarring his teeth. Vernon was charged with assault.

At the hearing conducted in the Indian Agency Office, Tuffnell asked Vernon if he had indeed belted Big Doug.

"Damned right I conked him. Always calling me names. Calling me 'Hoary,' whatever that means. Now everyone's calling me 'Hoary.' Hitting him's the only way to get him to stop."

"That will be a $5 fine," Tuffnell pronounced, trying to sound like a judge. "You can pay your fine now."

Vernon withdrew a $10 bill from his pocket and plunked it on the table.

"You have anything smaller? I don't have any change," the judge told Vernon.

"Smallest I got," Vernon grumped.

"Doug? ... Mr. Pitwaniquot (the Cape Croker constable in attendance)?"

Doug and Percy shook their heads. They all looked at each other with the question, "What'll we do?" in their minds.

Vernon, who had taken back his $10 bill, after some moments in silence, finally ventured, "Would you say that the fine for a punch is $5, Mr. Tuffnell?"

"Yes, I guess you could look at it that way."

Wham. Vernon belted Big Doug, knocking him ass over tea kettle. "There!" Vernon growled with satisfaction. "Here's $10 for two punches," and he walked out of the agency justified, leaving Tuffnell and Percy speechless and Big Doug bleeding and rattled.

Never was Tuffnell without a shirt, a tie, and a business suit. No one ever saw him without a scowl; he never spoke to anyone.

In his office alone, Tuffnell sweated. Each time the phone rang he jumped as his nerves jangled. He looked at each letter that came from Ottawa as if it were a court summons or a writ.

He studied the Indian Act, parliamentary procedure, directives, policy statements, the council minutes. "Adeline! What does this mean?"

At the end of every month he had to send in his monthly reports and a copy of the council minutes for the month.

"Adeline! Would you write the report for me?"

It was humiliating to have to ask his wife to read and write for him. Suppose something were to happen to her. What then? Suppose someone were to find out that there were adults, even children on the reserve who could out-read, out-write him? Tuffnell sweated. He was afraid of the higher-ups from Ottawa.

He had no such help from anyone in the council meetings with questions that he couldn't answer, and it seemed that the councillors deliberately asked him questions that he could not answer such as "so-and-so bought a lot from so-and-so, five, maybe six years ago; he's still waiting for his location ticket." Would the agent find out what, if anything, is being done? Would the agent expedite the issuance of the document? Would the agent find out under what circumstances White Cloud Island was sold? Has Ottawa ever received payment for the sale? Tuffnell looked in the files, found no records, then asked his wife to write a letter for him.

The letter went to Ottawa, was stamped, filed, misfiled, refiled, deferred, rerouted. As in the famous case of Jarndyce versus Jarndyce in Charles Dickens' *Bleak House*—which dragged on for years, generations, in the courts—letters, requisitions, and applications went from the reserve to Ottawa where they lingered, rested, moved from one desk to another, from department to department. In the meantime, chiefs and councillors came and went in election and defeat. They grew old and died. Agents were transferred or retired. The matter lay somewhere in Ottawa awaiting action.

Tuffnell waited in his office. He wanted to be there, if only to make it appear that he was on the job. While he waited, he practiced writing, but found it taxing, boring. To write as elegantly and as stylishly as the letters he received from Ottawa would take years of practice. "This is in response to yours of the second instance .... Your faithful servant." Tuffnell couldn't get David McLeod out of his mind.

"Don't go around by the agency. Take the short cut. I don't see why you have to go down to 'the other side' anyway," was what Rosa told David every night before he set out. "Stay out of that man's sight." David wasn't allowed to forget "that man."

And David frequently looked behind him to see if anyone was following him, then forgot.

222

Even though Liza spoke up for David by telling everyone who cared to hear that she saw the boys who had put the logs on the road that Halloween night, Casimir Taylor and that Ernest Lamourandiere, nicknamed Red Ryan, Rosa and Walter were uneasy.

Walter passed on what Liza told him about Casimir and Ernest to the chief, the priest, and the Indian agent. Tuffnell's only comment was, "I saw what I saw. My eyes don't lie. I have to do what I have to do."

It was around noon when Rosa glanced up from her work. A wisp of smoke wafted into the sky from the vicinity of the Catholic neighborhood. Someone was burning rubbish. The smoke grew thicker and blacker, spuming into the sky as smoke from a burning building. A house was on fire. Oh my God! Walter's house? Andrew Akiwenzie's? The church? The school? The little hall? The livery stable behind the church? It was hard to tell from where she was. As Rosa looked on she relived her own experience with fire thirty years before; she saw flames licking the wood, heard the boards and rafters crackle, and smelled the burning pitch and paint.

Rosa called David away from the organ to look. One glance and David was gone, forgetting that it was almost time to eat.

Hours later David returned, soaked in sweat, out of breath. Over and over he said, "Lee-lee! Lee-lee! Mikth! Mikth! Makakaeyauh. Kik!" He took hold of his mother's wrists and pulled her toward the door. "Woosh!"

Fear licked at her being like flames. "Stanley! Are you sure?" David nodded. Questions tumbled out of her mouth; others followed upon David's answers and gestures. "Where? At Walter's house? What was he doing? Lying down? Sleeping? Coughing? Sick? Whose house burned?" Rosa went through the names of all the people who lived near the church. She put her shawl on.

David led Rosa to Walter's and Frances's house fifty yards from the building that had burned. Walter met them at the door.

"Mother! Stanley's in a bad way. He came home this morning. He didn't look or sound too well when he came in. So we fed him. He started to tell us that he'd been working in the Guelph Stove Foundry for the past four years sweeping fine dust from the factory's floors, but before he finished his meal or his story someone yelled, 'Fire!

Fire!' Stanley was gone. He helped the fire brigade try to put out the fire, but it was too late. He came back to the house and collapsed, coughing and bringing up blood. He's in bed." Walter led his mother to the bed on the main floor where Stanley lay moaning.

"Son!" she said, her voice cracking as she sat down on the edge of the bed. She took Stanley's hand and looked into his face. "Oh, my Stanley, what's wrong?"

"Mother! I'm … going to … die!" and he broke into sobs and tried to take his hand away from hers. He began to cough violently. He twisted in bed so that he could lean over the side and spit and bring up into a pail that Walter and Frances had put there for him. He moaned and cried in pain.

Rosa, too, began to cry. She stroked Stanley's arm to give him whatever comfort she could with her touch. Walter brought a chair for her. "Frances has gone for her mother; she should be back any time now." David stood at the foot of the bed looking on.

Presently Kitchi-Low-C (Lucy Nawash) came in. "Hello, Rosauh. I guess sickness is the only thing that brings us together in someone else's house," Kitchi-Low-C remarked. Taking the chair that Walter had offered her, Kitchi-Low-C set it next to Stanley's bed. "Stanley! Look at me," she said quietly, and she read Stanley's tear-filled eyes. David started to talk to Walter. "No talking," she said, so that she could listen to Stanley's breathing and coughing.

"Leave me be," Stanley groaned. "I don't want to live. I can't stand it!" And he broke out into coughing that hurt even Kitchi-Low-C and Rosa.

"Be quiet. Don't talk," the medicine woman said quietly. She said little else. She and Rosa stayed by Stanley all night.

Twenty-four hours later Kitchi-Low-C gave her diagnosis: a lung disease that was curable, provided it had not settled in for too long and had not done too much damage. Stanley's answer, "Quite a while," to Kitchi-Low-C's question, "How long have you had this cough, this pain?" was disheartening. With medicine, prayer, and will, Stanley could recover.

Kitchi-Low-C took charge. Walter, Frances, and David would have to move out of the house until Stanley recovered. Only she and Rosa would tend to Stanley. The house was to be thoroughly cleaned and made fit for the Manitous of good health. When everything was washed—walls, floors, windows—the doors and windows were opened.

Cedar and sweet grass were hung about the house to freshen the air.

Taking Frances and David with her, Kitchi-Low-C went into the woods, marshes, swamps, and meadows to collect herbs, roots, leaves, berries, and resins. From this collection she made a beverage, a pail at a time. Stanley was to drink three cups every day. She also made a compound of roots, leaves, and berries that was commingled in Stanley's meals.

"Make sure that Stanley takes his medicine. Don't let him give in. Don't you give in. Scold him if you have to. To give in is what he'll want to do; it's the worst thing that he could do."

Rosa tended to Stanley as mother and nurse. At night she half-slept, waking up at the slightest motion, the least of sounds, as a mother of a newborn child does. By day she cat-napped.

Every morning Frances returned with David to the homestead to tend to the family garden, the chickens, and the pigs. David was to do whatever chores Frances assigned, sawing and splitting wood for the stove that was set outside, carrying water from the creek or the school pump. When he wasn't doing anything in particular, he was to serve as a sentry to keep strangers and unwanted visitors from the house.

For most of the day David had little to do but keep watch, a duty he diligently carried out from his seat astride a sawhorse just outside the front door. He smoked "makin's" and watched.

David couldn't stand Stanley's cries and moans and complaints. "I can't stand it anymore. Just leave me be to die." It pained him to hear his mother's own anguished weeping and her hiss, "I didn't raise you to preside over your death. Stop your whining." Each time he heard their voices in sadness or in anger, David moved his sawhorse out of hearing.

Once David was just outside the front door when Stanley cried louder than he had ever done before. Usually Stanley's cries were followed by his mother's voice. This time there was only Stanley's voice. David looked in. Rosa wasn't in the house with Stanley. David went in directly to Stanley's bed. "Lee-lee," he said, and he touched and patted his brother's leg.

The next moment Rosa came back into the house. "Eeeeyooooh! What are you doing in here? Get out! You're not supposed to be in here. Out! Out!" and she shoved and pushed David out the door. "I don't want to have to take care of two sick people. Stay out where you belong."

Stunned, David went out. He was confused; he was only trying to help.

While David was on duty he took his job seriously. "Don't let anyone come into the yard." As soon as he heard or saw anyone come along the road from either direction, he immediately took up his post at the gate, telling people in his own language that no one was allowed on the premises and that "Lee-lee" was sick in bed. People didn't understand him, but they smiled at him in condescension. Most times it was Enoch Taylor going home next door.

On learning that Stanley was at home gravely ill, Father Labelle came to visit and determine what sacraments, besides the Eucharist, the patient might need.

David was sitting on his sawhorse watching the road when he saw the priest come along. He went immediately to the gate and told Father Labelle that he was not allowed to come into the yard. He stood directly in the middle of the narrow gateway, his arms extended to show that he wasn't going to allow anyone to pass the gates, layman or clergyman.

Father Labelle smiled. "Good morning, David! What's this all about? You're not trying to get back at me, are you? You've got a long memory, haven't you?" David didn't move. "Come! Come! Cut the nonsense and let me by. I've no time for games." And he smiled some more as he tried to slip around David, first to the left, then to the right, but David effectively blocked him.

"Mrs. McLeod! ... Anyone!" Father Labelle eventually had to shout to attract attention. His shouts drew Rosa to the door. She let David know that the priest was welcome in the house.

By now Father Labelle spoke enough of the Indian language to understand and be understood by Rosa and others who spoke only Indian. To be able to speak the native language of the parishioners of their missions was expected of priests. By studying mightily, Labelle spoke passable Anishinaubae, conducted some prayers in Indian, and could read the gospels in the native language.

Father Labelle gave Stanley the Holy Eucharist, prayed, and gave him Extreme Unction, the last rites. On his return home the priest called Dr. Wigle in Wiarton to come to the reserve to examine Stanley McLeod. Every morning after mass Labelle came to the house to administer Holy Communion.

Some days later a car pulled up on the road in front of the gate, and two men and a woman got out. Seeing the car and the strangers, David scudded to his post. "No! No!" He stood in the middle of the passageway, his arms spread.

But before the visitors and David came together, Rosa, who'd heard the car draw up, was at the door watching. She called David away from the gate and sent him to get Frances.

Before doing what he was told, David stared at Fred Tuffnell. The agent glowered. To the doctor and Mrs. Tuffnell David paid not the slightest attention. Both asked David how he was.

Frances came along within a few minutes; Walter was in the woods, a couple of miles away, nowhere within easy reach. When she found that she had to speak English with White People, Frances, shy, was tempted to run off and hide. But there was no backing out of the situation.

"She says," Frances said, mixing up her pronouns when referring to the doctor, "that Stanley's got 'con-some-shin' and that he should go to a hospital in 'gravyn hearse' (Gravenhurst, Ontario)." Mrs. Tuffnell explained the meaning of consumption, and that there was nothing the doctors in Wiarton or Owen Sound could do.

"Stanley's not going anyplace. He's staying right here. Tell them, Frances, that we'll look after Stanley here, at home," Rosa said with iron in her voice.

After the doctor, the agent, and Mrs. Tuffnell had gone, David was nowhere in sight. Frances called and called for him, but David didn't answer or appear. Choc, too, was absent. Frances whistled and called for Choc. The dog, drawn by thoughts of food, came trotting into sight from the back. "Where's David?" she asked. Choc turned and, with Frances right behind him, trotted to the little barn in the back.

There she found David. "What are you doing in here? Come on, I need you to split some more wood."

"Where was he?" Rosa asked.

"Hiding in the barn."

For months Rosa sat at the foot of Stanley's bed keeping watch, giving him Kitchi-Low-C's medicine, stroking his head, bidding him not to give in. She cried when he cried, prayed when he slept. Her hopes that Stanley would recover mounted the longer he survived.

With Kitchi-Low-C's Indian medicine and Rosa's prayers and will, Stanley recovered. But keeping vigil for months, with her own spirit often at the breaking point, wore Rosa down. At the end of six months, she also needed Kitchi-Low-C's medicine to rebuild her body, which had wasted away to ninety pounds, and to restore her strength, which had failed her so that she could walk for no more than ten minutes without sitting down to rest.

By the spring of 1936 Rufus had soured on stevedoring in Depot Harbour on Parry Island. There was less work than before as other ports drew shipping away from Parry Sound, and demand for goods declined in the Depression. There were rumors among the Cape Croker men working at the docks that there was more work at home, and that the people were making a good living by fishing and cutting pulpwood. "For some, but not for all," Mac (Alfred) McLeod warned Rufus. Still, Rufus listened to the rumors. Fishermen could sell all of the fish they could catch. Everybody was better off than they had been in years. "Not true; some are just as poor as ever," Malcolm McLeod seconded his brother's remarks.

Rufus called the priest to arrange to have his cousin, George Keeshig, come to Parry Sound to pick him and his family up and take them "home."

George relayed the message to Rosa. "Rufus is coming home. I'm going to get them ... sometime in June."

Except for a couple of months after his release from residential school in Spanish, which he'd helped construct in 1913 as an assistant to Abe Gignac of that village, Rufus had been away from the reserve since 1912. His mother and his brothers had little meaning for him; during his absence the community lost whatever importance it might otherwise have had. The residential school, in priming Rufus for assimilation by alienating him from family and community, may well have made him care more for himself than for others.

Soon after Rufus left Cape Croker in 1917 he went to the recruitment station to join the army, and was turned down for being too young. To hell with them, he sputtered. He went on to the Christian Island Indian Reserve, where he worked in the pulpwood-cutting camps.

As assimilable as he was molded to be by the Jesuits—able to read, write, do arithmetic, and speak two languages fluently—no one assimilated Rufus. Too Indian. He tried Boston, Detroit, Chicago, and New York, where he was condescendingly greeted with "Hello, Chief. How are you, Chief?" At least it wasn't "goddamned Indian." He rubbed shoulders and sat with White People at Yankee Stadium, Briggs Stadium, Fenway Park, Comiskey Park, and Wrigley Field. But there were no permanent jobs. Rufus was not meant for the city.

Around 1925 he made his way to Parry Sound to work as a stevedore at Depot Harbour. Already there were some men from the Cape there, Gregor Keeshig, Lawrence Keeshig, his uncle Louis Lamourandiere, Mike Johnson, his brother Bobby, and Frances Nadjiwon, a cousin. The job was to load and unload trains. The men, many of them Poles from Depot Harbour and Parry Sound, worked ten and twelve hours a day, sometimes having to relay one hundred-pound bags of flour by hand from one man to the next, all for 40 cents an hour. For the men who worked at the docks, life was hard but good.

The stevedores worked hard and drank hard. Rufus excelled at both. On "pay days," Saturdays, the Cape Croker contingent, none of whom was as yet married, partied noisily, too noisily for the sensibilities of the Parry Island residents. In one of their meetings the Parry Island band council discussed the behavior of the Cape Croker Indians, and issued a warning that if they didn't tone down their celebrations, the council would declare them "Undesirables" and deport them to the mainland. To make sure it wouldn't have to take these extreme measures, the council allocated a partying place some distance from the main village where the Cape Indians might conduct their festivals without annoying the local residents. It was an eminently sound and fair arrangement, the Cape Indians agreed, worthy of Solomon.

Rufus and Bobby roomed and boarded at their Uncle Louis's home, not a particularly happy arrangement for a lover of festivals such as Rufus, considering that their Aunt Mary was opposed to festivals and happiness in any form of expression.

What drew Rufus to Joe Lafreniere's, his Aunt Mary's brother's place, no one knows, but the most likely reason was that Joe and his wife, Philomene, had two attractive daughters, Kate and Mary, both adopted. Rufus was one of two suitors; the other was Leo Phillips, whose origin was unknown.

Mary, the younger of the two girls, was born to Sarah Tobey of Honey Harbour. According to one story, Sarah gave Mary to her sister Philomene for adoption. According to another story, Sarah entrusted the baby to Philomene for baby-sitting for a month or so, but when the term was up, Philomene refused to return the baby to her mother.

That is how Mary came to be in Parry Island.

My mother, Mary, recalled the two men who visited her father, Joe. "There was this White Man, Leo. He started to come to our house before your dad. The thing that I remember most about him was his hands ... so big, just like mitts. Used to scare me the way he moved them, as if he'd like to put them round somebody's neck. And when he went back home to Parry Sound in his rowboat, he'd yell like an Indian; his voice would echo back and forth along the rocks and the islands and sound like there were dozens of Indians in the bushes.

"One night we were all sitting around the kitchen table, and my father said to Leo, 'I know why you've come here. You've come here because you like Kate. You can have her. She's old enough to get married. She's a good cook, can sew, look after a garden. She's a good worker, make a good wife.'

"Just like that my father give my sister away, like she was no more than an old coat. He didn't even ask her if she wanted to get married to this man, and he never asked my mother what she thought. But that's the way it was in those days.

"And my sister. She didn't say nothing, as if it didn't matter. That night when we were in bed, I ask her how come she never said nothing. Did she like that man, Leo Phillips? She said anything would be better than living at home, getting yelled at, nothing to do except work.

231

"The band council gave my sister and her husband a little bit of land about a mile from our place where this Leo Phillips build a house—you couldn't call it a house, it was more like a shack. Our own barn was bigger. My dad, mother, and me went to visit my sister a few times before she had her first baby. That's when my dad fix their house so that the roof didn't leak and the wind didn't blow through the cracks. Leo get mad at my dad for repairing the house, told him to mind his own business, and not come around the house again. You know, I never saw my sister again after that. She had three boys, Lawrence, Mervyn, and Kenneth. She got sick when Kenneth was born. My dad brought her medicines but they didn't make her better. But there was all kinds of talk about how my sister died, and why.

"Went crazy, that man. Leave those kids all by themselves and go out into the bush at night, right into the swamp, and yell like a wolf and scare the people here. People thought that it was a Bear-walker or Weendigo. Kept their doors locked at night. At last some policemen from Parry Sound and some men from here went after that man. It took more than ten men to hold that man down and tie him up. They lock that man up in Pen-tang (Penetanguishene). My mother and dad had to raise those boys.

"Only one who never stay home like the rest of the peoples was your dad. He wasn't scared of Bear-walkers or Weendigoes. 'That's a man yelling out there, some nut,' he told my dad. Your dad, he kept coming to our house; sometimes he bring some wine and try to give some to my dad. Once in a while my dad would take some when he wasn't making medicine or going hunting. He used to tell your dad that the Manitous might not give healing power to the medicines as punishment for drinking too much wine.

"That's when I found out that my dad was a medicine man. I used to always help him go pick plants in the bush and dry them outside, but I never pay much attention to what my dad did with them afterward.

"Everybody around here say that my dad was a Frenchman because his name was French. Maybe he was half, maybe not even that. But I think that my dad was more Indian than all the other Indians around here. The only thing that he carry with him, ever, was an ax when he go into the bush to pick medicine plants or make sugar in the spring; no matches, no knife, no blanket. He could do everything in the bush. He could understand the clouds, the moon, the sun, the stars, the birds, the insects, the animals, and the fish."

What my mother didn't know was that her stepfather, Joe Lafreniere, was on the Wooster Roll, which listed all of the Indians of Pottawatomi descent who had surrendered their lands in and around Green Bay and Manitowack in Wisconsin, but who instead of relocating in Indian Territory, emigrated to British-controlled Canada. In their exodus from their traditional home, Joe Lafreniere's ancestors took the northern route; some were even interned on Drummond Island in the 1840s, along with the traders and trappers of the Northwest Trading Company who had refused to go to work for the Astor Trading Company.

"Your dad," Mother told me, "he kept coming to the house. I don't know why he never go anyplace else. Only times he didn't come was on Fridays and Saturdays. I didn't like him. He was old ... and ugly. I used to pray that he would stop coming, but God never answer my prayers. That Rufus kept on coming to the house.

"One night my dad said to your dad, 'Rufus, you must like Mary. That's why you keep coming here. That's alright. She's young, fifteen; pretty; and she's a good girl. You can have her. I'll give her to you. ...'

"It was like a slap in the face. I screamed. I ran upstairs and threw myself on my bed. I cried. My mother, she came upstairs and held me to make me stop crying. She told me that my dad wasn't giving me away just to anyone. Rufus was a good worker and would look after me. But that only made me feel worse. I pushed my mother away from me. She didn't want to keep me, just like my real mother had let me go. I cried. Nobody wanted me. My mother went downstairs.

"I made up my mind to run away, someplace far. Never come back, never see the people who didn't want me. I'd steal my dad's boat. I really went down to my dad's dock and got in the boat. But I couldn't start the boat. It was against me, too.

"I cried because I didn't want to marry that man. Every night. I cried because I couldn't run away. I didn't know anybody. Only place I knew was Honey Harbour and Beausoleil Island. I didn't have no money. I didn't know how to speak English too good. I didn't know anything except how to cook and do housework. You see, all I had was grade three in Spanish. I was only fifteen."

Mother was actually nineteen. But she didn't learn this until she applied for her old-age pension and had to provide her baptismal certificate, which was eventually tracked down in Peterborough, Ontario. The date of my mother's birth, as shown on the certificate, shocked her.

"After a while I couldn't cry anymore. I gave up. It was no use going against my parents. Better to listen to them and do what they wanted. Because that's the way it was in those days.

"Me and your dad got married in 1928 and you were born in 1929. Up to that time there was lots of work for everybody, summer and winter, but after that there wasn't so much. Your dad, he was one of the lucky ones working at Depot Harbour, but he wasn't working every day anymore, just two or three days a week. Your dad liked to work and have money and it bothered him to sit around with nothing to do. It was work, then wait and watch for the next boat.

"And that was how we lived in Parry Island. Work and wait all summer; wait all winter for the summer and live on the money and the preserves until they were all used up. It wouldn't have been so bad if your dad had been able to hunt and trap like the other Indians, but he couldn't. All he knew was how to lift bags and cut trees.

"People said I was lucky to have such a good husband, always working, making good money. But I didn't feel very lucky in March when we didn't have nothing to eat and I had to go and borrow some grub from my mother. I was ashamed. Your dad, he was supposed to look after me.

"But after your sister Gladys was born I start to love your dad. I felt sorry for him when he wasn't working because he feel that he was no good. Then he'd get drunk with that Harry Medawayash and that Baepaesh, and blame me for all his troubles and say that he didn't want to marry me in the first place. That's the way he was, blame somebody else; never his fault.

"At last he said that he couldn't live like that anymore, he wanted to live a better way, he wanted something better for all of us, especially you children. He said that you and Gladys were going to be something.

"He kept talking about what Mac and Malcolm (McLeod) told him about how some people made a good living fishing and cutting pulpwood. It was just the kind of talk that your father wanted to hear. He said that he was going home ... to a better life.

"I didn't want to go. I was afraid. I didn't know anybody at Cape Croker, and I didn't know if life would be any better on your dad's reserve. I often think that if your dad had tried he coulda made a living just like my dad, but your dad, he wouldn't try, would give up and say, 'I can't do that.' Maybe that school done something that make your dad forget old Indian ways.

"He call the priest in Cape Croker for his cousin to come and get us."

I recall little of that trip that began early in the morning. Two incidents stand out in my mind, the rest of the ride forgotten in the monotony of sitting in a car all day. The first occurred just south of Parry Sound. A man stopped us on the road and wouldn't let us pass. Father and George Keeshig got out of the car. Up ahead were some men on the road; they scurried off the road and disappeared into the woods. A short while later the road and the earth in front of us exploded in a blast of thunder, light, and a cloud of smoke. Rocks and gravel shot into the air and showered down like hail. The men came out of the woods and cleaned up while Gladys wailed, "They broke the road, now we have to go home." I was afraid that she was right.

Not long after we went through a town whose name sounded like Australia, but must have been Orillia. Gladys and I fell asleep in the back seat. A shot rang out under the car, sending Sis and me almost to the roof of the car. The car stopped and leaned over. It was only a busted tire, one of many the car suffered that day, a common ailment of all cars in those days. While George and father were removing some of the cargo to lighten the car, Gladys, aged four, took the hems of her blue dress and spread her garment as if she were modeling it for an audience of fashion buyers. George mended the tire as if it had suffered a cut; he scraped the wound clean, dabbed some ointment upon it, and then covered it with a bandage. After the operation the tire was wound round the wheel and reattached to the car. We continued on our way. How many times did the tires bust that day? Who knows? The only one who seemed to relish these accidents was Gladys, who played little model, Shirley Temple, each time we had to stop. Even without the delays caused by the bursting tires the trip would have been formidable, as the routes were few and labyrinthine, service stations scarce and far between. We must have resembled the Judd family in their trek from Oklahoma to California in John Steinbeck's *The Grapes of Wrath*.

It was dark when we arrived at Grandmother's house in Cape Croker, though it may have been June, when it remains light until 10 p.m. We must have been on the road for about sixteen hours.

Rosa was up waiting for us, had been waiting since early afternoon, anxious to see her prodigal son and his family, her first grandchildren. She would have killed a fatted calf had she had one, but the best she could provide on this occasion was fried salt pork, gravy, potatoes, and scone, the local name for bannock, a fast-food bread.

When we went into the house, Gladys modeled her dress immediately, "See my new dress." Rosa cried, kissed us, and drew us into her arms. She looked ancient and half-starved; her hair was wound in a roll at the nape of her neck; her features were classically "Indian," making her look wise and indestructible; her thinness made her look taller than she was. She wore a black dress that made her look somber.

But my attention lingered only long enough on Rosa to gather these impressions. My eyes were drawn to and then locked on the man who was sitting on a chair against the wall on the opposite side of the room. His eyes were locked on mine, watching my every wink, blink, and movement. He didn't blink, and he looked as if he wanted to stare me out of the house.

He was a sorry-looking man; his short hair bristled and swept forward instead of backward as with most people. His eyes were small, and there were little half moons over and under each eye. And he was chewing his tongue as if he were chewing something deliberately, as cows masticate their cud, without hurry. I wanted to squirm out of his sight.

Meanwhile, Rosa, Mary, and Rufus were talking and making a fuss about this and that and arranging our bundles on the floor to one side.

After Rosa had greeted us, she introduced the strange man. "This is David," she said to our parents, and then presented my sister and I to "your Uncle David." This tubby man was as reluctant to shake our hands as Sis and I were to shake his.

During the meal I kept a wary eye on David. I didn't know what "uncle" meant. He, too, kept an eye on our every movement, even when he dunked his scone in his tea. From time to time I would look down into my plate to avoid his stare, but was drawn again and again by some magnet to look at him. Gladys must have been doing the same thing. Mother noticed not so much our stares but the slowness of our eating; she gave each of us a sharp crack on our heads for neglecting our meals, and bade us to, "Hurry up, eat your supper."

Just before we were shepherded upstairs to bed, Mother made us give our uncle a hug. Gladys was willing enough. She flung her four-year-old arms around David's neck and planted her lips on "Uncle's" cheek. David looked pained; he wiped his cheek as if it had been contaminated. When my turn came I refused to touch him. David recoiled, shook his head, "No! No!"

In the dark I closed my eyes but I could not shut out my uncle's glaring face. It kept appearing and when it faded away it was replaced by the image of a cook in a Parry Sound restaurant who had glared at me as he clashed his carver's knife on a sharpener as if he had intended to slice me. I now wished that I had not come on this trip. Fortunately for me, the Sandman (Weeng in the Anishinaubae language) was stronger than these images, for he put them to flight and me to sleep.

The next morning David, Gladys, and I resumed our staring match, while Grandmother and Mother cooked breakfast and got acquainted. Father was already gone, presumably house or boat hunting.

David squirmed under our double-barreled stare. He'd stop in the middle of stirring his tea with a chunk of scone. Finally, unable to withstand our withering stares, he sat bolt upright, pointed a finger at me, and uttered a moan that sounded like a whine, "Ook! Ook!" His name for me was "Ook."

"Aah," Grandmother exclaimed. "What's the matter with you? He's not doing anything to you. Now! Cut it out."

Before I could rejoice, Mother pulled my ear as a signal to stop whatever I was doing to annoy David. I yowled "Eeeeyoooh!" as I rose with my ear.

For a moment, but only for a moment, there was a glint of "serves you right" in David's eyes. His look doubled the hurt in my ear.

David accelerated his meal, shoveling his porridge into his mouth as quickly as he could swallow it. Lastly, he put his scone into his teacup, then fished out the soggy mess and put it into his mouth. He had no teeth. Before he got up and went out, David shot a withering glance at me.

Sis and I hastened our meal. To hurry her along even more, I kicked her knee to get her to whine to earn us quick dismissal from the table.

Sis whined.

"Go outside and play," Mother commanded us, and added as an afterthought, "and don't bother your uncle."

We went out the front door and to the road to see where our uncle had gone, and at the same time to look over our new home. How dull and flat it was compared to our Parry Island home. It was flat all the way to the distant bluffs, flat fields, flat bushes, some cedars, not like our old home, which was rocky and hilly and covered with pines and spruces. The only feature that grabbed my attention was the line of chalk-white bluffs in the distance. But they were far away and made no difference to our lives.

But we weren't as interested in our surroundings as we were in our strange uncle.

Grandmother, suspecting our intentions and interests, came outside with our mother. "Don't you go across the road into the woods; there are snakes there. Don't go into the bush over there," she said, pointing to a grove of cedars that grew in an adjoining lot just to the north of the house, twenty-five or so steps away. "There's poison ivy all over the place. And don't go across the road to that house. The people who used to live there left some ghosts to look after the place." She took us to the back of the house where there was a sawhorse, poles, and a pile of stove wood. There was also a clothesline. Not too far away was a barn, to which Grandmother pointed. "Don't go any farther than the barn; that's where the toilet is." Still farther back, two minutes by foot, was the verge of the poplar woods. There we could see and hear David chopping trees down. "Never go back there. A wood chip might fly up and hit you in the eye or a tree might fall on your heads. The ax and the saw are very sharp; they might cut you. Stay around the house where we can see you, hear you. You've got more than enough room." By this she meant the field in front and to the south of the house that was covered with grasses, thistles, crickets, and all sorts of other hostile creatures.

Grandmother's place was surrounded by danger. Our new world that appeared so vast had shrunk under a boundary of "don'ts."

Sis didn't say so in so many words, but her expression betrayed what was on her mind. "What will we do? Where will we play?"

"David's not used to kids," Grandmother said as she and our mother went back into the house.

But Gladys and I didn't play as bidden; we weren't so easily wound up as tops, ready to spin. We pretended to play, enough to satisfy the adults that we were disturbing no one. Instead of amusing ourselves, our attentions were on our uncle at the back of the property. He was not only working, he was talking to someone we could not see.

Sis and I drifted to the back of the house where we stood atop the pile of poles to get a better look at Uncle and the person or persons he was talking to. "What is he saying? Who is he talking to? Can you see?" we asked each other. Such strange language. It must be English or another foreign language. Look we did, except we saw no one.

We didn't stand there for too long. Burning with curiosity and suspense, Sis and I raced into the house. "Uncle David is talking to someone. Come! Listen!" We took hold of Grandmother's hands and pulled her outside.

Grandmother, amused by our excitement, smiled, "Oh! He always talks when he's working."

"Who's he talking to? Is he talking English?"

Grandmother explained that David had his own language, neither English nor Indian, because he couldn't talk like other people. Only God, the Manitous and the Little People listened to and understood him.

What effect Grandmother's words had on Gladys I don't know, but I was staggered … trying to sort it out. God. The Manitous. Little

People. And David's remarkable ability to communicate with unseen beings.

"Do they talk to him?"

"Well! They must, because he keeps talking to them."

"Why does he talk to them? About what?"

"Because ordinary people won't talk to David and they can't understand him."

"Stop pestering your grandmother with so many questions," Mother said as she shepherded us outside with the magic words, "Go play outside."

Outside Gladys and I went back to the summit of the pile of poles to watch and to listen. My mind drifted about, caught in a whirlpool of vague notions and conflicting images. God. My other grandmother, Philomene, had told me about God and taught me to pray. I had heard Grandfather Joe talk as he ground leaves, roots, berries, and stems, but I had never connected his talk as anything special. I had thought it was just an adult peculiarity.

Over the next few days I asked my grandmother dozens of questions. "Who is God? Who are the Manitous? Where do they live? What do they do? What do they look like? Have you, Grandmother, ever seen them? Do you talk to them?" Grandmother was hard put to answer these questions. The best she could say about them was that they could be friendly or vengeful. It was always best to win their goodwill instead of their enmity. The Little People dwelled in the forest and were the special friends of children.

After learning about the Manitous I envied David for the special kinship he had with these magic beings. I wanted to learn Uncle's language so that I, too, could talk to his friends.

I now looked on David not as someone odd but as someone special, possessing something that ordinary people didn't have, and I tried not to stare at him. I now wanted him to like me so I could be his friend. When David went out in the evenings, Gladys and I received permission to accompany him as far as the corner, Sis on one side, I on the other, holding Uncle's hands with affection.

At night we prayed even more piously than before, but God didn't speak to us. During the day I often led my sister near the cedar grove to peer into the underbrush and call out in quiet, friendly voices to the Little People, inviting them to make an appearance. But, like God, they didn't answer or show themselves.

Our behavior won David's friendship and trust. We tried talking to him in his own language. He frowned and shook a finger in our faces as if disapproving of our efforts, but more likely it was his way of expressing his opinion of what he thought of our silly attempts.

Mother sometimes played hide and seek with us, a strange sort of play to David. He watched us as we dashed out of the house and hid behind a door or woodpile. He looked on as Mother came out in search of us. To help our mother he told her where we were hidden. We got mad at David for spoiling our game.

One evening after supper when the dishes were done, Mother asked us if we wanted to play hide and seek. Turning to David, she asked, "Do you want to play, too?" David nodded yes. Mother explained the object of the game and some of its rules. Whether David understood the niceties of the game is moot. In the very first session David was hooked, becoming a hide-and-seek addict without ever developing into a skilled, adept player. He played the game with passion and diligence well into his later life, playing with our younger sisters Ernestine and Janet and their friends.

Uncle loved this game more than any other. Believing that he couldn't be seen or found, he laughed aloud to attract the attention of the seeker, and laughed louder as he raced home. He played until sweat poured down his face.

Alas, our stay at Grandmother's house ended all too soon. Father found a house, a small log cabin belonging to Alfred "Indian Act" Jones.

When we moved to our new home that stood at the edge of a swamp and was shielded from the skies by a canopy of limbs and leaves of immense elms and oaks, I thought I'd never see David again, but though I didn't know it, we were no more than a fifteen-minute walk from Grandmother's through the woods.

Much to our delight David came over often, sometimes in the morning, sometimes in the evening. He came over to play hide and seek; he also came over, sent by Grandmother, to help Mother with the wood and other heavy chores. Mother was in a family way again, and she needed all the help she could get during the day while Father was out on the lake from dawn till dusk.

Despite her pregnancy Mother did what she could to help Father bring about a better life. She planted a garden with vegetables and potatoes, picked raspberries, blackberries, and strawberries, and persuaded father to buy a piglet, whom Gladys and I promptly adopted as a pet, naming it "Coosh."

When David arrived in the mornings we immediately set into hide and seek, playing until David was soaked in perspiration and unfit for the work he'd been sent to perform. In no time Mother, with maternal cunning, extorted work from us before she would let us play. We carried water unwillingly from a spring that bubbled up just behind the house, pulled weeds from the garden, picked potato bugs from potato plants; nothing onerous, but backbreaking and demeaning for children. Only when we were done did Mother allow us to play. By then, soured by work and life, we had lost our zest for anything.

David soon caught on. He didn't like picking potato bugs or weeding any more than we did. Instead of coming to our place as directed by Grandmother, David took Bert Ashkewe's short cut that led through Will-ee's front yard, and went to Walter's. If David thought he was going to loaf and lounge at his brother's place, he soon learned otherwise. At least he didn't have to weed the garden or pick potato bugs. Instead, Frances conscripted David to wash and dry dishes, sweep the floor, and take clothing down from the clothesline. He soon quit taking refuge at Walter's, preferring to come to our place where he could play hide and seek.

Ever since Isaiah and Mary Jane had sold their home to the Francis Nadjiwon family, who had not yet moved in, Grandmother had had no neighbors and few visitors other than Walter and Frances, and Back-a-haw on occasion. Mother, knowing no one in the community, had no one to turn to except Grandmother for comfort and companionship.

We often went to Grandmother's, sometimes staying for several days, because Father himself was spending more time elsewhere. Whenever Grandmother wanted to see us and felt sorry for my mother, she sent Uncle David to fetch us and to help Mother carry a bundle of baby clothing.

It was at Grandmother's place during one of our visits that I developed a fascination for cars and the trail of dust that they raised. Since coming to our new home I had not seen cars and had all but forgotten that I had ridden in one. But at Grandmother's house I occasionally saw one go by, dragging a cloud of dust behind it. It was magic. How was it done?

Cars excited me. Each time I saw one I ran into the house calling out, "Car! Car!" But instead of sharing my excitement and rushing to see the car, Grandmother seemed nervous. "Where's David?" she asked.

"Out in the back. ... Why?"

"Because the man in that car doesn't like David."

I didn't ask why; too absorbed in the car and the dust. It was the agent's car.

The other vehicle that was a familiar sight around the reserve was a small, faded green pickup truck with a roughly constructed wooden enclosure covering the back. It belonged to George Ewald, a ped-

dler who sold tainted and untainted meats, bones, and stale bread
that were covered with a fine coating of dust gathered from the road
from Wiarton, fifteen miles away. Ewald enjoyed fondling or trying
to fondle women, who had to be deft in evading Ewald's groping
hands when they were handing over money.

I wanted a car, to be a car, at least to raise dust like a car. I exper-
imented with different articles. Finally I settled on poplar saplings
that were lush with foliage. Dragged on the dirt road, the saplings
raised a fine cloud of dust. At first I ran alone dragging the sapling
behind me, but the result was not car-like enough. So I asked David
to join me. Together we were more car-like.

Down the road we raced side by side, then back again in front of
the house, roaring like a car to draw attention. We had to stop now
and then to replace the leafless saplings with fresh ones that Uncle
cut down.

The afternoon was too hot for playing car; we resumed our sport
after supper, racing back and forth in front of the house until our
mothers called us into the house to get ready for bed.

My mother looked at me with disgust. "Look at you! Filthy! You
can't go to bed like that. Get some water. You're going to have to have
a bath." Grandmother agreed. "Get some water from the well across
the road."

"But Grandmother said there are ghosts there!" I protested.

"They're sleeping right now. Do what you're told."

David and I drew water for our baths. Slave work, like gathering
wood for one's own funeral pyre. But the ordeal for David had not
started. It began when Grandmother told him to undress. He whined,
he covered himself, he pointed at me and at the water. A big man like
that crying and carrying on like a baby! I couldn't figure out why
Mother and Grandmother went to so much trouble. All they needed
to do was to shake our clothes out.

Next morning we were once more playing car and raising dust
that drifted like a noxious cloud toward the house, driven there by
an easterly breeze.

Grandmother came out. There was an edge to her voice that
demanded obedience. "Go play someplace else. The dust is coming
into the house."

David and I sprinted up the grade in second gear to play in front of the neighboring house. To make sure that it was a safe place to play in front of and that there weren't any ghosts on patrol, I cast an anxious glance at the yard, in the windows. An object wedged in the fork of a large maple grabbed my attention and wouldn't let go.

"Daybit!" I called. "Look!" I pointed at the object. All thoughts of ghosts vanished.

To get a closer look we went up to the fence. It wasn't a nest, nor was it a bird.

To learn what the object was deserved an even closer look than could be gained from the road. Yet I had some misgivings about going onto property that was watched by ghosts; I also had a feeling that trespassing wasn't quite right. But the curiosity to know what the object was was stronger than my vague moral feelings or my fear of ghosts. David and I squirmed under the fence to save time and to outrace any third party who might have seen the spoils and snatched them from us in front of our noses.

At the foot of the maple we saw that the object was a brown paper bag lodged where brown paper bags usually are not lodged. Surprise! popped immediately into my head, so much had I learned about brown paper bags that father had brought home on occasion. Best of all, the brown paper bag was all by itself but out of reach.

Desperation, the mother of invention and resourcefulness, inspired us. I talked David into giving me a boost so that I could inspect the bag and see what it held. I opened the bag. Sandwiches! Tea! Cake! I gathered the bag into my arms tenderly, affectionately, to keep it from slipping out of my grasp. "Let me down," I whispered to David.

As soon as I set foot on the ground I hissed, "Come on! Hurry up!" I ran, wiggled under the fence, and scrambled to the road, with David breathing heavily behind. I looked up and down the road. The coast was clear. The next instant we scudded across the road to the other side, climbed over the fence and into the shadows of the cedar grove.

Breathless with excitement and hunger I dropped to my knees to open the bag and divide the spoils. David also plopped down. Buttered bologna sandwiches garnished with a spread, soft white bread, a large wedge of cake, and a jar of sugared tea; the meal was of the well-off. David and I sat on a log.

"Ook!" David said, and he cleared his throat noisily to smooth the passage of the goodies into his stomach.

"Shshshsh!" I shushed David, who looked frightened. "Keep quiet, don't you say anything."

We ate quietly and slowly, the way the well-off eat their meals, sensually savoring every flavor borne by every morsel, not bolting it down or spoiling it with chatter. We should have roared in triumph as did Archimedes when he discovered the self-evident truth that water rises when one gets into a tub to take a bath. Nor did we think of inviting friends, such as Gladys, to share in our bounty. Instead we acted as thieves do, afraid of being found out.

After we polished off the tea, I hid the brown paper bag and the jar under leaves, moss, and twigs. Before going out into the open world, I told Uncle to say nothing of our discovery to anyone, not even to his friends the Manitous, and to make sure that he understood I put a finger to my lips while making a shushing sound, "Shshsh." David put his own fingers to his lips as his way of letting me know that he understood. Still, I was uneasy; I didn't fully trust him.

When we emerged from the grove and stepped out on the road, there was Sis a little farther down.

"What were you doing in there?" she bawled. "You're not supposed to go in there! There's poison ivy in there! I'm going to tell on you!"

"I went for a poo," I told her.

"You're supposed to go in the toilet, dope," she wailed, but she didn't say anything else, thank goodness.

Sis was dangerous, but David more so. Throughout the rest of the day he put his fingers to his lips and said, "Shshshsh" while looking at me so that Grandmother asked, "What have you been up to?" and Sis echoed the same question.

It didn't do any good to tell David to "cut it out." The only way of keeping David from spilling the beans was by keeping away from him, which was difficult to do because he now wanted to stick by me. My nerves were on edge all day.

I was no different from other finders of treasures or recipients of windfalls in expecting providence to smile a second time and to bestow upon me a second favor. The next morning David and I bolted down our food and raced out the front door and up the grade.

Providence had smiled on us once more, and so had the good fairy. Maybe it was David's friends, the Little People, who had left a present for us the second time.

We bore off our booty as we had done the day before to our hideaway. Ham and mock chicken sandwiches, butter, mustard, pie, and a jar of milk. David and I feasted without guilt.

Before going back out in the world I sternly warned David not to say or do anything that would give away our windfalls, otherwise the Manitous might never again leave anything in trees for us. And if others knew that we had received gifts from the Manitous, they would get jealous.

Good old David. He kept his fingers from his mouth, and avoided doing anything that would have let the kitty out of the bag.

That evening we ate supper, coarse compared to what we, David and I, had eaten at lunch. To eat quietly was not unusual, of course. We were constantly reminded, "Eat! You can't taste or enjoy your meal when you're talking." Nor were we allowed to leave the table until everybody was done. Gladys and I were done before Grandmother, Mother and David. We fidgeted and squirmed in impatience.

"You know, Percy came over here today, this afternoon, while you were gone for a walk," Grandmother started to tell Mother. David and I had gone on a walk with Mother, Gladys, and Baby Marilyn. "He came over and asked for a cup of tea. The first time that man has set foot in this house. Scared me at first. I guessed that he didn't have anything to eat, so I made him some porridge and some of our leftover scone.

"After he ate and thanked me he told me that someone had made off with his lunch today. Same thing happened the day before. At first he thought it might have been a raven or a raccoon that had taken his lunches, but they wouldn't have made off with the bag and bottle; they would have left those articles behind. He figured it was a person that took his lunch. He shouldn't have left his lunch where it could be taken, but he never thought anybody would take it because nobody around here takes what belongs to someone else. He couldn't blame anyone but himself. He should have hidden his lunch better." Grandmother paused.

"Isn't that terrible," Mother said.

David looked at me. I shot back a dirty look and then fixed my eyes on my empty plate.

Grandmother continued, deliberately letting each word fall like drops of water dripping and then sinking into sand. She enunciated the adjective "poor" each time she uttered the name "Percy," as if "poor" were synonymous with and related exclusively to Percy. "That *poor* Percy has to get up earlier than anybody else on the reserve in order to cut hay; that's quite a long way, five miles at least. Then that poor Percy has to work all day in the hot sun. Then after cutting hay all day, that *poor* Percy has to go home late in the evening and has to do more chores before he eats and goes to bed. People like that *poor* Percy have to eat, otherwise they can collapse from starvation. And someone had the nerve to steal his lunches."

David, I noticed from the corner of my eye, chewed with even greater deliberation, as if the salt pork were too salty and he wanted to spit it out. He cast a furtive glance my way. I looked elsewhere, almost feeling sorry for "poor Percy." To deflect suspicion I agreed with Grandmother that taking "poor Percy's" lunch was a foul deed. David looked at me again.

Mother asked, "Who's Percy?"

"Percy Pitwaniquot. A farmer. But he's also a policeman. As soon as he's finished cutting hay, he'll be looking for the person or persons who stole his lunches. He carries a club and handcuffs. First he conks thieves over the head with his club, then he clamps the handcuffs on their wrists." And here Grandmother brought her hands together to show how handcuffs locked wrists together. David stopped chewing. Grandmother went on. "And then Percy will march that scoundrel to jail, lock him up, and he won't give that culprit anything to eat or drink. ..."

"Ook! Ook!" David blurted out, pointing a shaking finger in my face. At the same time he rose from his chair without first moving it back, so that he sent it clattering to the floor. "Ook! Ook!" he repeated, and he let loose a torrent of words of condemnation, then stomped out of the house without finishing his meal.

I was stunned. I reeled in my chair. My vision blurred. My own friend, my uncle betraying me like a Judas to save his own skin. I stammered my pleadings, "He made me do it. He lifted me up to get the bag. He was going to hit me!"

Grandmother didn't bat an eyelash, much less look at me. She continued to talk to Mother as if she hadn't heard a word of what David or I had said. "I hope that poor Percy doesn't catch them; they must be very poor to have to steal."

Miserable, I went out. I didn't know what a policeman or a jail was, but both filled me with foreboding. David was in the woods, ax in hand, but he wasn't working as much as he was denouncing me to the Manitous and to the Little People, who surely relayed what they'd heard to Percy.

I wished that I'd never met David. Never again would I speak to or play with him. I'd find a new friend.

Over the next days David and I avoided each other like mortal enemies, as much as it is possible for two people living in the same household to keep out of one another's way.

David didn't go to "the other side" or down to the village in the evenings as was his habit. Not wanting to be collared by either the agent or Percy, he went instead to the back where he cut wood and denounced me for coming into his life and causing him grief. Every night I thanked Kitchi-Manitou for having kept "poor Percy" from thundering at the door and demanding our surrender that day. In the next prayer I beseeched Kitchi-Manitou to keep Percy on his farm in Sidney Bay where he belonged.

Since David and I had become estranged, I had no friend. I longed for someone to play with. The friend I'd been longing for arrived when Francis and Ethel Nadjiwon moved into the house across the road with their children, Clifford, Vera, Dorothy, and Ernest. Ernie, two years younger than me, became my friend.

Eventually David and I outgrew our enmity, and resumed living with less and less fear with each passing day as the specter of Percy faded from our minds. We no longer hid whenever we heard a car. Kitchi-Manitou had answered my prayers by keeping "poor Percy" away from our neighborhood.

Just before I started school in 1937, Father found another unoccupied house: Norman McLeod's house, just a bit farther up the road near the trail's end. Since Norman had gone to Longlac in Northern

Ontario to work in the lumber camps and had not come home for four or five years, no one was sure how long he'd been absent, and Stanley had moved into his father's house. Stanley, not needing such a large home, now lent the house to Rufus and moved in with Rosa. It was a two-story house with a large room downstairs and another on the second floor. There was also an unfinished addition that had a bright, undefined future. It was a mansion compared to Alfred Jones' log cabin. Downstairs was a stove, a cupboard, a table, two chairs, and two blocks of wood that served as chairs. Upstairs was uncluttered; no beds, just mattresses on the floor.

For the first few days I followed Benjamin, Bessie, and Hilda, Bert Ashkewe's children, to school. They took the short cut across a meadow, through some woods, across another meadow, and through more woods, emerging at Will-ee's and cutting in front of his house. The distance was close to a mile and a half, a half-hour walk.

One morning they ran ahead of me and hid behind a rail fence in the middle of the first wood. As I climbed over the fence I was deafened by an outburst of shrieks and yelps. Terrified, I ran home. It was the Manitous, the Little People, Uncle's friends.

The next day I took the main road to school, stopping at Grandmother's house to tell her what those dreadful Ashkewes had done.

Grandmother sent David to escort me to school.

At school I invited David to come in to see the classroom and my desk. Never having set foot in the school, David came in willingly. While I was showing David my work books, Miss Burke, our teacher, came into the classroom. She clapped her hands smartly to draw our attention and, although it was not yet 9 a.m., told us to settle down. "This is not a barnyard," she declared perspicaciously. And spotting David, she asked, "And who are you?"

"Oh! He's a new kid," someone in the grades seven and eight rows piped up before I had a chance to say a word. "His name's David," the same voice chimed.

"Please be seated," Miss Burke directed, pointing to an empty desk behind me. David sat down. Miss Burke went out and rang the bell to summon the children still outside to come in. The older students sniggered.

"David! Go home! Hurry up!" I hissed.

"No! Stay!" the older students, mainly boys, insisted; their words overwhelmed mine.

Actually David started to get up, but sat down when the voices told him to "stay."

The rest of the students trooped in, arching their eyebrows when they saw David sitting in the grade one row.

As for me, I was deeply troubled. It was now too late to regret having invited David to my school.

Miss Burke took her command post behind her desk. We recited "The Lord's Prayer." Next in the opening exercises was the singing of the national anthem: "God save our gracious king ... a noble king." David, knowing no more than the rest of us about the king, nor caring one straw about His Majesty's well-being, sang not a note.

Last in the sequence of exercises was the issue of cod liver oil, an elixir believed to prevent plagues, pestilence, the Black Death, and whatever ailed one. There was not a student in the school who did not dread this concoction.

When David came forward to receive his tablespoon of cod liver oil, Miss Burke looked at him quizzically. "What's your name? How old are you?"

"He's a new kid; doesn't speak English," a boy's voice volunteered.

Miss Burke poured the cod liver oil into a tablespoon. "Open your mouth." She poured the stuff into Uncle's mouth. We waited.

Instead of grimacing like the rest of us, David grinned in immense satisfaction. Miss Burke looked gratified, almost smug, as she looked around before asking, "Now, why can't you take your cod liver oil without fuss like this boy? ... David, you may take your seat." Miss Burke had to point to the seat behind me to get David to understand.

Miss Burke was new to the school but old in life; at least she looked old. She was the classic schoolmarm: petite, gray-haired, sallow-complexioned, hawk-nosed, and hawk-eyed behind round, silver-rimmed glasses. There was not an iota of humor in her. She inspired fear.

When she said, "I am vexed," she meant that she was getting ready to shift into the next gear of anger and that the source of her vexation had better desist. One warning was all she issued to get compliance. "Millicent (Solomon)! What are you chewing? ... Gum? Get it out of our mouth!" Millicent knew better than to cross Miss Burke.

In these first few minutes of school after the exercises Miss Burke had to work fast to keep all eight grades occupied. She went from row to row checking homework and assigning seatwork. Grade one was immersed in the mysteries of the alphabet through the "phonics," coughing, hissing, and blowing sounds. After the sounding exercises, we printed letters, forming balls and sticks between lines.

Behind me I heard Miss Burke explain to David how to hold a pencil properly and that he should form the letters as they were formed on the blackboard. "Now print neatly. I'll be back to check your work."

While assigning seatwork to the higher grades, Miss Burke returned to the grade one row to check our progress once, twice, three times. Each time she inspected David's work she found his pencil point broken. "What's the matter with you?" she demanded. "You're pressing too hard, you big oaf." She slapped David's hand. "Not so hard. ..."

David started to rise to his feet. To prevent him from getting up, Miss Burke put a hand on his shoulder to press him down, but nothing could keep David from getting to his feet. "God-dab, sudlabitch," David stomped out the door.

"You come back here. Where do you think you're going? I'm going to report you!" Miss Burke fumed.

Turning to the class for help, Miss Burke appealed, "Who are his parents? Where does he live? Who brought him here?"

My heart jumped.

The senior grade eight girls told Miss Burke about David. "He can't talk right, never went to school. He wasn't right in the head."

David did not escort me to school again. He and I drifted apart once more. I was nothing but trouble to him.

He never set foot in the school again, though he often stopped by when he was in the vicinity to watch a game called "pig," played by the children during the lunch hour.

David sat on the shoulder of the road, leaning this way and that, imagining that he was the batter. His eyes followed the ball and the scramble of fielders who chased down and picked up the ball. Then he focused on the batter, who ran to the other goal line, chased by the player who had fielded the ball. He riveted his eyes next on the fielder bearing down on the runner, ball in hand, ready to strike the runner down and "out," the runner zigzagging like a water bug to avoid being caught. There was nothing on the reserve or anywhere else to compare to this game for generating joy.

This is what school was all about. And there was no teacher present to spoil the fun with rules and right ways. David looked on, and played the game in his imagination. He too could do that: hit the ball, run, and throw.

The boys and girls noticed Crazy Dave watching them, but paid no more attention to him than they did to any other passerby. But there were a few, less selfish than the others, who felt sorry for him for being left out of the fun. "Let's let him play, let him try," they said.

"No," the others grumbled. "He doesn't know how to do anything."

"Let's give him a chance anyways. Just once. Let him have one turn at bat. If he can't hit, we won't let him bat again. It won't last long."

"Alright then," the objectors relented. "Just once."

"David! Do you want to play?"

David was taken aback by this invitation, which he had not expected. He wasn't sure if it was genuine or feigned. Of course he wanted to play. He hesitated, unsure whether he had heard right.

"Come on over. It's alright, the teacher won't come out; she's having lunch right now."

David went over the stile into the school yard.

The captain of the team at bat was generous, handing David the bat.

David didn't know which end to hold or which shoulder to rest it on or how to stand in line with the pitcher. The players at bat had to show David how to do all these things, while the fielders waited and grumbled. "See! I knew it. He doesn't even know how to bat properly."

But once David was briefed on the techniques of batting and was set to face the pitcher, he swung, as did mighty Casey, as soon as the pitcher tossed the ball into the air, even before it came down. He grunted, such was the force of his swing. The batters on deck gasped, "Holy mackerel! Stand back. If he ever lets that bat slip out of his grasp ...."

Even the pitcher was rattled by the force of David's swing. "Not so hard! Don't you let that bat go!" he pleaded.

Seven, eight, nine times the pitcher cast the ball into the air, jumping back with each pitch to avoid a flying bat. He now regretted that he had invited David to play. To top it all off, David had not even come close to hitting the ball and, from all appearances, it looked as if he wouldn't. The players in the field sat down. "See! We told you! Take the bat from him or we won't even get our game in today."

"Okay! David. You've had your turn. You struck out. Now it's somebody else's turn," the pitcher explained as he extended his hand to take the bat from David, who refused to give it back. The pitcher tried to wrest the bat from David's grasp. David clung to it. Had the pitcher not told him not to let go? David looked at the pitcher, bewildered. He didn't know what to think or do. The pitcher had asked him to play, had given him the bat, and now he was taking it back. David had not struck the ball, he had not run yet.

"Give me the bat." The pitcher's voice grew louder and less friendly as he repeated the demand. Other voices joined in. "Give us the bat. It's our bat. Go on home. You don't know how to play. You're spoiling our game."

Miss Burke, drawn from her lunch by the commotion, came out of the school to see what was going on. Seeing the crowd of children milling around this David McLeod, she marched directly into their midst. "What's going on and what are you doing in the school yard?"

"He's got our bat and he won't let it go," the players whined.

Miss Burke held her hand out for the bat. "Give me the bat," she demanded sharply. David let the bat go. He too was scared of Miss Burke.

"Get out of the school yard. You don't belong here. Go on."

David left the yard. "Get out! Go on home!" burned and resounded in his ears. They wanted him and then they didn't want him. They asked him to play and then they changed their minds. And this woman had taken the children's part. He too wanted to play like the children; he too wanted to laugh, to be part of something. But no one wanted him.

Kids! How can one trust them? Nice to you one minute, turn on you the next. Almost as bad as adults. "Sudla-bitch." All he had to do was to hit that ball. "Cheewi Cwise!" If they had given him time, he would have been able to hit that ball. "God-dabit." Always in a rush, hurry.

David told Frances, Walter, the Little People, and his mother.

Grandmother, while sympathetic, reminded David, "See! I told you. Stay away from kids and they won't hurt you."

Except there was not much point in telling David what to do or what not to do. He was a kid himself. He'd forget or, if he remembered, would defy the fates, trusting that what happened the last time wouldn't happen again.

On my way home I stopped at Grandmother's for a short visit. "What happened to David at school today?" she asked, but I was unable to say. Because I was in the primary class, confined to another yard on the other side of the school, I didn't know what went on in the senior yard.

One evening not long after that incident, Walter came to our house to visit Father.

"Must be something very important that brings you all the way out here," Father teased after he and his brother had drunk a pot of tea and discussed baseball, their school days, and, of course, fishing.

"Actually, there is," Walter answered. "Some people have asked me to speak to you about running for council or even for chief."

"Gee Whittaker!" Father cut in sharply. "I've never done that sort of thing. Never thought of it. You've got to be smart to be a councillor. I don't have enough ability." And Dad went on about his intellectual shortcomings. He always took this way out to avoid undertaking any task or project that required mental effort. He never pushed himself. "No. I don't want to do that."

"Tom and Alfred are going to be disappointed when I tell them you won't run," Walter explained. "They thought you'd be a good councillor. I thought you would make a good councillor ... with your experience outside the reserve and your education."

"Tom Jones?"

"Yes."

"Why does that Orangeman, of all people, want me to be on council? Why doesn't he run himself?"

"Actually, he's going to run for chief and he wants a strong council to stand up to the agent."

"Can't understand that man," Dad shook his head, expressing his bias. "Him a Protestant, and an Orangeman to boot, asking Catholics to vote for him. He's got to have something up his sleeve. He's got enough money already and he's raking in more and more. What's he running for anyway?"

"He doesn't like the agent. Ever since Tuffnell told Tom that he couldn't speak for Ruben (Ashkewe) in council, Belcando (Tom's nickname, evolved from his reply, 'Bes' I can do,' in setting a limit on people's lines of credit) hasn't had a good thought or a good word about the agent. You should have heard and seen Tom that day, scolding the agent and the council … and the agent adjourning the meeting.

"With elections coming up, Tom's been going 'round the reserve drumming up support. He's been saying that the reserve needs a change, someone to stand up to the agent. Oliver's too soft, too nice to put that agent in his place. If no one stops that man, he'll be running the reserve. Indians should be running their own show."

Father thought about what Walter said, then gave his opinion. "I don't trust Tom. He's an Orangeman, got no use for Catholics. He's got two faces, one that he puts on when he wants your business and your vote, the other that he puts on behind your back. No. I'm for Oliver." Father was no less tolerant of Orangemen than he was of the slothful and the profane.

Tom campaigned on the primacy of the chief and band council in reserve affairs. "I'll see to it that I and the council manage our community's business as we are supposed to," Tom thundered.

"Fine words spoken by a man in fine clothing," Oliver countered. "Don't be fooled. You may well find that the tree you have chosen to cut down as planking for your home is decayed in its core. Don't overlook the tree that is crooked, bent, and gnarled; it may well be sounder and stronger than your good-looking tree. I am your crooked, gnarled tree."

The Cape people were won over by the crooked, gnarled tree analogy. Oliver was reelected.

There was trouble at home and trouble brewing anew in civilized Europe.

At home, Father was seeing another woman. But neither Gladys nor I were aware of what was taking place between our parents. We were too young to be concerned about marital tensions, too young to understand them, too absorbed in our own little worlds and dreams. But our mother's world and her dreams were crumbling.

She did what she could to shore up her marriage and save it from ruin. Mother now wanted to cling to the man whom she had not wanted to marry in the first place. She had come to love this hardworking, impetuous, selfish, self-deprecating man, even now when he was ditching her and me, Gladys, Marilyn, Ernestine, with another baby (Janet) on the way. She fought and beat the woman who was wrecking her marriage and her life. She asked the priest and the chief to intercede on her behalf. At nights she cried and prayed to Kitchi-Manitou for compassion.

Twice before as a girl she had been given away, abandoned. Mother was to be cast aside once more, without money, home, support, or much education, and with only Grandmother, Aunt Frances, and Ethel Nadjiwon as friends.

She begged for a little money to feed my sisters and me. She appealed to the court for child support. The magistrate scowled as he dressed Rufus Johnston down in the Wiarton courtroom, calling him irresponsible and indifferent, with little capacity for love except for himself, and ordered him to pay $5 per week to our mother for child support. A payment was made to the court that day but no others were made, in contempt of the order.

Grandmother sent word that she wanted to see Rufus, but her request had as much force as the court order. He stayed away. Father Labelle accosted Father on the road and commanded him to abandon his life of sin. Father laughed at the priest. Oliver Johnston, the chief, attempted to reason with Rufus, but Father would have nothing to do with him.

Did Father lose whatever capacity to love he may have had during his confinement in Spanish? Did he ever have much to begin with? Was he really as indifferent to law, church, and family as he seemed to be?

Besides publishing news of local auctions and the teas sponsored by the Women's Institute, the shooting of a marauding bear in Keady, and the blaze that destroyed a barn in Tara, the *Owen Sound Sun Times* now carried reports of events in Europe.

There had always been trouble in Europe. The civilized nations were once more standing toe to toe, jaw to jaw, glaring at each other eyeball to eyeball, hands at their hips ready to draw swords or pistols and to slit each other's throats or blow their brains out. Dictators were itching for living space, "lebensraum." They felt cheated in treaties and settlements. They were stocking up arms, ready to strike. Kings and queens, emperors and empresses, rulers of kingdoms and empires made up of lands arrogated from the weak and the unarmed allowed their foreign ministers to keep the malcontents appeased with understandings, treaties, and protocols. The West-European Christian clergy prayed to God to keep the Red Menace from spreading. At the same time they clashed over dogma. White churchmen prayed for peace; seditionists fanned the fires of bitterness and revenge. They wanted nothing to do with peace.

The League of Nations took note of the disputes and invited the wrangling parties to settle their differences in a civilized manner. The Great Powers sent their ambassadors and diplomats to Geneva to iron out disagreements. In the headquarters of the League of Nations, mediators and plenipotentiaries with medals, ribbons, and sashes adorning their uniforms and tuxedoes met in grand halls and smoothed over their irritants. In the evenings they drank, dined, and danced with their bejeweled spouses in civilized elegance.

On the day that these plenipotentiaries signed treaties, pacts, accords, or other high-sounding documents they smiled and shook hands for photographers. But within hours of signing protocols, some of them cried "double deal," and indeed there was as much under-the-table dealing as there was above board.

It was back to square one. The civilized nations built fortifications; the big powers increased the size of their armed forces. The smaller nations blustered, the bigger nations wagged their fingers. But under the civilized trappings and refined manners were human warts, the waft of foul toilet smells, primal feelings and instincts, wounded pride, fear, distrust, envy, ambition, suspicion, avarice, greed, selfishness, misperception, conceit, pique, revenge, impulsiveness.

The civilized nations could not let bygones be bygones in a civilized manner. They had never settled their misunderstandings except by war.

War for Europeans was not a function of the past. It was in their blood, recorded and glorified in their histories and embodied in their standing armies. They were spoiling for war, walking around with chips on their shoulders, daring someone to knock them off. For the victorious, war was glorious; for the defeated, it was needing vindication and revenge.

Europe was created and shaped from bloodshed, destruction, invasion, occupation. There were wars between Portugal and Spain, Spain and France, Spain and England, France and England, Poland and Germany, Turkey and Greece, every country. War was a tradition in Europe, going all the way back to the time when Rome used it to subdue, subjugate, and civilize the "wild tribes" that owned and occupied what is now the greater part of Europe, plus the Middle East and North Africa. Ever since then there has not been peace for any length of time in Europe, only periods of truce during which the victors gloated and the vanquished licked their wounds and planned revenge.

Adolf Hitler was itching for war. He couldn't get over the many slights, some real, but more imagined, that he had suffered as a youth. The humiliation of defeat as a German soldier lingered. He wanted to get even. He wanted to restore the Reich to its rightful place of honor among the ranking nations of Europe and the world. He dreamed. He dreamed of war, but no one would knock the chip off his shoulder.

When no one would accept his taunts, Hitler manufactured an incident on the Polish border that gave him an excuse to declare war on Poland and to unleash his armored corps and motorized Panzer divisions against Poland's cavalry forces.

The civilized nations were at it again.

On Sundays Father Labelle and the minister spoke of the war in Europe and led their congregations in prayer for victory of the forces of good over the forces of evil. The Indians prayed fervently to God to instill sense and reason in the White People to keep them from slaughtering themselves and everybody else. Indian prayers were futile; the White People longed for war.

After church the people asked, "What are they fighting about this time?" No one knew, not even the Cape Croker veterans who had fought in World War I. "Didn't they just finish fighting no more than twenty years ago?"

Within days of Germany's invasion of Poland, England, France, and Canada declared war on the enemy. The issues at stake, as defined by the nations' leaders, were freedom, democracy, justice, Christianity, and civilization itself, not to mention the preservation of the British Empire. Every person was duty bound to serve "King, Flag, and Country" and to lay down his life.

Prime Minister King's announcement that Canada had declared war on Germany had hardly echoed down Parliament Hill in Ottawa than the men and boys from the Cape hurried to Stratford to enlist in Canada's armed forces, mainly in the Perth and the Grey and Simcoe Foresters regiments.

John came home in uniform, his tunic and wedge cap sporting the badges and flashes of the Perth Regiment. He had always been a sharp dresser, but now looked sharper than before, with shiny brass buttons and gleaming black boots. No longer did he just walk; he now marched smartly, head held high, chest thrust out, body erect as if he were going somewhere to meet someone of importance.

David looked at his brother. He too wanted to wear a uniform, a wedge cap, shirt, tie, tunic, trousers, and black boots.

"Like it, Mom?" John asked Rosa, modeling his uniform. "You proud of me?"

"Of course I'm proud of you. But I wish you hadn't joined the army."

"But, Mom, I had to. We had to. If we didn't join, people would look down on us. We have to keep the Germans from coming here and taking over everything that we have, everything that this country has ... and besides, what's there to do around here except fish and cut wood? We never have any money."

"Our men went overseas in World War I. Some never came back, some came back wounded. They change anything? We're just as poor as before."

"Mom!" John persisted. "It was different then. Our chief said now is our chance to show what we can do. Show the White Man what we can do."

"Don't believe everything the chief says. The only thing you're going to do is to give me sleepless nights."

Whether John believed in what he said is moot, but it was the thing to say, the line pushed by the government of Canada. Younger men and women in their late teens such as Clifford Nadjiwon, Randolph Keeshig, Jackie McLeod, and Alexandra Desjardines, perhaps most of the youth, gave as their answer for joining up, "For adventure ... travel, to see the country and go overseas ... and earn a little bit of money. Life is so boring on this reserve ... nothing but fishing, cutting wood ... and shooting pool."

"Back-a-haw!" David called his brother's name to draw his attention, and he talked and gestured. John took David's talk to mean, "What's the uniform for? What do you do? Where have you been? Where are you going?"

"There are bad men afar off," John explained, "beyond the bluffs. They are fighting and hurting good men, good women and children." He stated that he and the other men from the Cape were going to stop these bad men before they came to the reserve.

As David listened to John's explanation, his brow knitted and he shook his head ruefully, as if he could see men on the ground, their faces bloody. David shook his head, clenched his fists, flexed his muscles, and felt his brother's biceps. He swung his fist in an arc to show John that he understood.

Within two months of joining the army, John was promoted to the rank of corporal. On his first leave after his promotion, John brought home a discarded uniform for David, but no badges or flashes.

While Rosa altered the uniform to fit David, John armed David with a broom and led him outside to the road for drill exercises.

"Tenshun!" John bellowed. "Now, David! Stand up straight. You're going to be a soldier. Pull your belly in!" John pushed David's paunch in. "Arms at your sides, like this. Feet together. Chest out! Jaw out. Eyes to the front .... Look at the Sidney Bay bluffs. Look like a soldier!"

David was going to be a soldier, just like Back-a-haw; he was going to fight bad men. He tried to follow the commands. He pulled his belly in but when he did so his rear end stuck out. He stuck his chest out, but his belly came out as well. It was either do or fail. From David's pursed lips and set eyes, he was going to succeed. It wasn't play, it was the real thing.

Despite the grave look that he put on, David looked like a chubby dancer doing the hula dance in slow motion. John grinned. "Attaboy, David," he said as he went around adjusting David's alignment.

"At ease!" John showed David how to stand at ease.

"Tenshun! ... At ease! ... Tenshun! ... At ease!" The commands echoed outside, over and over as they must echo on parade grounds.

After half an hour John told David, "If you're going to be a soldier you have to know the commands."

"Tenshun!"

"Chichin!"

"At ease!"

"Cheem!"

"That's good for the first time, but that's enough for now. When I'm not here you practice what I showed you."

So encouraged, David practiced. He was going to be a soldier, just like his brother. "Chichin! Cheem!"

Of course, I couldn't let him go on believing that he was good lest

262

it go to his head. I had to save him from falsehood and tell him the truth. "Uncle David! You walk like a duck. You're not a soldier."

Wham! I saw stars. I heard thunder. I felt as if a firebrand had been pressed upon my face as I lay on my back, dazed.

As the stars faded and the thunder died away I saw David standing over me. He was pointing a quaking finger in my face. "Ook! Ook!" What he said after that I could not make out, but the gist of his tone was, "Let that serve as a lesson to you, twerp. Get off my back."

I cried out for sympathy, for someone to put an arm around me. Instead I heard, "Serves you right. We told you to leave your uncle alone."

What I had said had no effect on David. He continued to practice diligently. My words, compared to those of John, were meaningless.

Next day John taught David how to salute and march. "Tenshun! Forward march! Hup, two, three, four! Halt! ... Tenshun! ... At ease! ... Fall out!" Back and forth in front of the house my two uncles marched. At the end of each drill John patted David on the back and complimented him. "You're going to be a fine soldier ... if only you could talk."

David smiled a toothless smile of immense satisfaction. He had done something to please Back-a-haw.

From the basic drills John led David to another stage, "presenting arms."

Saluting was easy enough, but presenting arms was more difficult for David, for the exercise demanded some fancy footwork with a weapon, a broom. John showed David how it was done. He barked out commands and slapped that broom to his shoulder, gave another command and slapped that broom back down to the ground next to his feet. Finally, after John had gone through the exercise a dozen times, with David gaping in concentration, John handed the broom to David. "Your turn."

When David had the broom resting at his side at just the right angle, John bawled out, "Present arms!" David's hands were in instant motion, slapping the broom from left to right, in no particular order, as if he were slapping bees. Again and again John showed Uncle David.

"Tenshun! ... Present arms!"

David looked ahead, his jaw set. His hands and arms were locked. His mind commanded them to move, but his hands and arms didn't know which was to start first and which way to go.

I couldn't understand how David was unable to perform these simple exercises. How stupid could he be? I would have given up trying to teach him by now. But not John. He made David do the drill again and again, without getting tired or angry. In fact, John seemed to derive a great deal of pleasure from these drills.

"At ease!"

"Sudla-bitch! Cheewi Cwise!" David muttered while he shook his head in frustration and disappointment.

Another time, "David. Tenshun! Seig heil! Heil Hitler!" John taught David the Nazi salute.

Weeks later, with his mother's help, David was able to perform the "present arms" exercise, after a fashion, though his feet could never follow the same pattern twice in succession.

"Chichin! Cheem! Pup! Pup! Pup!"

David's military wardrobe grew. His father, Norman, who had come back from Longlac and joined the home guard, brought shirts, ties, trousers, caps, and boots. As his wardrobe grew, it created more work for his mother.

In the evenings when he went out, David put on his uniform. He didn't amble anymore; he marched. He would make John proud. One day Back-a-haw would say, "Let's go, David," and they'd go together.

John, Rufus, and Norman were but three among the large number of men, boys, and young women, some as young as fifteen, who enlisted in the Canadian army.

When the soldiers came home on leave, they were smartly dressed. They marched wherever they went. They jingled money in their pockets and smiled as they explained the meaning of the insignia that was affixed to their uniforms. When the men were home the women smiled lipsticked smiles.

Almost overnight the Cape changed. Tom Jones and Lennox Johnston closed their stores early and the brass band practices were suspended, as there were not enough musicians. Fishing boats were drawn up, turned over onshore, some never to be launched again;

trawling equipment and nets were stored away, some for good. Saws and axes were retired. Threshing bees were discontinued, never to be revived. On Sundays the churches were only half full. Funerals were sadder because there were fewer mourners to mourn. Cape Croker became a half-dead, half-alive village, lonely and apprehensive, expecting the worst.

There was little to do.

Fourteen- and fifteen-year-old boys squirmed in impatience and glowered at the calendar, anxious to celebrate their sixteenth birthdays. At sixteen they could "register" without knowing what the term meant, work, or go to a recruitment office and try to lie their way into the army. Fourteen- and fifteen-year-olds wanted to do something, go somewhere farther than Wiarton and Owen Sound.

While life slowed down for most people, there was more work for the men who did not enlist, mainly the overaged and the underaged. There were as many households to heat as before.

For David life changed little. By day he cut, sawed, and split wood for "tet tsets." He pitched horseshoes and played the organ. He played solitaire by the hour, putting the cards aside gently when he grew weary of playing, or slamming them down on the table if he felt his invisible opponent was cheating him. And as often as he thought of it, he practiced the drills that John had taught him. In the evenings he'd put on his uniform and march to "the other side," saluting soldiers whom he met. Nothing made him prouder than to have soldiers return his salute. He was like them ... no, he was one of them.

Too often nowadays it wasn't worthwhile going to "the other side." No one was around. Even Lennox pined for company and customers. He kept his store open a little later than did Tom in hopes that the extra hour might draw in an extra 20 cents or even a dollar. Then he'd retreat into his living quarters, there to compose and arrange music till 4 a.m.

David went to Walter's place more frequently, putting up with the chores that Frances assigned him. There he learned about Hitler and Mussolini, Franco and Stalin, Germans and Italians, Nazis, Fascists, and Reds. He sat next to Walter with the *Owen Sound Sun Times* spread out on the table in front of them. He saw pictures of what the people in Europe were doing to one another. There were pictures of buildings aflame, charred and gutted skeletons of churches, streams of old men, women, and children clutching toys, horses drawing two-wheeled wagons packed with clothing and blankets, hideous corpses of soldiers and bloated horses sprawled grotesquely on the ground, soldiers on stretchers, soldiers cringing and cowering in a ditch. Beside these pictures Walter pointed to caricatured sketches of Hitler and Mussolini. He explained to David that the pictures in the paper represented what the enemy was doing to good people. Back-a-haw, Ish-ish, Tsibih, and Beeyah were fighting these men.

David shook his head in horror. Never had he seen such death and destruction, much less imagined it. "Too goot! Too goot!"

Under Walter's guidance, done more for amusement than to instill hate, David grew to detest the pictures and the names of Hitler and Mussolini. Not even David was immune to propaganda.

"Who's this?" Walter often asked David, pointing to a picture to test his memory.

"Sud-la-bitch! Cheewi Cwise!" David would almost explode. He'd point a damning finger at the picture and clench his fist and throw a haymaker. For good measure he'd extend his arms as if he were holding a rifle and bellow, "Pow." That's what he'd do to Hitler.

The pictures roused David. He didn't like to see dead horses, dead men, crying children, burning houses, and gutted buildings.

After these visits to his brother's place, David had a great deal to tell his mother and the Little People.

When Father left us, we were living in Charlie Nadjiwon's house, another borrowed home. In her isolation and desolation, Mother didn't know what was happening in the community. It wasn't until a week before his wedding that Charlie Nadjiwon came over to tell Mother that he and his wife would take possession of the house, and we would have to move. Charlie was very apologetic for having to force my mother out onto the road. Mother was devastated by this latest blow. She sent word to Rosa that to add to her woes she would have no home when the week was over. She had no money, nowhere to go.

Grandmother took us into her home.

Fred Tuffnell didn't like the situation at Rosa McLeod's household. There were too many people in that house; with Mary Johnston and her five children, there were eight altogether. And there was that idiot living with all those children, four of them little girls. Mrs. McLeod never went to church, more pagan than Christian, and couldn't read or write. What kind of example was she? She had no visible means of support. How were they all going to live? Sooner or later they'd come to band council to ask for relief.

But what disturbed Tuffnell most was the presence of "that idiot" in the household. If something happened, if that idiot touched or molested one of those girls, he, Fred Tuffnell, likely would be made to answer why he had done nothing to prevent such an incident. More than likely he'd be fired for neglect of duty. Before the unthinkable happened, Tuffnell acted.

He called Father Labelle to tell him of his fears and that he was going to defuse the situation. The priest, too, had been keeping an eye on Mary Johnston and her family: no home, no money, no husband, forced to live with her mother-in-law.

They agreed it would be best for everyone—the children, Mary, Rosa, and the community—to remove two of the older children from this unhappy situation and send them off to Spanish Residential School where they'd receive food, clothing, shelter, guidance, and training under the loving care of priests, brothers, and nuns.

Father Labelle delivered the bad news to Mary and Rosa. When Rosa cried, "No! No!" in Indian, Labelle put her in her place with, "Then David will have to go in their place." Mary cried. "They're my children; they need me." To console her and to stop her crying, Labelle gave her a glimmer of hope. Gladys and I would be returned home the moment that Mary and Rufus were reconciled. If, in the meantime, Mary and Rufus were to iron out their troubles, the arrangements for our admission to Spanish would be rescinded.

Rosa and Mary cried, but neither Gladys nor I saw or heard them. Rosa had gone through the ordeal before, the separation, the heartache that lingered and kept her awake at nights. And though it had been twenty-six years since her own children had been taken from her, it still hurt. Mary also cried. She remembered a baby that she had lost, a blue baby, Marceline. Now she would lose two more, because she was deemed unfit, unable to look after her children, forced to bear a hurt and a stigma. She paid the penalty; Rufus paid none. She needed money but Father had none to spare after he spent it freely on others. Yet she still loved him.

Mary grasped at straws. She asked Father Labelle for time. Two weeks he gave her. Mary asked the woman whom Rufus was seeing to let him go; when the woman refused, Mary cuffed her. She begged Rufus to come home for the sake of the children, only to be spurned. She cried and begged, demeaning herself. And grasping at a last-minute miracle, Mother told Gladys and me that we were going on a trip. Mother had been deluded; she now deluded herself and us.

Sis and I fell for it. We believed Mother. A trip? When? Where? We were both ecstatic and impatient, ready and anxious to start at once. We asked Mother where we were going, but she wouldn't say.

It was a secret, to be a surprise. We asked when we were to leave, but that too was a big secret. Every evening we asked, "Is it tomorrow?"

"Is David coming?"

"No."

"Ha! Ha! David, you're not coming with us. Ha! Ha!"

"Ook! Ook!" David said, pointing a warning finger in front of our noses, muttering something that most likely meant, "Knock it off or else. Remember what happened last time."

Fred Tuffnell issued an ultimatum that Mary Johnston had "stalled long enough. Tell her to get her children ready next week." Father Labelle delivered the word.

Gladys had visions of wearing a blue dress and having picnics along the way, just as we had had many picnics along the route when we came to Cape Croker four years earlier. A few days before we were scheduled to leave, Gladys caught poison ivy. She tried to relieve the itching by scratching, but she succeeded only in spreading the rash and the itching further. The next day Mother and Grandmother put her to bed with her arms and legs bleeding. Mother was frantic with worry about Gladys's condition, but relieved that Gladys would not go on the trip.

Mother broke the good news that I was leaving on my trip the next day. I couldn't understand why she was crying as she told me.

After breakfast the next morning I dressed in the clothing that mother had culled from the boxes of old clothes that Father Labelle had in the little hall. In a small cardboard suitcase Mother had packed extra clothing. Christine Keeshig, Grandmother's sister, had sent over a small shoebox that I was to give to Eugene Keeshig, her grandson and my cousin.

Eugene was there? Charley Shoot? Kitchi-Meeshi-Hec? They were already there? Where was I going? I thought my trip was special. But my mother used the term "trip" in a sense similar to being "sent up the river."

David was at the back cutting trees, sent there by Grandmother. Marilyn was at the back of the house with Choc.

I waited by the road, Mother next to me holding my hand.

At last a green car hove into sight at the corner. As it went by I waved frantically to flag it down, almost panic-stricken that it might leave me behind. To my relief it turned in the Nadjiwon driveway and came back, stopping next to me.

I broke from my mother's grasp and grappled with the front door latch. Mr. Tuffnell, dressed in a suit, growled, "You sit in the back! ... Where's the other one?" he turned to my mother.

"In the house," Mother mumbled. "Sick."

"Are you sure?" the agent demanded. "Or are you hiding her? Go, get her ready. I'm in a hurry." He glanced at his watch.

"But he's sick," my mother wailed, mixing up her pronouns. "He's in bed, got poisin ibey, him."

Just then my little sister Marilyn, then four and a half, came running around the corner.

"Her, then," the agent growled. "I'll take her; get her ready."

"No!" Mother wailed. "He's just a baby, he's only four, he's too small."

"Get her ready ... or else I'll take the whole family. It's up to you." And the agent placed the burden of sending all of us away on my mother's shoulders.

Mother and Grandmother cried while they dressed Marilyn, who didn't know what was going on. She, too, began to cry, not wanting to go anywhere.

I couldn't understand why Mother and Grandmother were crying, making such a big fuss. It was only a trip. I'd be back in just a few days. Hadn't Mother said so herself? I couldn't understand, but it was unsettling. I tried to comfort my mother. "Don't cry. It's not like we're going away for good. We're coming back. Me and Mirleen will be back soon. You said it's just a trip, like a holiday."

I went outside to avoid the crying, and around to the back to wave to David, but he didn't wave back in return.

Marilyn was ready; Mother carried her to the car.

"Get in." The agent's tone was sharp as he opened the back door for Marilyn and me. He didn't allow any time for parting embraces.

Had I looked behind I might have seen my mother and grandmother wave feebly, and gather each other in embrace to hold onto what little that life, the fates, and men had doled out to them. I might have seen David shake his fist at us for making my mother and his mother cry. But I didn't look back; I looked only ahead.

After the car bearing Marilyn and me disappeared from view my mother and grandmother returned to the house, Mother to cry some more and to nurse Baby Janet, Grandmother to hold Ernestine, who was crying because Mother and Grandmother were crying.

David, who had stolen back to the house, looked on. Something had taken place, something connected with "Ook!" and the man in the green car. That man had done something to his mother and to Wha-Wha (David's name for our mother). He was upset. He didn't know what to make of the tears and the wails, whether to go back outside out of sight and hearing, yet he felt he must do something to get his mother to stop crying.

He put his hand on Rosa's shoulder and patted it. "Woosh," he said softly and shook his head to get her to stop crying. Then he went to the Nadjiwon homestead to fetch someone to come and see what was the matter with Grandmother and Wha-Wha. Ethel came over almost immediately, thinking someone was sick or some accident had taken place.

"They've taken my children from me," Mother sobbed the moment Ethel walked in the door and asked what was wrong. "It's me that they're punishing, not him. It's them, the agent and that Rufus, that want to see me suffer. I never done anything to them. It's that priest, too. They take it out on me, but they don't do anything to that Rufus; they let him get away." And Mother wailed on about never having had anything—no house, no money—all the injustices that she'd suffered.

Ethel stayed with my mother and grandmother until noon, listening and providing whatever comfort she could. Meanwhile, David had gone back to his work.

At the poplar grove David spent more time talking and smoking than he did working. Sounds came out of his mouth, sprinkled with salty words. For emphasis he shook his fist in the direction of the departed car. Then he'd turn, facing the woods, talk in a quieter tone and at a normal pace. If David was directing his purple language and fist at the Indian agent, he wasn't the only one who wished that Fred Tuffnell had never been born.

John Bucket may have expressed it best when he complained, "I'd like to rub that man's nose in his own piss. He don't like us. I don't know why they sent him here in the first place! ... Supposed to look after us! Humph! He don't care two farts for nobody! ... I don't know how his wife can stand that little runt, or anyone for that matter."

But there was one person who thought enough of Fred Tuffnell to call on him from time to time. Every second week in the summer, Abe Mitchell and his wife came from Owen Sound to visit the Tuffnells at Cape Croker. Abe, like his friend, had become a gentleman after years of pitching manure and slaughtering pigs, chickens, and cattle for farmers around Markdale and Durham. To make ends meet, Abe brewed moonshine and sold his product in Markdale and Flesherton on Friday and Saturday nights. It was a risky business but it earned him extra money.

Abe was frugal and ambitious. And the money he made peddling hooch fed his ambition. After a few years he moved his operations to Owen Sound. There business was even more rewarding, and his move paid off.

By the late 1930s he had a fine home, a car, a farm, and membership in service clubs. Moreover, he contributed to local temperance unions and opposed the opening of any liquor or beverage room. He and other bootleggers campaigned mightily to close Duffy's Tavern in Hepworth and the Chatsworth Hotel in Chatsworth, towns nine miles north and south of Owen Sound, respectively. These were represented as institutions of corruption, undermining the morals and sensibilities of the people of Owen Sound. The campaign never succeeded. Owen Sound residents flocked to Duffy's and "the Chatsworth" every night. Tourists bypassed Owen Sound in deference to its reputation as a model of sobriety.

As a registered and respected farmer, Abe avoided conscription and received extra gasoline allowance that enabled him to ignore his country's obtuse pleas to conserve gasoline and to go to Cape Croker to visit his friend.

"Good life, ain't it, Fred? Beats pitchin' fuckin' cowshit, don't it," he was fond of saying.

"Please don't swear," Fred frequently begged his friend. "There are ladies present, and we're not in a barnyard anymore."

"Sorry about that, Fred," Abe apologized without remorse. He could not cast off certain aspects of his more humble beginnings.

Soon after Abe began visiting Tuffnell he saw some boys with a string of perch and bass. His interest and passion were immediately roused, as Betty Grable slinking by would have aroused other men.

"Where'd they get those?" he asked, his eyes round.

"Right there in the bay … probably at the Point or by the wreck of that old barge near the Point." Tuffnell gave his friend the rundown. "There's lots of fish. On 'the other side' too … at the dock, perch, bass, and trout."

"Hey, boys!" Abe called out. "What kinda bait you use?"

"Jis worms, only."

"Take you long?"

"Nah! Not even half a hour. They're bitin' real good." The boys didn't stop.

"Fred, there's nothing I like better than fishin'. Can't very well do that in Owen Sound. You know what people are like in that town. I'd like to do some fishing here."

"You'd need a guide though."

"What in hell for?"

"It's reserve land, reserve waters. Only the Indians can fish here."

"What in hell is this 'only Indians' crap? Why in hell can't I go out there and fish like I should be able to do in Owen Sound?"

"Because it's in the Indian Act," Fred explained. "And I have to see to it that everyone obeys the law, Indians and Whites. That's my job. But you don't have to hire an adult to be your guide; you can hire any one of them kids. That would be the same thing. Give that kid a dime, a quarter … make his day."

"Well, next time I come in, I'll bring my tackle."

From fishing and Indian privileges Abe and Fred turned their attention to the war. Abe was upset about the "copulating" Germans, and the "copulating" British doing next to nothing to stop the "copulating" bastards.

"Abe! Stop using that word."

"Sorry, Fred. But I get so goddamned mad … and worried about them copulating Huns. You know, Fred, if they win, they'll come over here, take everything we got, change everything. Have Gestapo ruling over us. No sir! I'd never knuckle down to no copulating foreigner, Fred. I'd sooner die. I'm doing my share, buyin' them War Bonds."

The next time Abe Mitchell came to Cape Croker he brought his tackle and went fishing at the Point, with a boy as his guide. He caught, as fishermen are fond of saying, "a mess" of perch and bass. Thereafter, whenever Abe came to visit Fred he spent more time at the Point and the dock than he did in Fred's company.

In the meantime Tom Jones had been smarting from his election defeat at the hands of Oliver Johnston, who had implied by his cedar trees analogy that Tom was insincere and shallow. In the spring of 1940 Tom ran for chief and was elected. "We'll see to it that this reserve is run by people from this community in a democratic fashion, not as a dictatorship," he proclaimed in his victory speech.

Right from the first Tom Jones and Fred Tuffnell clashed. The new chief let the agent know that he and the band council would conduct the community's business and meetings in the Indian language, and hear petitions as in the old days. Both men glared at each other.

In council Tom got his way. Tuffnell glowered and stewed, alternately drumming his fingers on the table and doodling in his black notebook.

Tom wasn't afraid of the agent. He had, as they say, the agent over a barrel. Through his wife's friendship with Tuffnell's wife, he knew the agent was barely literate. To Tom this was galling. For a government to appoint a man with only a grade four education as an agent in charge of a community of four hundred people, its monies, and its future wasn't right. There were a great many people on the reserve who had more education and more ability than the agent.

In the first council meeting Tom told Tuffnell to quit acting like a dictator, otherwise he hinted he would let people in Ottawa know that the agent's credentials in Cape Croker should be examined.

Tuffnell boiled, publicly humiliated. He had to be wary of this Tom Jones. The bastard was stepping on his toes because he had a better education, taking advantage of him. He'd show the son of a bitch; he'd learn how to write. Sooner or later he'd turn the tables on the upstart. This Indian! Bigheaded, just like people with an education.

Tuffnell asked the local member of parliament, who had sponsored his appointment as an agent, about the security of his position. The honorable member assured Fred that his job was safe and that he, Fred Tuffnell, not the chief or band council, had the authority in Cape Croker.

After a couple of months of fishing on the reserve, Abe grew bolder, no longer bothering to hire a guide. No one said anything to him except, "Hello, Sir!" or, "How are they biting today?" Everybody thought the agent's visitor was a high-ranking government official.

One day while Abe was casting from the dock, Tom Jones came to check his boat.

"Where's your guide?" he asked Abe.

"Who in hell are you?" Abe shot back testily.

"I'm the chief of the reserve," Tom answered.

"What t'hell am I supposed to do! Kiss your ass for that?" the man grinned.

Tom, stung and shocked, limped away without another word. If he were younger he would have rushed at that man and throttled him. His heart raced and he spat contemptuously every third step on the way to the car.

He drove directly to Sidney Bay to fetch Percy Pitwaniquot, the reserve's big, burly, barrel-chested, dark-visaged constable. Percy, some said, could scare beasts and even ghosts just by looking at them.

On the way back to the main village Tom explained that an outsider was fishing in reserve waters without a guide, and had acted as if he had no respect for the people there, or the laws. "I just want you to scare this damned fool, Perce."

"What will I say?" Percy asked nervously. "You know that I can't speak English too good."

"You don't have to say anything. I'll do the talking. All I want you to do is clamp the cuffs on him if he gives me too much lip or any trouble. Then you can take the cuffs off him."

"Tom, you're going to get the White People mad. I'm nervous. I don't like doing this."

"Percy. Yes, I know that we're going to get some people mad at us, but some are mad already anyway, so it's not going to make a great deal of difference. But we have to do something, otherwise that man will continue to come and fish here as if he owns the place. Next thing, he'll bring in other people and, before we know it, they'll just take over what little we have left, just like they did when they first came here."

Fifteen minutes later Tom and Percy arrived at the dock. The stranger was still there fishing. Tom and Percy made straight for the angler.

Very calmly Tom told the stranger, "These are reserve waters. You may fish but you need to have a guide. If you're unwilling to abide by our regulations, I'll have to ask you to leave or have you arrested and charged for trespassing." Behind Tom stood Percy, caressing his truncheon.

The stranger looked contemptuously at Tom. He wasn't cowed. "You ain't got no fuckin' authority or nothin'. This is a free fuckin' country and I can fuckin' fish any fuckin' place I fuckin' want. I don't need no fuckin' Indians to tell me what I can do."

"Ahow, Perce."

Percy clamped an iron grip on the man's arm and spun him around. In two motions he had the handcuffs locked around the surprised angler's wrists.

"What t'fuck do you think you're doing? Get these goddamned things off me if you know what's good for you. I got friends in the government. You'll pay for this."

Neither Tom nor Percy interrupted the stranger. While the man ranted and raved Tom spoke to Percy in Indian.

The man changed tack. "What t'hell are you talking about? Why don't you talk English like civilized people?"

"Certainly, but not the way you speak it," Tom retorted. "I've never heard so much verbal diarrhea. Perhaps that's the extent of your vocabulary and mind."

"Fuck you, old man."

"Okay, Perce! Put him in the car and we'll lock him up until he cools down and buttons his trap. Then I'll call the RCMP and have him transferred to Walkerton County Jail." Percy lifted the man's arms. The man whined and moaned. "Ouch! Okay! Okay! Don't break my arm."

"Now. Are you going to listen?" Tom asked.

The man said nothing.

"Let me explain your situation, my friend. I'm Chief Jones of this reserve. You're breaking the law, my friend. You're fishing in our waters. You can fish anywhere from Wiarton to Owen Sound to Collingwood to Midland, anywhere. You've got more fishing grounds than we have. But you can't fish here."

The man looked at Tom with contempt. "This is supposed to be a free country, people all equal."

"Yes, you're right, my friend, it's supposed to be. People like you never cease to amaze me. How you invoke rights to suit yourselves, yet never stand up for the rights of others. My friend, why aren't you in the service fighting for the rights of the people now being slaughtered? … What's the use of arguing with a bigot." Tom was exasperated. "I have the law on my side. We can lock you up, my friend, impound your car and all your equipment. We can turn you over to the RCMP, or we can let you go. Your choice. We'll let you go if you agree to go quickly and not fish these waters again without a guide."

"Okay! Okay! I'll go, but take these goddamned cuffs off!" The angler was unrepentant, surly. Tom would not have been far off the mark if he thought that the two "okays!" also carried a second meaning: "I'll get even with you, you bastard."

"Ahow, Perce. Unlock him, but take his fishing gear." In English he told the man what they were going to do with his tackle.

"Please, Mr. Jones. Let me keep my rod and lines; they're hard to get. It's my recreation. … I've got a bottle of whiskey in my car that you can have if you let me keep my gear."

"Whiskey?" Tom asked. "You can't bring that on the reserve. Another offense. Perce! Take the whiskey."

"Give me a break," the man pleaded.

"You're already getting a break. Just consider yourself lucky. If you hadn't been so huffy in the first place you might have kept everything."

As the man drove off, Tom took note of the license plate. "A real tough nut, that one," he commented to Percy.

That night Tom Jones received a phone call. "You fuckin' old bastard. You're goin' to pay for what you and your fuckin' black grizzly did today. You're not getting away with nothin'." Before Tom could tell the caller that he'd taken down the license plate number and the make of the car, the man hung up.

"Who was that?" Nellie asked.

"Some man who thinks he can run roughshod over Indians; some man who's got nothing better to do in his spare time than fish."

The next morning Tom received a call from Fred Tuffnell asking him to come to the agency office to explain what he and Percy had done to a visitor the day before.

Tom refused. "If you want to see me you can come to my store anytime, or we can discuss the matter at the next council meeting. You're not my master."

"I may not be your master," Fred Tuffnell retorted, "but as agent … I call the shots in the community, not you."

"That may be so," Tom broke in, "but that's going to change. Just remember that some people in Ottawa are going to learn that you can't write, can't read. Now, if you tell your friend to quit threatening me, and you stop hounding people on this reserve, we'll get along; otherwise I'm going to have to complain. Goodbye!"

Fred slammed the receiver back on the hook.

Later that month Tom received a letter from Ottawa, Indian Affairs Branch.

1940
Dear Chief Jones:

We have recently been informed by our agent in Cape Croker that you and the local constable forcibly detained a visitor to your reserve and seized his fishing equipment. This is a serious breach of law and constitutes an usurpation of the authority vested in our agent under the provisions of The Indian Act.
We have instructed Mr. Tuffnell to conduct an investigation into this episode and to report to this office. Your co-operation is expected.

Yours truly,
Lionel Chevreaux
Deputy Minister

S hortly after Marilyn and I were taken to Spanish, Mother, under pressure from the priest, rented a house belonging to Beulah Pitwaniquot. We had occupied that house once before in happier times; now Mother lived in it a second time, evoking memories of what was supposed to have been. She began to receive an allowance from the army for Rufus's military service.

When the house and its memories were more than she could take, Mother bundled up Ernestine and Janet, packed a bag of diapers and baby food, and went to Rosa's, taking the short cut at the back of the house. Mother carried Baby Janet. Trailing behind was Gladys, a bag over her shoulder, her hand closed about Ernestine's hand. Sometimes, when Ernestine grew tired, Gladys carried her, not for long distances, but far enough to prompt Gladys to wish that she had gone to Spanish.

After the visit Rosa bade David, "You go with Mary and give her a hand."

David breathed in heavily and breathed out noisily to show his distaste for escorting Wha-Wha and her babies. Gladys he liked, but Ernestine, then three, and Janet, ten months, or any other baby, David had little use for. They cried, they made "Choo-a" and stink. If David had foreseen what he had to do in helping his sister-in-law, he might have put his hat and coat on and gone elsewhere whenever they came over. But he didn't foresee these things until it was too late.

When the babies were bundled up, Mother gave Ernestine to David to carry. She placed the bundle in David's arms so that the baby's head was resting on David's right shoulder. "Now, be careful,

David. Don't drop her. Don't hold her too tight." David was reluctant to carry such dangerous cargo. But he had to.

"Don't drop her! Don't hold her too hard!" stuck in his mind, and he held the bundle so that he wouldn't drop it.

Two minutes before they arrived at Mother's home David whimpered, "Oooh! ... Eeeeeeh! ... Babeesh! Babeesh! ... Uh! Uh! Uh!"

"Settle down! We're almost there," Mother assured and encouraged David. But David whimpered only longer, more pitiably. "Stop it!" Mother spoke sharply.

"He's just standing there, Mom. He's not coming!" Gladys blurted out.

Mother went back to where David stood, gave Janet to Gladys, and checked what was troubling David. "Babeesh! Babeesh!" David wailed.

Mother felt the bundle. Ernestine was upside down, kept from dropping on her head by David's arms pressing her legs against his belly. "Babeesh!" Mother took Ernestine, rebundled her, and carried her in her own arms.

In the house David exhaled like a deflated tube and wiped his brow. He shook in relief, having survived as harrowing a situation as a person could experience. When he recovered his breath and composure, he pointed to Ernestine. "Too goot!" he said.

In December 1941 the German armed forces were within forty miles of Moscow; the Afrika Korps was pressing the British back to Cairo; the German U-boat fleet was sinking hundreds of tons of Allied shipping. On December 7, 1941, Japan attacked Pearl Harbor, destroying almost the entire U.S. Pacific Fleet in a couple of hours. Canada at once declared war on Japan. She took on another enemy: Japs, the Yellow Peril. And to prevent sabotage and the establishment of a fifth column, the Canadian government rounded up all Canadians of Japanese ancestry, seized their properties, and locked them in concentration camps.

Canada's propagandists were industrious and imaginative in stirring up fear and hatred of "Japs" or "Nips," while nurturing pride and patriotism in the country. Posters urged citizens to guard what they said, with graphic illustrations of eavesdroppers listening to loose and careless talk over captions that read, "The enemy may be listening." Other posters encouraged citizens to keep their eyes open, with the message, "Watch for and report all strangers." These posters were affixed to telephone poles, hydro poles, doors and walls of public buildings. There were caricatured illustrations of Hirohito, Tōjō, and Japanese soldiers, all wearing horn-rimmed goggles, slit- and slant-eyed, buck-toothed and yellow-complexioned. Comic book authors created Johnny Canuck, the Canadian archetype, who single-handedly defeated the enemy, almost as often as John Wayne overcame thousands of Japanese on film.

Tom's store and the council hall were plastered with posters. Levi Chegahno, who had sloshed and slugged through the mud in France in World War I, looked at the posters and asked Tom what the pictures meant. Tom explained, "I didn't know them enemies could understand Indian ... I don't see no sense in keeping quiet about anything; CFRB can't keep quiet, them enemies will know everything. All they have to do is listen to her."

David now had another enemy to hate. The Japanese were going to fight Back-a-haw and Ish-ish and Tsibih.

The women bought radios and listened to them every day. It was depressing, nothing but bad news. There were bulletins and communiqués from the BBC in London. The Huns controlled most of Europe; the Japs were overrunning Asia, the South Pacific. For the Allies, there was nothing but losses, defeats, surrenders, retreats.

Letters began to arrive postmarked "Somewhere Overseas." Many of the ninety-five Cape Croker servicemen and servicewomen were now going overseas.

A letter arrived from John.

"David, go get Walter."

Hours later Walter arrived to read the letter that Rosa had received. The letter said little except to tell everybody that John was in good health and in good spirits. Was he fighting? He didn't say. Where was he? He didn't say. What was he doing? He didn't say.

"Walter, will you write a letter for me?"

"Sure. What do you want me to tell John?"

"I don't quite know. What do you put down in letters? There's so much I want to tell him. Tell him that I think of him every day and pray that he'll be alright. Tell him that David's busy cutting wood and putting his uniform on every evening and practicing the drills that

John taught him. He'd go with John anytime. I don't have a neighbor anymore since Ethel (Nadjiwon) and her family moved back to Parry Sound, maybe to some big city. Jack Martin (Lavalley) was rejected from service because he didn't pass their physical; he and Irene have moved to Toronto where he's going to work for Massey-Harris. Miss Burke's gone and there's a new teacher, Miss Odriscow (O'Driscoll). Father Labelle was transferred up to northern Ontario and we've got a new priest, Father Howard (Howitt). Tell John that we're putting his money away and buying War Bonds."

After Walter had written the letter Grandmother asked him to tell her what news the *Owen Sound Sun Times* had to report.

Walter read the paper silently before summarizing the news for her. "There's a story here about how the Japanese forced American soldiers to march in the hot sun without any food or water or rest (The Death March at Bataan, 1942). Shot them if they fell down, wouldn't give any medicine to the sick. Four thousand killed ... out of twelve thousand. Awful, Mother. That's what could happen if the Japanese won the war and took over this country."

"Walter!" Rosa said after a long moment of silence. "That happened to our people, our ancestors, a long time ago. But nobody remembers that, nobody on this reserve cares. The White People don't want to think about it. But when something like that happens to White People, they act and make a big issue out of it, as if they'd never do such a thing, as if they're the only ones who've been subjected to this kind of atrocity."

"Oh?" Walter exclaimed, surprised.

And Rosa told him about the troubles the Indians went through and how they had been hunted and hounded by the American army as recently as sixty years before. "The Americans did the same thing to our people. It was alright for them to do it, but if others do it to them it's a crime, an atrocity."

Up to this time Walter had heard nothing of Indian history. What knowledge he had was confined to snippets of incidents in British and Roman history carried in the public school readers for grades six, seven, and eight. The Battle of Hastings, the Crusades, St. Joan of Arc, the Battle of Thermopylae, the Battle of the Plains of Abraham, the Black Hole of Calcutta, the Battle of Trafalgar, and Magellan's first trip around the world. There were no comparable stories about

Indians in any of the books that he'd read. Walter was curious and skeptical at the same time.

"Where'd you hear this?" he asked.

And Rosa told Walter that she had heard her grandmother, who had come from the Green Bay area of Wisconsin more than one hundred years before, speak of the anguish and the flight of the Indians.

While the enemy was circling, poised to deliver the knockout punch, the Americans, reeling and punch-drunk, were hanging onto the ropes to collect their senses. The Russians dug into the snow and took shelter in blizzards until relief and supplies were sent.

The Allies needed arms, arms, and more arms. Mines coughed up iron ore twenty-four hours a day. Mills forged steel around the clock, but what they produced fell short of what was needed. The armies needed more. Metal, even scraps, came into demand.

On Oliphant Road, which formed the boundary of Wiarton, lived Jim Cook, who operated a small stone quarry that furnished fine stone for fine homes in the district. Before the war broke out, cutting and delivering slabs of rock provided Cook with a modest living. But after the war started the demand for fine quarried rock petered out, leaving Cook short of funds and desperate. Little could be grown on the rocky soil. Too old for military service, Cook cast about looking for work.

While he was looking for a job near home, Cook learned that the government and a steel company in Hamilton were looking for scrap metal. An enterprising man, Cook asked Carl Whicher what he should do to supply the steel company with scrap metal and how to corner the supply of scrap metal in the county. With Mr. Whicher's advice and help, Cook received exclusive rights to all the scrap metal piles in the Bruce Peninsula north of Oliphant Road.

It was a solid business. There were thousands of farms in the peninsula, all with their own junk piles where tin cans, pails, stoves, stovepipes, bed frames, wire, old cars, car parts, haymowers, rakes, tools, and utensils were cast into a great heap to gather rust and provide shelter and comfort to snakes, mice, and skunks.

Cook no longer had to worry about making ends meet. Yes, he'd do even better than merely get by. He'd help himself and contribute to the war effort at the same time. Not only that, but he'd clean up the countryside of unsightly heaps of rusted metal and restore the fields and meadows to their pristine states. He'd demolish these eyesores and drive the snakes, mice, and skunks into the wilderness like refugees.

Cook and his helper were on the road every day collecting the scrap metal that had been piled on the side of the road for ease of pickup. There were scrap metal piles in Oxenden, Big Bay, Keppel, Clavering, Hepworth, Purple Valley, Colpoy's Bay, and Adamsville, a one-house village. There were more in Mar, Ferndale, Lion's Head, and dozens of other hamlets, all clamoring for recognition of some kind. Cook delivered loads of scrap either to Wiarton or to Park Head, another village whose mention raised eyebrows with the question, "Where's that?"

By the spring of 1944 Jim Cook, his helper, and other scrap metal dealers had pretty well depleted the scrap metal piles in northern Bruce County. They had done their share to push the enemy into retreat.

The news from the war fronts was good. The Allies were now on the offensive, delivering blows that were sending the Axis reeling back on all fronts. But the war was still far from over. The demand for scrap metal was as great as ever. There was still money to be made.

Scrap metal piles were growing scarcer. Since he had gone into the scrap metal collection business, Cook had set Sunday afternoons aside for exploring the countryside for scrap heaps. In all that time he had not driven to Cape Croker.

But now that he had plundered most of the junk piles in the area, he ventured into Cape Croker. He did so with some misgivings. It was a reserve, set aside and meant for Indians. He'd heard about Indians; he'd seen a few in town on occasion, but he'd never spoken to one before. He didn't know what to expect, whether there'd be tepees and hostile Indians. He decided that if anyone asked him what he was doing on the reserve he'd say he was lost and wanted to get back to Wiarton.

Cook entered the reserve via Coveney's Road into the Little Port Elgin neighborhood, driving slowly, watching for junk piles and hostile Indians. Of the former he saw many that spelled dollars, of the latter, none. The Indians that he saw, old people, women, and children, waved at him and smiled. They looked friendly, dispelling his vague fears of ambush and assassination. He was surprised that Cape Croker looked like Barrow Bay or Stokes Bay, any other village in the peninsula; two-story wooden homes, log houses, barns, gardens, rail fences, livery stables, mailboxes, two general stores, churches; no tepees. And the people that he saw were dressed just like the people in the rest of the peninsula, although there was a marked preference for rubber boots by men and women alike. If Cook hadn't known that Cape Croker was a reserve, he might have mistaken it for Purple Valley.

On his way out after making a circuit of the reserve, Cook stopped near the school to speak to a man walking on the road. It was Levi Chegahno.

"Sir!" he addressed the surprised Levi. "Can you tell me how to get to Wiarton from here?"

Levi was flustered because his understanding and command of English was very limited. To be called "Sir!" made him shift his feet, for he now had to talk like a gentleman. This exercise caused Levi to lisp and stammer.

"Tir! You 'tay on dit road; don' turn no plate. You git to Wighton, Tir!" Levi was scared. He hoped that his English had been good enough. "Did you under'tood?" he asked.

"Yes, Sir! Thank you, Sir! I appreciate that. By the way, who's your chief?"

"That Tom Joneth."

Levi stood on the side of the road looking at the car. He wondered what the White Man was doing on the reserve. Probably coming to steal more land. That's the only reason White People came to the reserve. To look at the land first, then take it. Never satisfied, them people. Twenty-five years earlier he had fought in France. He had fired at White Men and they had fired at him. Sometimes he'd hope that he'd hit one of them and kill him. The next moment he'd hope that he'd miss. He wouldn't be able to sleep if he had killed somebody, even a White Man. Maybe he should have killed, but he couldn't. Maybe that was part of being a coward. He had been scared every moment; shots had frightened him, explosions had made him jump, flashes of light had forced him to cower. Did fear make him a coward, he had wondered? He had thought better of himself when his comrades had confessed that they too were afraid for their lives. He watched the car pull away.

The next day Jim Cook went back to the reserve to look for Tom Jones to ask for permission to collect the scrap metal lying in heaps in the fields. With the directions given him, Cook found Tom's store, its front designed like that of a frontier town store.

As Cook opened the door he tripped the overhead bell that tinkled like a sleigh bell.

"My name is Cook, Jim Cook, from Wiarton. I'd like to see the chief. Is he in?"

"Just a moment, sir," Nellie purred before she went to the entrance door that led into the store's living quarters. "Tom! There's a White Man here. Wants to see you about something."

Jim Cook fidgeted anxiously, not knowing what kind of Indian chief he was about to meet.

Tom lurched out of his living quarters. Behind rimless glasses his eyes trained on the visitor, straight into the man's mind and heart. Tom's eyes were cold, his face hostile, his tone hard. "Yes! You want to see me?"

"Yes, sir! My name is Jim Cook, from Wiarton. I'm in the scrap metal business and I would like the scrap metal on the reserve, if it's for sale. How do I go about doing that? I pay top price for the metal, $1 a ton, cash on the spot. Whom do I see?"

"Been in the business long?"

"Since '42. I've got a contract with the steel company in Hamilton."

"How do you arrange your purchase of scrap metal from other people?"

"I go to them directly, in person, ask them if they'd sell me their scrap, work out dates for pickup, get them to pile it on the side of the road."

"You do the same thing here. Go from house to house and ask. I don't suppose there's anyone that'll refuse. When do you mean to start?"

"I was set on starting today."

"If you can put off starting for a few days it'll give me a chance to let the people know what you're doing on the reserve, that you have my permission … and do you have a hired hand?"

"Yes, I got a man from Wiarton."

"You really should hire one of our people. In fact, I insist on it before I will give you my consent to remove the scrap from the reserve."

"That's fair enough, Chief. I don't know the people in this village, so you'll have to hire a man for me. But he's got to be strong, 'cause some of that scrap is heavy. I'll need a good worker."

"All of our able-bodied men are in the army, more than ninety so far; the rest are just kids and old men," Tom explained, boasting about the reserve's service record while borrowing time to think. "The only one that comes to mind is David ... David McLeod. I don't know if you'd want him or not; he's Mongoloid."

"What's that? I thought everybody was Indian on this reserve."

Tom explained. "But despite his disabilities, he's a good worker; strong as a horse. You should try him first and if he doesn't work out, get your own man."

"So long's a man can work, keep his temper, and don't hurt no one I can work with anybody," Cook declared. "Where's he live? I'd like to look him over."

"If you can spare the time I can take you there now."

On the way to Rosa's place, Tom hinted that if Cook needed anything, such as gas, oil, cigarettes, luncheon meats, or refreshments, his store was well stocked with such goods and he'd be pleased to serve him.

"Ahnee, Rosauh!" Tom greeted Rosa, and he came right to the point of his visit.

"I guess it's up to David. You'd have to ask him."

They called David from the back where he had been working. Rosa explained what Tom and the visitor wanted, and that he would earn money, "tet tsets." She also let Tom know beforehand that David rested whenever he felt like it and for as long as he felt like it. The visitor should know this before hiring David.

"Try him for a day; see how he works out. If you're not satisfied with him you can bring your own man."

"I'll give him a try," Cook agreed reluctantly, but underneath the surface he had grave misgivings about David. He was short, chubby, and not built for heavy work. Maybe the chief was pulling a fast one on him.

Cook would call on David the next Monday.

Word went out to every household that a scrap metal collector would come by to pick up unwanted metal. Payment would be made on the spot. "Good old Tom! He knows how to bring in business! Wonder how much he gets out of it?" the Cape Croker Indians asked one another, suspicious as always.

During the next few days heaps of scrap metal disappeared from the fields and meadows, appearing on the sides of the roads in front of every household. Muggs' old car parts vanished from his garage. Parts of Aesop's old cars—hoods, doors, and bumpers that he had intended to use on his other old cars—were there one night, gone the next.

Early on collection day Jim Cook picked up David.

"Good morning!" He greeted David with a warm smile as well. "You all set for a good day's work? Good morning, Mrs. McLeod. A grand day, isn't it? It's really too nice for working, but one has to make a living. David all ready?" Small talk. He had to say something to show his breeding, even though he knew that neither Rosa nor David spoke English.

David grinned and flexed his muscles.

"Let's go. See what you can do."

"Don't forget to work hard, David," Rosa reminded him.

In the cab of the truck Cook told David, "Now we'll see what kind of man you are. I hope that you're as good as Chief Jones says you are."

David's first test came at Bert Ashkewe's homestead at the Benjamin Point turnoff. There was enough scrap metal to fill up the truck. Cook stood in the bed of the truck to arrange the scrap in some order as David, wearing leather mitts that Cook provided, put it on board. Tin cans, pails, wire, lanterns, chests, boilers, washtubs, washboards, bed frames, springs, and hoops pinged, thudded, grated, and clanged as David threw them on board. David grinned to hear the metal clash on metal. He grunted with the heavier hardware. A box stove gave him a little trouble, not because of its weight, but because of its bulk. His arms were too short to bear-hug the article and heave it on board. He wrestled with and swore at it until he caught and latched onto two of its legs and heaved it on board the truck. He cleared his throat loudly as an expression of great satisfaction, pulled a red polka-dotted bandana from his pocket, and wiped his brow. Time for a smoke.

Cook leaped down from the truck to join David. Taking a bottle of Coke from the cab of his truck, Cook gave it to David while he poured himself a cup of coffee from his thermos. "You're as strong as a bull," he said in admiration.

After the break David finished loading the truck. It had been a most satisfying morning of work for the scrap dealer, and it was only 10 a.m. He had time to make another trip that day. Before leaving, Cook paid Mrs. Ashkewe for the metal and then drove back to Wiarton slowly, scanning both sides of the road for little dumps. Through the new growth that was now starting to spread over lots that had once been gardens and orchards belonging to the Snake and Black families, now vacant, Cook saw two uncleared garbage dumps.

As he paid David his morning's wages, four dimes, Cook asked Rosa not to let David go anywhere. He was returning for another load in the afternoon.

Cook stopped briefly at Tom Jones' to let the chief know that he couldn't have asked for a better man. "He can work with the best of them. Too bad that he can't talk. He'd be good company. Would you let Mrs. McLeod know that I'll be in twice a week until all the scrap iron is picked? I told her, but I don't think she understood."

"That I can do," Tom promised.

In the weeks that followed, David was a familiar sight riding in the back of Cook's scrap iron truck. Shortly after he started working for Cook, David found riding in the back of the truck more to his liking than sitting in the cab. He liked the feel of the wind blowing in his face and through his hair, and it cooled him off and dried the perspiration from his brow. To top it off, he could yell at and taunt the dogs that barked at, chased, and tried to bite the tires of the truck. "Sib-ae! Sib-ae! Come on, dogs! Bite! Run! You're too slow!" And he loved to wave at people along the way to draw their attention. "Look at me! I'm riding in a truck! I'm working, making 'tet tsets'." Without knowing it, David was doing his bit to turn the tide against the enemy and save civilization.

Since Ethel Nadjiwon had gone back to Parry Island and Shawanaga, there to wait out the war and the return of her husband, Rosa had no source of local news except David. And he brought home all sorts of news, local and foreign.

David's first major news report unsettled her.

He had seen pictures of the remnants of the defeated German 6th Army at Stalingrad, marching in columns in the snow, feet bound in rags, heads wound in rags, hands wrapped in rags, terror in their eyes, death in their faces. There were pictures of corpses locked in grotesque positions in the snow, their faces twisted and contorted by terror, hunger, and the brittle cold; masks pleading for life, a crust of bread, a little warmth.

"Back-a-haw?" David asked, his eyes wide in fear.

"No, that's not John," Walter assured David.

But these pictures were etched in David's mind, haunted him.

"Woosh! Something terrible happened. There was a man in the snow, lying down like this, all curled up. There was a horse as well. There were lots of men," David explained in his own way, referring to the picture that he had seen.

"Where?"

"Over there."

"In the snow? Sleeping? Who were they? Were they drunk? Were they hurt? Was it Budeese? Edgar? Herman? Aesop?" and Rosa recited a litany of names to which David shook his head negatively. "Where?" she tried again.

David scowled at his mother. Why couldn't she understand? He couldn't get through to her.

Rosa had trouble falling asleep thinking about what tragedy had taken place and who the victims might be. She recalled some of the tragedies that had occurred in the past on the reserve. Was the terrible scene that David described something like the tragedy that took place in 1906 when six fishermen decided to return home on the evening of December 1 and, instead of walking, elected to come back by boat to McGregor Harbour? The north wind, a gale really, blew them off course onto the shoals at Partridge Point, where the sailboat floundered, pitching the heavily clothed men into the frothing, ice cold waters. Their bodies were recovered one by one during the following summer. The men had taken a short cut to the next life. Was what David had tried to tell Rosa comparable to that disaster?

Rosa recalled as well the experience of Snake and Black, who had gone ice fishing off the Cove of Cork one February day. While they were fishing some distance from shore a blizzard developed. Before the men could come ashore, the ice cracked and the men were marooned on a floe of ice. They gave themselves up for dead; the community gave them up for dead. But the other world didn't want them just yet. Their guardian Manitous summoned the winds and the currents, which drove the floe of ice onto the south shore of Owen Sound Harbour where a farmer found the survivors and took them to a hospital. The men recovered.

These men should have known better. Yet they went against common sense. Haste and greed nearly took their lives. Were Indians born for tragedy? Self-destruction?

The Allies, as they called themselves, invaded North Africa and, after chasing the Afrika Korps out of there, landed in Italy, the soft underbelly of the enemy. It was now just a question of time and casualties before victory would be theirs. On the Eastern Front the Russians, with massive help from the United States, were leaning on the Germans and forcing them back. Canada's armed forces were in action.

Within days of the invasion of Italy, the pictures and the names of the local soldiers killed or wounded in action were published in the *Owen Sound Sun Times* and in the *Wiarton Echo*.

Mac (Alfred) McLeod (one of nine members of the John McLeod family to serve in Canada's armed forces) was killed in action in Italy ... for King, Flag, Country; he was the first casualty from the Cape.

Howard Jones, killed in action.

Orville Johnston, wounded in action.

John Johnston, wounded in action.

John was lucky. Had it not been for Bun (Edwin Akiwenzie), his comrade, the caption with John's picture would have read, "Killed in action." While his company was running forward from building to building under heavy artillery and small arms fire in Ortona, Italy, John was cut down by shrapnel that burned into his knee. At the same time the building beside which he had fallen received a direct hit. Its walls teetered. Just before the wall collapsed Bun, who was across the road, turned, ran back, and dragged John to safety.

A few days after John's picture appeared in the paper Rosa cut it out and hung it on the wall, along with the telegram notifying her of her son's injury. The telegram, delivered by Father Howitt, s.j., did not detail the extent of John's wound. Rosa couldn't sleep or eat, fearing the worst.

David looked at John's picture. "Back-a-haw," he said as his imagination stirred up vague images. "Tenshun ... At ease." He'd been neglecting his drills these past months. He must have felt guilty, for he practiced his drills in front of the picture.

Only after Rosa received a letter from John telling her that he was fine and was hoping to come home soon did she feel some relief and tell David that John had been hurt by the enemy. David looked at the picture, studied it, and spoke to it. Rosa didn't understand what he said, but she sensed from the tone of his voice and the way he shook his head that David was upset.

Toward midnight Rosa heard David talking loudly and rapidly about Back-a-haw as he came home across the Big Meadow. He must have been telling the Little People that his brother had been hurt.

David didn't know that the enemy was being driven back on all fronts by rocket fire, mass bombs, waves of Russian soldiers, and all the might and fury of the Western world.

There was no longer danger of invasion, or even air raids. People felt relatively safe and secure, but uneasy about their men overseas.

June 6, 1944. The Allied Forces invaded mainland Europe, landing on the Cherbourg Peninsula in the early hours of the morning. Walter read of it, the people heard about it on their radios. David listened to Walter describe the invasion to Frances. Heavy fighting, heavy casualties.

"Woosh! Some men landed over there on the shore. They were fighting. Lots of them fell down and they didn't get up."

"Who, David? Who?" David said something that Rosa could not make out. "Where David? At the Point? At the dock? At the agency? I don't know what you're talking about."

The next time Walter came to visit he told Rosa the good news that the Allies had opened a second front.

But for some families it was not good news.

Jackie McLeod, killed in action.

Benjamin Ashkewe, killed in action.

At home, nothing was worth talking about. Dullsville.

"Anything new in council?" Rosa asked.

"Nothing really, except that Tom and the agent are at it again ... over the council minute book. Since the agent started keeping custody of the book, we've found alterations in the minutes, not much mind you, but enough to change meanings. I told Tom about these changes and we monitored the minutes for a while until we were sure that someone was making changes to them.

Tom accused the agent of altering official documents. The agent explained that the English had to be corrected so as to conform to government standards. Tom blew his top. He muttered that he was going to tell someone that the agent was altering government records.

*I*n mid-July Jim Cook told David, "In a couple of more days, my friend, we'll be all done. No more scrap. And the way the war is going, that's going to be over soon, too. There was an awful bunch o' scrap for such a small place."

David just looked at Cook and grinned, then talked. "Aehn-haehn! Back-a-haw Muk-uk-ayauh … muh … bitches. Sudla-bitch." David's mood clouded.

"God, how I wish I could understand you, fella. I'm sure that you've got a lot of things you could tell me. But I guess it doesn't matter, does it? I mean, it shouldn't matter."

As David got off the truck he motioned to Cook to wait so that he could go to the store to buy some tobacco.

"Hurry up, David. I want to get this load to Park Head this afternoon."

In less than ten minutes David came out, fully dressed in wedge cap, shirt, tie, summer tunic, khaki trousers, and spiffy black boots. He clambered aboard the back of the truck and sat on top of the cargo. When Cook called out, "You settled in? Ready?" David shouted back. Cook put the truck into gear.

At Edgar's Corner Cook stopped to pick up an aged hitchhiker, John Angus, who was returning to Little Port Elgin. As soon as the hitchhiker settled in the seat beside the driver, he told Cook about the time that he hoodwinked a White Man, a policeman, who had come to the Cape to arrest him for something that he had done, for being a vagrant. He evaded arrest by telling the arresting officer that the wanted man had just died and that he, as his surviving brother, was in mourning. Instead of getting off at Little Port Elgin, John continued on to the Purple Valley. Cook completely forgot about David, so engrossed was he by John Angus's stories.

As Cook drove away from Gilbert's General Store in Purple Valley, he glanced in his side-view mirror. Behind him the hitchhiker was waving his arms and his cane. Cook waved back, "You're welcome." And he shook his head in admiration, for he had never heard anyone with such imagination as the old hitchhiker.

At the bottom of Wiarton Hill, Cook pulled into the White Rose service station set back a little from Berford Street on the west side.

While the attendant was filling up the gas tank, Cook walked around the truck inspecting the tires, and then asked if he could use the washroom.

David got off and walked to the opposite side of the street.

Cook emerged from the washroom, paid for his gas, and drove off, not realizing that David was no longer in the truck. The service station lessee gave the hitchhiking "soldier" who had got off the truck a fleeting glance and went back to work.

In front of David was a whole new world. It consisted of huge buildings pressed one against the other, shoulder to shoulder, all constructed of stone, all of them bigger and taller than any of the buildings at Cape Croker. Dwarfing all the buildings was the Arlington Hotel. What David saw drew him like a magnet.

David could not resist the lure of the big city any more than a hummingbird could ignore hollyhocks. He made his way south, walking slowly, creeping forward warily as a cat entering alien territory where he didn't belong. He stopped in front of the stately Arlington Hotel, where Wiarton's upper class drank cocktails and took their out-of-town visitors for dinner.

There was little traffic on the street, few cars, and as many shoppers. After reading the posters urging the purchase of Victory Bonds that were affixed to the Arlington's doors, David looked to the other side of the street. There were neon lights, yellow lights that appeared as if they were chasing one another, then flashing on and off. These were the lights of the Berford Theatre. David crossed to the west side of Berford Street to examine the lights and the posters plastered on the walls and in the glass-enclosed cases. There were large posters of John Wayne single-handedly defeating the Japanese in battle after battle in the comfort and safety of Hollywood's studios. There were pictures of Betty Grable, the pinup girl, nice legs, nice ass, nice tits, that drew long, lingering looks and drooling lust.

Betty Grable's considerable charms and assets did nothing for David. On he went. At the end of the town block, four doors from the Berford Theatre, was Wiarton's other ranking institution, the Pacific Hotel, patronized by the town's less affluent. David stopped in front of it. From within he heard muffled laughter, the clatter of glasses, the scraping of chairs. On the hotel's doors were more posters. So much happiness within. That was the place to be.

David went up the short flight of concrete stairs. He opened the door to see who and what was inside but, because of poor lighting, he could not see clearly and, because of the lack of ventilation, the interior was rank with stale tobacco smoke and skunky beer. David closed the door.

One man inside had seen the face at the door. He pointed a finger. His lips and his mouth quavered.

"What's wrong, Russ?" the man's drinking companions asked. "You sick or something?" They looked toward the door where Russ was pointing.

"A-a, J-J-Jap soldier," Russ stammered, his finger still extended, now unsteady.

"What t'hell you talkin' about? A Jap soldier!" the other drinkers wanted to know. Despite their doubts, they twisted in their seats to face the door. "I think you're getting corked, Russ. Time for you to knock it off. Seein' Japs! Hell! The Yanks got them on the run. How can they be here?" Another drinker snorted.

"H-h-honest to God! I seen a Jap. It was a Jap ... just opened the door ... an' ... looked in. I swear. I seen 'im plain as day. Short an' stocky ... an' slant-eyed, just like in them pitchers. ... Maybe it's an invasion!"

While the drinkers roared and slapped their thighs in derisive laughter at the idea of an invasion, Bill, one of the regular patrons, got to his feet and lurched to the door. "I'm gonna see what a Jap looks like. Never seen one of them 'afore." He opened the door, then slammed it closed immediately. He bawled huskily. "It's true! There's a Jap soldier standing outside! Christ. Lock the damned doors!"

Chairs scraped and screeched as the drinkers, stricken into sobriety, staggered into action. They bolted the doors, leaned chairs against doorknobs. They hissed at one another, "Grab a weapon! Somethin', we gotta defen' ourselves."

"Other door, too, to the ladies' section," another voice wheezed.

The drinkers armed themselves with bottles, ashtrays, and chair legs, ready to defend themselves.

The bartender, Cliff, with Bill at his heels, burst into the lobby of the hotel. "Close the doors. ... Lock them. There's Japs outside. Call the police! Call the home guard."

"Hold on to your damned horses. What t'hell is this all about?" the innkeeper demanded truculently, taking his eyes off the ledger.

"Japs! There's a Jap soldier outside! For Christ's sake. Do something! Get on the phone!"

Vern, the innkeeper, his eyes narrow, leaned back in his chair. His dander was rising; the idea of his hired help telling him what to do! What t'hell was going on?

Cliff grabbed the phone, cranked it. "Get me the operator! Who? Using? Who in hell is this? Dr. Wigle! Get t'hell off the line. I don't give two farts if you're a doctor. This is an emergency." While Cliff was snarling into the phone, Bill led Vern to a side window to see if the Jap soldier was still at the corner. He was, just about to cross the street.

"See! Now, you believe me?" Bill demanded.

"Well! I'll be hanged!" Vern gasped.

David went across to the other side of the street. He stopped at Taylor Hardware Store for a minute to inspect the latest lanterns and washboard stylings. Next door was Levine's Clothing Store. Levine himself was on his knees arranging ties, socks, and shirts in the display window. David smiled at him, but the man didn't smile back. Instead, the man's mouth opened wide and he crawled backward like a crab, away from the window.

When he turned away from the window, David saw two soldiers striding toward him, their steps in unison, arms swinging, their jack-boots pounding the pavement.

David drew himself together and marched forward in his finest military bearing and style, flinging his arms back and forth. Several paces in front of the fuzzy-cheeked soldiers, David did a quick two-step and saluted smartly. The two soldiers returned his salute. David, hugely pleased with himself, stopped, looked back, and then continued on his way.

The two young servicemen from farther up the Bruce Peninsula looked at each other. "What do you make of that?" said one to the other. "That guy salutin' us privates."

"Oh, leave him be. I'm drier than an old buzzard. I want to drink. Coupla' cold ones will loosen me up."

At the Pacific the two young soldiers tried the door. It was locked. They tried the side door. That too was locked. "Shouldn't be closed; it's not 6 p.m. yet. Too early," they complained. Back to the front they went. They jiggled the latch.

Cupping his hands around his eyes one of the soldiers peered through the small, square window set in the door. "There's men in there," he wheezed. "Place looks as if there's been a fight in there. ... Open up!" Both soldiers pounded on the door. "What in hell's goin' on? Servin' zombies and civvies but not soldiers?"

"You goddamned Japs. ... You can go to hell," came a defiant voice from within.

"Japs!" the two soldiers bellowed. "What in hell's the matter with you, anyhow? We're from Lion's Head. Grey and Simcoe Foresters."

Cliff peered out another window. Instead of Jap soldiers he saw two Canadian soldiers. He opened the window and hissed, "There's Jap soldiers in town. One of their soldiers was here not more than five minutes ago."

The two Lion's Head soldiers looked at each other wide-eyed. "That soldier! ... He saluted us! ... Looked like a Jap, didn't he?"

"Yeah! That's him! *You saw him?*" Cliff asked, astonishment in his voice.

"A spy!" the two soldiers gasped.

"Ain't around here for nothin'," Cliff went on. "There's got to be more of them. Do somethin' … you're soldiers."

The two soldiers, neither more than eighteen and with less than six months of service, stood rooted where they were. They were awakening to the situation. They were unarmed. All they had were their kit bags. They were just two young farm boys against, who knew, an enemy that was armed and much more numerous.

"What's wrong? Scared?" Cliff taunted.

"We're not scared," the soldiers spat. "Oh, shit." The boys didn't want to appear to be shrinking but they remembered the images cast by comic books of Japanese soldiers carrying grenades in their armpits and performing other treacherous acts that civilized soldiers did not. The two soldiers mumbled and trembled as they descended the steps. They left their kit bags at the foot of the stairs, asking Cliff to look after them.

One of the soldiers took charge. "Come on! You stay on this side of the street. I'll go on the other side. Watch for my signals."

The leader dashed across the street. He flung himself into a doorway, flattened himself against it. His heart was already pounding. Ahead, the enemy strolled nonchalantly by Plante's Music Store. The soldier held his hand up as he had seen John Wayne do in movies. He checked the roofs of the buildings opposite, the sky, and the buildings behind him for other enemy soldiers. He hoped that Jap didn't have a grenade, a gun, a knife. The thought drew a prayer: "Our Father, who art in heaven …." The coast appeared to be clear. He waved his arm to signal his comrade to move forward. They ran.

As they sprinted ahead, the two soldiers nearly ran down aged shoppers coming out of shops. They snapped, "Get back inside! There's Jap soldiers!" Some people took cover. Others continued on their way, disinclined to believe drunks. Another signal, another scurry of boots on the pavement.

By the New London Café a patron, Abe Mitchell, Fred Tuffnell's friend, seeing a soldier on the far side of the street running from door to door as in the movies, came out to see what was going on. At that moment the soldier moving forward on the east side of Berford Street almost collided with him. Before Abe could ask what was in the wind the soldier hissed at him, "Get back inside. There's a Jap soldier on the other side." The soldier kept going, but Abe didn't go back inside as commanded. He watched, then followed.

When the soldier on the west side of the street was within thirty paces of the enemy, the soldier on the east side sprinted across the thoroughfare to join him. Sweat rolled down their temples. Neither said a word.

Just ahead was the Jap. Cool, he walked and looked about him. He didn't even bother to look back. And … he was talking in his own language. Stupid son of a bitch … so damned sure of himself.

The enemy was about to cross George Street.

The two soldiers looked at each other. This was it. "Let's go!" They charged. Boots clattered. They hurled themselves on the unsuspecting "Jap," sending him to the pavement. The enemy grunted.

In the next instant the soldiers had the enemy's arms pinned behind him in a hammerlock. "Get up!" they shouted at him. The soldiers forced him to his feet. The enemy was moaning from the pain that shot from his elbow to his shoulders as his arm was levered upward. He didn't resist.

At that moment Abe rushed forward. He struck David full in the face. Blood spattered. David's head jerked back. Abe struck again. He drove his fist into David's stomach. David's head pitched forward and he groaned. Abe spat. "You goddamned, fuckin' Jap. I'm going to kill you!" And he struck David once more in the face and drove his knee into his groin. David sagged, then went limp.

Before Abe delivered another blow, one of the soldiers barked out, "That's enough! He's a prisoner!"

"He's a goddamned Jap! You should kill the son of a bitch. That's what these bastards would do to you."

"Knock it off! He's our prisoner. I don't want no goddamned man being killed in my arms," the soldier protested. "Bugger off!"

The two soldiers looked at one another. "What do we do now?" they asked each other.

"Kill him. Shoot the bastard," the intruder insisted, but the soldiers ignored him.

"There's a jail up here," one of the soldiers recalled, referring to the courthouse that stood only steps from where they were standing.

"Damn, this guy's heavy. And we've got blood all over us." As they dragged their unconscious prisoner up the incline the soldiers groaned, "How we gonna get this blood off? What'll we tell our commanding officer? Will he let us off for getting our uniforms dirty?"

"What's this?" the warden asked as soon as the soldiers entered the reception area.

"A prisoner. A Jap. Just captured him."

"And ... what do you want me to do with him?"

"Lock him up," the soldiers answered.

The warden leaned over the counter that separated his office and the reception area. "You boys really did a job on this guy, didn't you? Can't tell if he's a Jap or not with all that blood .... But he don't belong here. He should be in a prisoner of war camp. Where'd you boys git him? Where'd he come from?"

But the soldiers ignored the warden's questions. "Cut the stallin', Warden! Lock this prisoner up! We gotta keep him someplace while we go out and check the area. You gotta do your share in this damn war."

Duty! That was something the warden understood. The prisoner started to stir and moan. Yet the warden was hesitant to lock someone up without the authority of the police of Magistrate McLevis. What would His Honor, Otto McLevis, say? Worse, what would he do?

The warden decided he'd take a chance. "Just wait," he muttered, then went to the far side of the office to fetch a ring of keys. He emerged from the office through a door that was marked "private." "This way," he said, and led them along a corridor and then down to the basement.

Behind him the two soldiers half-carried, half-dragged their moaning prisoner. On their heels tagged Abe. Who he was, the soldiers didn't know. The prisoner's boots clumped down the stairs. The warden unlocked a cell door that had two small, barred windows. Just before the soldiers dragged their prisoner inside, Abe gave the prisoner a violent kick. "You goddamned, good-for-nothing Jap! I hope they shoot you!" he hissed.

"What t'hell's the matter with you, anyway?" one of the soldiers demanded. "Enough's enough! The man's out. You don't have to hit him again. Or do you hit people only when they can't hit back?" The soldiers deposited the prisoner on the cell's cot.

The iron cell door clanged shut. No one said a word on the way up the stairs. The warden returned to his office.

The two soldiers stood and fidgeted uneasily in the reception room. "What do we do now?" one asked.

"You gotta go out and look, see if there's more of them bastards," Abe offered.

"Why in hell don't you mind your damned business?" one of the soldiers snapped. Neither of the two boys needed to be told what they were supposed to do. But the prospect of having to search for enemies who might be armed, and who knew the number, was daunting. The two boys didn't want to go out, but they had no choice.

"Keep a close eye on the prisoner. There may be more of them," the local soldiers advised the warden.

"Oh my God! Who's going to help me guard the prisoner?" the warden wailed.

"I will," Abe volunteered.

"And who are you?"

"Abe Mitchell, Owen Sound," the man said, extending his hand. The soldiers went out.

Downstairs, the other prisoners awaiting transfer to Walkerton County Jail were restless. "Hear that? A Jap prisoner? What t'hell's he doing here?"

The two Lion's Head soldiers combed the streets of Wiarton, checked the alleys and the back driveways of the main buildings. They looked aloft frequently. They asked people they met if anyone had seen any Japs. They succeeded only in causing alarm in some; others, thinking that the soldiers' questions were some kind of charade, a military exercise, continued with their business.

At the southwest corner of Berford and Division streets, the two soldiers met. "See anything? Think there's any more of them? No? What'll we do? Hell of a way to spend a short leave." Neither of the men believed that one Jap soldier meant invasion. More likely he was a spy. "What are we supposed to do? Why in hell did we get mixed up in this mess anyhow? Home just for a couple of days," they grumbled, "and now we have to wait around."

"To hell with it," the other answered. "I don't think there's any more. Let's go for a drink."

But the other was hesitant. "Let's take one more run around the area. I don't want to be accused of not doing my duty. People are watching us. We'll meet back here in five minutes." The soldiers ran off.

As agreed, they returned to the same corner five minutes later. "See anything?" … "No! You?"

Cliff, who had been keeping watch behind a window, now called out, "Pssst! What happened? Did you get him?"

"Yeah! He's in jail, locked up."

"There any more?"

"Don't think so. Better not be. We've checked the alleys and the streets a couple of times now. Didn't see anyone."

Cliff and the two soldiers argued for a while about continuing to search for more Japs, but the two soldiers didn't see much point in conducting a house-to-house search. "If there was more of them, they'd be out already. Might as well search the whole damned Peninsula for that matter. Besides, what would they be doing in Wiarton anyway? We want a drink and then to go on home."

Cliff relented. "Alright boys, come in. I'll have someone at the door to keep an eye on the street, just in case."

The patrons clustered around the two soldiers like a gaggle of newspaper reporters wanting to know the details of the capture and what was going to be done with the Jap. The soldiers' explanations only served to stir up more speculation. "What happens to spies? They're shot? Where they goin' to get a firing squad? Meaford? Camp Borden? Here? Who does what? Anybody get in touch with the army? Yes, the manager finally got in touch with the *Echo* man. He'll know what to do. Bring a round for the boys, Cliff."

Since he had received an urgent call from the innkeeper of the Pacific Hotel, Ted Duncan, publisher and editor of the *Wiarton Echo*, had not hung up the phone or stopped jotting notes on a pad of paper. At first he laughed at the absurdity of the call, but when he saw the Jap soldier across the street he could no longer doubt. His first impulse was to run and hide, but that was cowardly and unworthy of the journalists who remained at the scene of the action. He shook, he could hardly crank the phone, but he stuck by his post.

A soldier flashed by the front window. Another Jap? Ted rasped into the phone. "Using? Using? Operator! Get me the army! The home guard! Don't ask dumb questions .... They're not listed? There's a Jap soldier on the street ... another one just ran by. Get the RCMP ... What? The line's busy?"

The publisher tried the *Toronto Daily Star*, the Toronto *Globe and Mail* and the *Toronto Evening Telegram*, but the static was so bad that he hung up in frustration.

Then he called CFOS, the Owen Sound radio station. The receptionist laughed when he told her what the call was about, as if he were some kind of crank. "Sure! Sure! Hee! Hee! Hee!" she hung up on him. Typical big-town attitude. He cursed the system that urged vigilance but did nothing to provide phone numbers. "Go to hell," he spat at the phone. In his growing rage and fear, Ted dropped the receiver.

Did newsmen cower? Or did they cringe and feel like hiding, as he did? Or were they all like Ernie Pyle, who ran forward with the infantry, directly into enemy fire, leaping into trenches, hunching down and cursing the enemy, waiting for the signal to run forward again while shells and bullets whined and shrieked overhead? In those moments Pyle jotted down notes for another war story dispatched directly from the front lines.

Chagrined by his fear, Ted gathered up a pad of paper and stuffed a handful of pencils into his pocket. He wasn't going to be cowed into inaction. Still, he held back. He pushed the door open inch by inch. Damn! The thing squeaked. Ready to slam it shut if he saw an enemy soldier, Ted eased himself out onto the street. He looked to his left, then to his right. There were a few rash people walking about, a car coming down the hill from the south, another turning near the Arlington Hotel. Almost like any other day.

At the corner of Division and Berford were two Canadian soldiers. At least they looked Canadian, but it was hard to tell from the distance. They went into the Pacific Hotel. Ted drew his breath in and went toward it. He tried to walk without fear, but he couldn't help glancing from front to side to back, ready to run.

"Hey, Ted! What are you doing in this Den of Iniquity?" they greeted the publisher. By now the patrons were getting over their fear and feeling triumphant. "Wife kick you out? Come on, have a drink. Better still, buy a round. Caught a Jap spy bare-handed. But you know, Ted, even if these boys had not come by, we were ready to go after him ourselves."

"Never a story like this again, Ted," another patron offered. "Beat them stories 'bout the round of visits in and around the Cape, or them Women's Institute teas in Oxenden and Adamsville."

Ted sat down to interview the soldiers in preparation for writing the biggest story of his life about the most singular event ever to take place in Wiarton.

*I*n the cell, David came to. He moaned. His mouth and his face throbbed. His stomach ached. His body hurt. His soul and his spirit chafed. He moaned, "Woosh! Woosh! Mother! Mother! Kik! Kik! Walter! Walter!"

The other prisoners heard him. "Shut up, you goddamned Jap. I hope they shoot you! You no-good son of a bitch."

David didn't know what the men were saying, but sensed from the tone of their voices that they wanted to hurt him. He tried to stop moaning so as not to offend those men any further. He cringed on the floor, afraid the men would come in and beat him again.

Even when he swallowed his hurt and cried for his mother and Walter to hold him and to take him home, no one came, not even the Little People. The other prisoners taunted him and roared at him. "I hope they shoot you, you slant-eyed son of a bitch." If they couldn't fight the enemy, they could at least hurt his feelings.

An hour and a half after David had been beaten up and clapped in a cell, Constable Robinson from the Owen Sound RCMP detachment, accompanied by Constable Johnson, a provincial police officer, arrived at the Wiarton courthouse.

Constables Robinson and Johnson didn't need to introduce themselves to the warden; they merely explained that they were there to investigate a report that a Japanese soldier or spy had been apprehended.

"Yes!" The warden confirmed that the Jap soldier was in custody and, pointing to Abe, who had remained in the courthouse, said, "This man helped capture him."

The officers looked at Abe. They were already familiar with him. "And what are you doing around here?" Abe explained.

"Long way to come for lunch," Johnson commented sarcastically.

"You officers treatin' me like a suspect?" Abe complained. "I just helped capture a Jap spy, a goddamned Jap. Them soldiers wouldna captured that guy by themselves."

"You're excused. You may leave ... and keep your nose clean."

Abe was pained by the officers' attitude. He felt like arguing but held back. Best not to stir them up. He got up as slowly as an old man and, just as slowly, dawdled out. "Christ! I'll never get any credit for helping capture a Jap spy. Fuckin' stupid sons o' bitches," he spat out to the grass outside.

Inside the warden led the officers downstairs to the cell block. He opened the cell door.

"Get up!" Johnson ordered.

"Kuh! Kuh! No! No!" David cried out. He flinched.

The officers pulled him up by his armpits. They clamped handcuffs on him and conducted him forward. "Move," they barked at him. They pushed and shoved him so that David missed his step and banged his knees and elbows on the stairs. "Get up! Move!" There was no pity. The officers jerked the cuffs upward so that pain stabbed David in the shoulder. He screamed. It didn't matter. He didn't matter. He was just a prisoner, a nothing who deserved only to be beaten, pummeled.

As the officers went upstairs with David, voices, loud and belligerent, came from the other cells. "What t'hell's going on! Cut the racket!"

"RCMP here to take custody of the Jap prisoner," the warden shot back.

"Kill the son of a bitch! Shoot the bastard!" the voices demanded, reminiscent of another time, another place, under other circumstances when a mob cried, "Crucify Him! Crucify Him!"

There was no private office where interrogations could be conducted as needed. The warden opened the door to the room that magistrates used as judges' chamber.

First the officers frisked David. Instead of weapons, codes, maps, poisoned capsules, and identification papers that spies are presumed to carry upon their persons, the officers found a package of Turret tobacco, a packet of cigarette papers, several sticks of wooden matches, and two dimes.

In the judges' chambers there was a table, one chair, a garbage container, a spittoon, and a coat rack. The warden brought in another chair.

"We won't need you," Johnson dismissed the warden. "We'll call if we need anything."

When the door closed behind the warden Johnson took charge. "We're police officers. We're going to ask you some questions. You must answer! Do you understand?" His tone was rock hard.

David shrank back.

"What's your name? Where did you come from? How did you get here?" A pause. "What are you doing here?" Another pause, no answer. "When did you arrive?" A moment of silence, no reply. "Who came with you?" A blank stare. "Where are the others?" A dumb look. "Do you speak English? What language do you speak? ... Or are you playing dumb?"

David cowered. When were they going to hit him? What were they saying? What did the men want? What were these "soldiers" going to do to him?

After the third series of questions elicited no response from the prisoner, Johnson snarled, "So, you won't answer!" He nodded to Robinson, who was standing behind David's chair.

Robinson lifted on the chain that linked the handcuffs.

David yowled as he rose to his feet.

"Now! ... What is your name?"

There was no answer. Robinson, on a signal from Johnson, jerked the cuffs upward. David screamed, threw his head from side to side.

"What's your name?"

No answer. Another upward thrust. David screamed again, but the scream died in his throat as he passed out. Robinson let David go. He slumped to the floor. There he lay, gasping and twitching in pain.

"Sons of bitches can't take their own brand of medicine," Robinson commented contemptuously. "What do you think? Think the son of a bitch can't understand, or is playing dumb?"

"If we had an interpreter," Johnson suggested, "this bastard wouldn't be able to play dumb for long."

"Where do we get an interpreter with all them Japs locked up?"

"You know, if this Jap can't speak English, or won't, there's not much point in trying to get answers out of him. We better lock him up again."

The two officers dragged David back downstairs.

"You stay here," Johnson told Robinson. "Call headquarters in Owen Sound. Ask for instructions. I'll go downtown and look around."

Outside the courthouse a small crowd of men were gathered. As Johnson emerged from the building he almost collided with Ted Duncan, who was on his way in.

The *Echo* man introduced himself, though he was known to the officer, and asked if he might ask a few questions about the prisoner, but Johnson declined; the officer himself asked the journalist if he knew anything about the capture of the Jap prisoner.

Duncan directed the officer to the Pacific Hotel, where he'd left the soldiers and the other man who had taken part in the capture.

Johnson hurried away through the small crowd that gave way to let him through.

"Can we see the prisoner?" someone in the crowd called out, expressing what was in the crowd's mind. But the officer hurried away without a word.

"What did he say? He didn't say anything. He didn't say no, same as saying it's alright." The crowd agreed, then turned to Ted Duncan. "Ted! Would you ask the warden if we can see the prisoner?"

Ted went inside, asked, "Can we see the prisoner? ... Johnson didn't say we couldn't."

The warden didn't know what to do. The prisoner was not a prisoner like the others who were entitled to visitors. He looked at Robinson for guidance, but the officer was busy on the phone.

"Well?" Ted asked.

"Guess there's nothing wrong with that. Just a couple of things, though. There's not much room down there. Don't stay too long and don't stir up the other prisoners."

Ted went to the door and relayed the word that they could see the prisoner on a one-at-a-time basis, and only for short periods.

The men lined up outside the courthouse as patrons line up at a theater for a show.

They went in, stayed a minute or two, and came out. "What's he look like?" those still waiting their turn asked those coming out.

"Like a Jap. He's all beat up and bloody."

"What are they going to do with him?" was the question on everyone's mind and lips. Each one hoped for death for the intruder by the worst manner possible. "Shooting's too good for him. Better that they hang him up by the balls."

Constable Robinson was on the phone trying to get through to his headquarters in Owen Sound, with little success. Crank the handle. Lift the receiver. Ask, "Using?" Then listen to, "Yes, I'm using. Can't you hear, sheephead? Get off the line." He wished there was a better system.

Ted went back to his office to write the biggest story of his life.

It was around 8 p.m. that Fred and Jim Jones, sons of the venerable C.K., arrived in Wiarton on furlough. They had hitchhiked from Camp Borden and were on their way home to Cape Croker. The motorist who had picked them up dropped them off at the outskirts of town. As they walked into town they came upon the crowd of people assembled outside the courthouse.

"What's going on?" they asked.

A dozen voices garbled the story at the same time.

"A Jap! A spy! A soldier!"

Fred and Jim gasped in disbelief. "You gotta be kidding!"

"No crap! You can see him if you want. He's locked up. RCMP are guarding him."

"Can you believe that, Fred?" Jim shook his head.

"I gotta see it to believe it," Fred declared, as doubtful as St. Thomas. "Come on!"

As they awaited their turn in line, the crowd was full of goodwill. They heaped Fred and Jim with all kinds of good wishes for being such nice boys from the Cape, serving in the army for the country. And the crowd asked them if it were true that spies were shot.

"Yes, they are, aren't they, Jim?" Fred answered.

"That's right, Fred," Jim confirmed.

When their turn came to go in, Fred and Jim both entered. The prisoner was on the floor, so Fred and Jim had to get down on their knees to see the Jap.

"Jesus Christ!" Fred swore. "Goddamn! I could almost swear that's David. You remember Crazy Dave? And they beat the crap out of him. Those sons of bitches!" And Fred spoke in Indian to David. David answered something that Fred didn't understand, but was able to make out "Kik."

Jim bent down.

"Yeah, that's him, Fred. If it ain't, I'm not Jim Jones."

"What in hell you guys talkin' about?" voices from the other cells croaked out.

"None o' your damned business," Fred barked.

Fred and Jim stomped upstairs. At the counter Fred demanded, "You better release that prisoner. That's not a Jap! It's David McLeod from our reserve. An Indian. He's one of us. He's, what do you call them people? ... a Mongoloid. Let him out and we'll take him home."

The warden looked up. "You sure?" he asked incredulously.

"You damned right I'm sure, ain't that right, Jim?"

"That's right, Fred."

"Well!" Fred exclaimed belligerently.

"I can't let him out just on your say-so. Only a person in authority can do that."

"Like who?"

"A magistrate."

"Who's the magistrate?"

"His Honor Otto McLevis."

"Where's he?"

"At home in Walkerton, I guess."

"Well, let's get in touch with him."

"I don't think I want to do that."

"Why not?"

"You don't know His Honor," the warden told Fred and Jim, who were not familiar with Otto McLevis's well-known bark and bite. "The magistrate's office hours are nine to five in Walkerton. He don't like to be disturbed. You'll have to wait till tomorrow."

Constable Robinson came forward, introduced himself, and asked Fred and Jim what their names were and what their interest was in the prisoner, as if they weren't to be trusted. At the end of the brief interrogation Fred pressed Robinson to do something. "You people made a mistake. You gotta set it right; let David go."

The officer made excuses. "We don't have the authority. Johnson, the provincial officer, and I came here to investigate reports that there was a Jap soldier in town and that there may have been several others. The prisoner was already in custody when we arrived here. Sorry, but the prisoner must remain in custody until the authorities set him free."

"Ain't that a son of a bitch," Fred ground his teeth, meaning to say, "What a stupid justice system." Then, almost in the same breath, he asked if he could use the phone. "I want to call my uncle, Tom Jones. He's the chief at Cape Croker. He'll know what to do."

"Don't be too long. We're waiting for calls from our headquarters."

While Fred was cranking the phone Jim told the warden and the constable that, if they had not already done so, they should call a doctor to tend to David.

"Uncle Tom! It's me, Fred. Yeah, just got back from overseas a few weeks ago. Me and Jim, we're on furlough. Listen, Uncle! We're in Wiarton at the courthouse .... No, Uncle, it's not what you think .... Listen! They got David McLeod locked up in jail ... and they beat the hell out of him. No, they won't let him go. You better come on out here and see what you can do. Nellie's got the car? Okay! Me and Jim will go over to the Pacific Hotel and wait for you there. Bye!"

Just before leaving Fred and Jim received permission to speak to David in Indian to tell him that help was on the way.

After Fred and Jim left, Constable Robinson returned to the phone to report the turn of events to his superiors. How far beyond the detachment's headquarters in Owen Sound had the news of the capture of a Jap soldier gone, Robinson wondered.

On their way to the Pacific Hotel with their kit bags slung over their shoulders, Fred and Jim grew meaner and hotter as they thought about David. "You know, Jim, I never felt like this during the whole war while we were fighting them Germans. I'd like to get my hands on the son of a bitch who beat up on David ... and this is what we were fighting for."

At the Pacific Hotel Fred and Jim were greeted as conquering heroes and invited to join the cabal of drinkers. "Come on, boys!

Come and meet a couple of heroes from Lion's Head. Just captured a Jap spy this afternoon."

"That was no Jap," Fred spat the words out. "That was David McLeod of our reserve ... a Mongoloid who can't talk or think like us. You're not goddamned heroes for beating up a guy that can't help himself."

One of the young soldiers stammered, "It wasn't us, Sir! That guy done that. It was that man." And he pointed at Abe, who had been basking in the hero's limelight. "It wasn't us that beat up that Jap ... I mean that soldier from your reserve ... we just caught him ... and while we were holding him that man came over ... hit the prisoner over and over ... we had to tell him to stop, Sir! Honest to God, we never hit that man."

"Grab him, Jim," Fred commanded.

Jim grabbed Abe by the collar.

"Not in here," the bartender pleaded.

"I didn't do anything," Abe whined. "It was a mistake. The man was wearing a Canadian soldier's uniform; that's illegal." Abe's voice trembled as Jim conducted him outside. "Give me a break ... I'll get even!"

"Shut up!" Fred barked. "Cut your whining!"

"I got a wife and kids," Abe wheezed. Jim pushed and manhandled him so that Abe stumbled on the way to the back of the hotel. The drinkers came along to witness the beating. They smelled blood; they wanted to see blood flow.

Only one of the young soldiers from Lion's Head found his voice. "Just don't kill him!"

"Don't worry, we're just going to give him what he gave David McLeod .... Okay! Jim, hold him still."

Jim slid his arms under Abe's armpits and locked his hands behind the man's neck, a full nelson.

Fred drew his arm back. Abe closed his eyes and screamed, "Noooo!" Fred tapped Abe's face once.

"Alright, Jim! Let the son of a bitch go. He ain't man enough," Fred snorted contemptuously.

Abe staggered away.

*A*round 9:30 that Monday evening, Tom Jones hobbled up the steps of the Wiarton courthouse and into the reception area, where he identified himself to the warden and the police officers.

After he saw David and spoke to him, Tom demanded his release but was turned down. They didn't have the authority, the officers said.

While Tom was considering what to do next, Dr. Wigle came in.

"Well, Tom, how's the chief?" the doctor inquired. "Heard one of your boys was in jail and needed attention."

"Yes! Maybe *you* can get David to the hospital for treatment!"

Tom went downstairs with Dr. Wigle.

"Damn, damn, damn," Dr. Wigle exclaimed when he saw David. "Get some water, soap, and towels ... and get these cuffs off this boy." While the warden ran upstairs to fetch these articles and to relay the doctor's message about removing the cuffs to the officers, Dr. Wigle ran his fingers over David's face. He pressed here and there, on stomach, arms, legs. Each time Dr. Wigle pressed, David winced and cried out.

"Yes! Yes! Yes!" Dr. Wigle sympathized. "I know it hurts. Sorry about that, but I can't help it. At least there aren't any broken bones. Yes! Yes! Yes! Yes! You're going to be just fine, just fine, just fine."

After Constable Johnston came down and undid the handcuffs the warden brought soap, a facecloth, a towel, and water. Both Tom and Dr. Wigle talked to David to comfort him during the washing.

"This man should be in the hospital," Tom suggested.

"Yes! Yes! Yes! Yes!" Dr. Wigle agreed.

"Sorry," Constable Johnston said, "but as much as I'd like to oblige, I don't have the authority to grant the prisoner's transfer to a hospital."

"Chief!" Dr. Wigle spoke to Tom. "This lad needs a change of clothing. He's all wet and he's crapped in his pants." Turning to the constable, he asked if the officer would go to the hospital for pajamas. The constable went out.

"Tom! I'll look after the boy. You can go home or do whatever else you need to do."

Tom thanked the doctor and left. On the way home Fred and Jim talked of nothing else but what they had seen and heard in Wiarton. "You know, Uncle, never did I feel such hate and anger as when I saw David and what they did to him, not even when I was in Italy fighting the Germans and the Italians. They were supposed to have been our enemies. But when I had the chance to hurt that man for David, I couldn't bring myself to do it."

It was late, 11 p.m., well past Tom's bedtime, and his arthritic leg was throbbing. Tom still had one more errand to perform, one that he would have preferred to avoid.

What would he say to Rosa? He had to tell her about David in such a way as would diminish her grief and alarm.

When she came downstairs, she called through the door without opening it, "Who is it?"

Only when Tom identified himself did Rosa light the lamp and open the door. "It's David, isn't it?" Her voice broke. "Is he alright? I've been on edge since 11 p.m."

"He's in Wiarton, in jail. I just came from there. I saw him. Someone beat him up but he's going to be alright. The doctor is looking after him. Now, try not to worry too much. I'll come by tomorrow to take you to see him and bring him a change of clothing. I've had a long day, Rosauh; I must be going."

Rosa cried, "I knew it. I knew that some day something would happen. My poor, poor David."

Tom, now in his sixties, was tired and relieved to go home. There was nothing more he could do that night. Tomorrow would be a busy day for him, getting David's release. "Nellie!" he whispered. "It's hard dealing with people who will not accept responsibility. It's always someone in authority and when you ask them who is in 'authority,' they don't know for sure, and if they know who is in authority they will not call on that authority because it is after hours. They're afraid. I'll call McLevis in the morning and ask him what we have to do to get David out."

In the morning Tom glanced at the old grandfather clock every few minutes. He wished he could call without having to wait for the proper time. But he was well aware of Magistrate Otto McLevis's strict obedience of conventions and his reputation as a no-nonsense judge who gave the impression that he hated the world and the people that appeared before him in his courtroom. Tom didn't want to antagonize McLevis for nothing. He would appeal to the magistrate as a fellow Masonic Lodge member.

At 8:15 a.m. Tom rang the operator and got through to the McLevis residence in Walkerton. "Your Honor. This is Tom Jones, chief of Cape Croker, calling."

"What do you want, Chief?" The words snapped as twigs snap when bent too far.

"I need your help, and I come to you as a fellow Lodge member." Tom explained David's predicament. "What can be done? What should I do?"

"This is a delicate situation, Chief. It's going to depend on a number of factors, on the RCMP, on the Department of National Defence. But if the situation is as you've described and explained it, you must get a sworn affidavit duly signed and executed by a lawyer or your agent and bring it to the court at its next sitting this coming Friday. Your agent must be in court to vouch that the person in custody is a member of your community and is not what he is accused of being. However, Mr. McLeod's release will depend on who has legal custody. Beyond that I cannot say, Mr. Jones. Good day!" And Otto McLevis hung up.

Tom heaved a sigh of relief and then muttered, "Dammit."

"What's the matter, dear?" Nellie asked.

"I've got to see that little runt. I've got to ask him for a favor ... kiss his damned feet."

"Who?"

"Tuffnell!" Tom spat out the name, then told his wife he would be busy working for David's release that day.

First Tom drove to Rosa's place to fetch her. She was ready. As they drove to Walter's home, Tom let Rosa know what he had done. He broke the news to Walter, who offered to do whatever Tom wanted.

Next he stopped at Father Howitt's manse. "Walter, would you go in and ask your priest if he could come to Wiarton on Friday to vouch for David's identity." Walter was back out in a few minutes with word that Howitt would be in attendance.

On to the Indian agency. Tom was curt and brief with Tuffnell. After explaining David's situation, Tom told the agent that he was to draft an affidavit and notarize it for presentation in court that Friday.

"I just can't write a document like that on your word," Tuffnell was defensive. "The man must have done something, as I thought he would all along. Police don't arrest people for nothing and clap them into jail."

"If you're refusing to do what you're supposed to do, then I must report you to Magistrate McLevis."

"Chief Jones! I didn't think that you'd stoop so low."

After Tom left, Tuffnell asked his wife if she knew how to draft an affidavit. She didn't. He called his friend Abe in Owen Sound rather than call head office in Ottawa to ask what he should do. Mitchell knew nothing about affidavits except that lawyers drew them up. Tuffnell would have to go into Wiarton to have one made up for him.

At the courthouse the warden took Tom, Rosa, and Walter to the cell block downstairs. Dr. Wigle was already there checking on David. With a cry, Grandmother collapsed when she saw David, his face swollen and discolored. Walter caught his mother as she fell.

Dr. Wigle gave Rosa smelling salts to revive her. "Yes! Yes! Yes! Yes!" he said. "You're going to be alright Mrs. McLeod. Your boy's going to be alright. A bit tender here and there, but he'll come around."

Rosa sat weakly on the cell cot and drew David to her, cradling his head and stroking his brow. She cried silently. Afterward she bathed David and changed his clothing.

Later, when Tom came by to take her and Walter home, Rosa told him that she would not leave David, but stay with him until they let him go. She didn't want "them" to beat her son again. It was against regulations for anyone but prisoners to remain in the cells overnight, the warden said, but Rosa refused to leave, and there was nothing that he could do except bring an extra cot for her. She remained in the cell from Tuesday until Friday.

An hour before the court sessions began people started to gather in clusters outside the courthouse. Tom Jones, Walter, Father Howitt and Rev. Burgess; Catholics and Protestants stood together unwillingly. Fred Tuffnell stood alone.

Magistrate McLevis arrived. He glowered at the bystanders, but nodded to Tom Jones and remarked, "You've got your documents and witnesses, I trust. Get your constituent's name on the docket."

From 10 a.m. to noon there was a succession of minor charges: drinking, disorderly conduct, break and enter, assault and battery, cattle rustling, and bootlegging preferred against the citizens of Mar, Ferndale, Purple Valley, Hepworth, and Oxenden. As each one entered a plea of "Guilty, Your Honor!" Thirty-Day McLevis, as he was known for his predilection for meting out a $30 fine or thirty days, intoned the sentence "thirty days" to those not having the money to pay the fine. Most chose thirty days of free room and board and good companionship in Walkerton. No one but the foolhardy or those who did not know McLevis dared to plead "Not Guilty." No one trifled with His Honor, as Dennis Akiwenzie found out. After His Honor had pronounced "thirty days" with no option to pay the fine, Akiwenzie wisecracked, "That's nothin' ... I can do that standing on my head." His Honor rejoined just as quickly, "Give that man an extra thirty days to get him back on his feet."

At noon Magistrate McLevis declared a recess.

When the court resumed after lunch, David and Rosa were brought into the courtroom. There were only ten cases still to be heard. McLevis didn't waste any time. The last case was disposed of at 2:30 p.m.

His Honor looked pleased as he glanced at the clock on the wall. "People in the Bruce Peninsula are improving," he remarked wryly.

He looked at the docket. "I understand we have one other case, an unusual case, one concerning David McLeod."

"Yes, Your Honor!" the clerk answered. "His name was just added this morning."

"Call David McLeod."

"Mr. McLeod! Come to the stand!"

David and Rosa went forward, accompanied by Walter.

"What's he charged with?" His Honor's tone was soft compared to what it was earlier.

"There's no charge, nothing here, Your Honor!" the clerk answered.

"Then why is he being held?"

"I don't know, Your Honor."

"Bailiff?"

"Yes, Your Honor."

"How did the prisoner come into your custody?"

"Two soldiers and a civilian brought him in."

"For what reason?"

"They said that he was a Jap soldier, Your Honor."

"Incredible," McLevis Honour commented, then turned to David, Rosa, and Walter. "Who speaks English?"

"I do," Walter answered.

"What's your relationship with the prisoner?"

"He's my brother, and because he speaks neither English nor Indian, our chief asked me to speak on his behalf."

"And the lady, I take it, is your mother?"

"Yes, Your Honor."

McLevis asked the clerk to swear in the prisoner. After the clerk went through the formality, he asked David to tell the court his name, his age, his occupation, and where he lived.

At this point the magistrate broke in, "Mr. Johnston. We need proof, a notarized affidavit, that establishes that the prisoner is who you say he is."

"Our chief has an affidavit, Your Honor," Walter let the court know.

"Is the chief present in court?"

"Yes, Your Honor," Tom replied, and he proceeded forward to the bench. He handed the document to the clerk, who passed it to the magistrate.

"I'm sorry, Mr. Jones," the magistrate remarked after examining the document, "but I cannot accept this affidavit as it is. Your signature, Chief, invalidates the document. As you and I know, Indians have no standing in court. Is there anyone else from Cape Croker present in court this morning who might have standing?"

"Father Howitt, Reverend Burgess, and Mr. Tuffnell, the agent, are here, Your Honor," Walter replied.

"Call Mr. Tuffnell to the stand."

His name being unexpectedly called, Tuffnell stumbled as he left his seat. His face was crimson.

"Do you know the prisoner?" the magistrate asked the moment Tuffnell was sworn in.

"Yes, Your Honor." Tuffnell hesitated.

"Well, tell the court," His Honor said coldly.

"His name is David McLeod. He is a member of the Cape Croker band. He's twenty-four years of age, a Mongoloid. He's also known locally as Crazy Dave."

"You are dismissed," the magistrate cut Tuffnell off. "The court orders David McLeod's release into the care and custody of his mother." The magistrate paused and glared. "This whole episode beggars belief and justice ... this poor soul ... this Indian ... a Mongoloid to boot, has been held in custody without due process." McLevis looked about the room imperiously. "I will not allow a miscarriage of justice in my court. And who beat this man up? ...That man, if such a person can be called a man, ought to be charged and horsewhipped. Court is adjourned."

A week later Jim Cook drove to Rosa's house, parking his truck and leaving it running while he delivered tobacco he had brought for David. Before he crossed the little bridge, Rosa came outside. She screamed, pointed down the road, and slammed the door shut.

Hurt and dumbfounded, Cook stopped by at Tom Jones' store, where he learned what had happened to his helper.

"Oh my God!" Cook exclaimed and muttered about not knowing and how the person who had beaten David should have every bone in his body broken. "What can I do to help?" he asked Tom, and he meant it.

"Nothing," Tom said. "Nothing until Mrs. McLeod gets over her hurt and is ready to forgive you, but I'll speak to her."

Eventually Rosa's hurt and resentment ebbed away. The scrap metal dealer wasn't to blame. Every Christmas and on David's birthday Cook delivered a present, always tobacco and some other articles of clothing—socks, shirt, a pair of mittens, something useful.

The marks, the bruises on David's face cleared up, but the memories lingered and fueled his rage, which he let loose to the Little People in the woods and to Walter whenever "Kik" mentioned the episode.

Back-a-haw came home on crutches early in that fall of 1944. He was lucky. The enemy had wounded him, smashed his knee so that he couldn't walk. For months after his return from overseas, Back-a-haw's home was the Crumlin Hospital in London, Ontario, where he underwent surgery and physiotherapy treatments to remove shrapnel from his knee and to give his joint some mobility. To the doctors, orderlies, and nurses at the hospital, John, the amputees, and the blind were heroes; to the manager of the Iroquois Hotel, where John and a friend sought a drink and a meal, they were just Indians, barred by the Indian Act from being served liquor.

Whenever John came home he once again filled the house with music and laughter during the day. In the evenings it was, "Come on, David, let's go."

David, who had not gone to "the other side" since his arrest and beating, began to venture beyond the Catholic neighborhood. But he did not put his uniform on again; he didn't dare risk another beating.

At nights in the bed downstairs John sometimes cried out in terror as his soul-spirit relived the shellings and bombings, waking both Rosa and David. David, too, relived the torments of his own beating.

The village was coming back to life. Each soldier who returned from service added more vitality to the community. Each soldier received a welcome home party, with greetings from the chief and a dance in his honor, just as their ancestral warriors used to receive a "welcome back" festival on their return from a raiding mission.

The orchestra and the brass band were resurrected; new members were being groomed—Cliff Nadjiwon and Wildore Lamourandiere on trumpets, Gary Johnston on clarinet and saxophone. Lennox dreamed of a ten-, even a twelve-piece orchestra.

The returned soldiers dreamed of picking their lives up where they had set them aside five years earlier. Bill Johnston and Allan Sky were busy constructing rowboats, from rails stolen from rail fences; a few, such as Leonard Nadjiwon, bought motor boats. Wilmer Nadjiwon began fishing with a passion, not in the traditional way, with a single line, but with three lines, one at thirty fathoms, a second at forty-five, and a third at sixty. Moreover, he rowed twice as fast as was considered normal. But that was Wilmer, ever in a hurry to catch up with time, not like those who got left behind.

Wilmer's attitude was a new one compared to the "what's the hurry?" outlook that had governed Indian thinking for generations. And every soldier had a new and different view of education. "What's the use of grade eight?" Frank Nadjiwon often said for my benefit when I worked for him as a farmhand. Through my father's efforts I had returned to Cape Croker from residential school in February 1944 to write my entrance examinations, as the grade eight finals were then called; the residential school grade eight program in Spanish did not meet the Ontario Department of Education standards. I had a lot of catching up to do, but I passed the examinations and then went on to Regiopolis High School in Kingston, Ontario, as Father had hoped I would. To Father's intense disappointment, I dropped out of school in early March 1945. My sister Marilyn remained at the girl's residential school until she completed grade eight in 1949. Except for the occasional visit, Marilyn did not return to Cape Croker. Instead, she accepted Angeline Copegog's invitation to go to Honey Harbour, Ontario, where she got married and settled down.

The North Star Club was revived. The returned soldiers had become accustomed to a life of motion; now they were restless. They organized a soccer league with Annan, Bognor, and Balaclava villages southeast of Owen Sound.

But within a year many of the returned soldiers were disillusioned, some bitter over the lost years, many soured by receiving less rehabilitation monies than their non-Indian comrades, all resentful of their relegation to a status of people without rights. They had fought for nothing, given five years of their lives for nothing, suffered wounds and disabilities for nothing. Rosa had been right. Many men, seeing no future in fishing except marginal existence, drifted away from the reserve to seek work in Sudbury, Sault Ste. Marie, Niagara Falls, London, and Toronto; others found ready work in the lumber camps of northern Ontario. Boys and girls began attending high school.

Back-a-haw was discharged, but he still commuted to London for treatments. He hired a housekeeper for his mother, whose strength and health, never robust, declined even further after David's beating. She could walk a few hundred yards, then would have to rest; she could do no heavy work. The doctors from Wiarton examined her, prescribed rest. Kitchi-Low-C made a tonic that Rosa was to take every day in decreasing amounts as her health improved, and it did improve. She took a mouthful of the medicine every evening from a small bottle that she kept in the porch.

In the early fall of 1946 John married Kate Debossige, house-keeper, and he and his bride moved to their own home near Will-ee's place. By now Rosa was strong enough to do her own housework.

It was already dark, but not late, in December when Rosa went to the porch to get her medication. She unscrewed the cap, put the bottle to her mouth, and swallowed.

She screamed, staggered, then fell. She clutched her throat to ease the fire that burned her mouth and stomach. "David! David!" she rasped.

David, who had not yet gone out, came to his mother's side. He took her hand and led her to the bed in the living room where she slumped, moaning.

As he had not run in years David ran, first to John's and then on to Walter's, to tell them that Rosa had fallen down and was in bed.

Walter limped across the Big Meadow. John was already at Grandmother's. "David, go get Stanley!" And David was off.

Less than ten minutes later Stanley arrived aboard his bicycle.

"Get Kitchi-Low-C and Maggie Bonhomme! Call the priest! The doctor!" Stanley went back out.

With the medicine woman's care and that of the doctor we were sure Rosa would pull through. We prayed.

But we all kept watch. David sat on a chair not far from Rosa's bed, chewing his tongue. From time to time he got up and walked to Rosa's bedside. He would look down at her and say something that she didn't understand. She had just enough strength to reach out to hold his hand. In a hoarse whisper she cried, "David! Who's going to look after you?"

"Don't talk like that, Mom!" John and Walter bade Rosa. "You're going to get better."

But the lye that had been switched, perhaps by children who used to come to play, and put where Rosa kept her tonic, had done its work. Rosa knew. But Walter, John, Stanley, David, Rufus, Kate, Mary, my sisters, and I, who kept watch and visited Rosa, didn't know. We didn't want to believe that Rosa would go on to the next world just yet. But the lye shortened her life. It made her last four days an excruciating physical torment. Beside her deathbed "Bushuh" lay, keeping Rosa company as he had done all his life.

My father and I were having supper. There was a sharp rapping on the door. Both Father and I sprang from our chairs. "Go around the back," my father snapped. I ran around the back; there was no one. We finished our meal in silence. A half hour later we heard the church bell toll the death knell.

As Father Barker, s.j., the newly appointed priest, cast a handful of gravel on Rosa's lowered casket he uttered the words, "Dust thou art and unto dust shalt thou return." A worthless thing, she was declared. Had she been buried in the traditional way, the celebrant would have said, "Kitchi-Manitou has called you home; your family that has gone before is waiting for you with a feast."

Of the members of Rosa's immediate family who lingered at the graveside on that bitterly cold December day until the grave diggers had completely covered the grave, Stanley was the first to go.

"Let's go home," he said to David. Stanley took David's hand to draw him away from the grave. Stanley had to pull him along. For David would not take his eyes off the grave. He looked over his shoulder until Stanley and he entered the woods and were out of sight of the graveyard. All the way home David looked over his shoulder and called, "Woosh."

David no longer had "Woosh" to look after him and to live for his sake. There were Stanley, John, Walter, Norman, his aunt Maggie, his cousins Alexandria and George Keeshig, and Mary, my mother. But they could never look after David the way Rosa had; they could only put up with David and provide what he needed: clothing, meals, and a bed.

With only himself to care for and look after, Stanley took David home with him. After all, he was David's brother, doing what brothers are expected to do for each other. For Stanley, looking after David was his duty, if an unwanted one. Every morning Stanley left the house to cut wood and set snares for rabbits and traps for beavers, muskrats, and raccoons. While Stanley was gone, David kept the fire in the stove alive. On the table was a pot of stew or soup that Stanley had made before he left for work. All David had to do was warm it up for his meals. But after David burned the contents and scorched the pot, Stanley discontinued providing ready meals. Rather than risk a fire, Stanley left fried salt pork, cold potatoes, bannock, and a small pail of tea. At the door Stanley's parting words were, "Don't you dare fry the potatoes ... or if you're hungry, go down to John's place."

Though Stanley was uneasy about leaving David alone in the house all day, he could not bring him to the trap lines. He had taken him twice before; twice was enough. David dawdled and dawdled.

To ease his mind Stanley tried sending him out of the house when he left for work. "Go to John's house. Go to Walter's. Go to Mary's."

At first David was willing enough to do what Stanley wanted him to do. But after a few days David balked, shook his head, and said, "Kuh!"

Stanley lost his temper. He snarled at David, "Go on. You can't stay in the house all day by yourself. You might burn the house down."

David stalled. He looked at Stanley, his eyes full of hurt and bewilderment, which made Stanley feel guilty.

Stanley gave in. He had to live with the anxiety of leaving David alone in the house, not knowing what David would do while tending the fire, or whether he would warm his meal on the sly, forget it, and burn the house down and himself along with it. The only thing Stanley could do was threaten David and hope for the best. To be as safe as he could, Stanley came home at noon every day to check David and the house.

Whenever he came back to check, both David and the house were intact. As far as Stanley could see or tell, David had not touched the frying pan. Other than a litter of bread crumbs and potato peelings on the floor and table, the house was still standing. There were times when Stanley felt like scolding David for his sloppy eating habits, but it would be useless. At least he didn't burn the house down.

In his new home David had little to do except sit and chew his tongue in sadness. There were no horseshoes, no organ, no cards. Bushuh, too, had gone and not returned; he had simply disappeared a week after Rosa's death. And David no longer sought the company of the Little People, as far as Stanley knew. But the Little People may have come to David when David was alone. Who knows?

David's sole company was provided by my sister Janet, my half-sister Eileen, Berdina, Rose, Ray, and a few other youngsters who came to play hide and seek. Then David's face lit up, broke into a smile. His laughter echoed in the woods. He played until his shirt was soaked in perspiration and he was gasping for air.

Fishing no longer provided a living for the fishermen of Cape Croker. Something had happened to the fish. By the late 1940s the trout were smaller, the number caught were fewer. No one could support a family on fishing. The old days were gone. It was the same with trapping. There were fewer raccoons, beavers, muskrats, foxes, and squirrels. The furriers on Spadina Avenue in Toronto paid less and less for pelts. "Demand for furs has declined," they explained.

Many men, young and old, took themselves to lumber camps in Northern Ontario, while others headed to Niagara Falls, New York, to work for chemical plants.

Stanley would have gone with them, except that he had to think of David. He couldn't just get up and leave. There were people who would have been willing to take David in for a while, but not permanently; John and Walter would have done so except that they had their own families to look after. Poor Walter had a hard enough time feeding and clothing his children. He, too, was working outside the community, slaving for farmers in and around Brampton. There were times when Walter brought home a bag of cabbages or turnips or carrots or onions, which he had accepted as part of his wages to make up for the shortfall in his employer's paycheck. No! Stanley wouldn't encumber Walter and Frances. The only family member who would not be too burdened was Maggie Desjardines, their aunt. She agreed to look after David.

With his brother provided for, Stanley went to southern Ontario, Brampton, Simcoe, Tillsonburg, St. Catharines, and in the fall to Meaford to pick apples. In late October he returned home to look after David.

Maggie Desjardines, as well as Alexandria and George Keeshig, who helped look after David, found David difficult to care for. If he had been trained he would have been easier. There was no doubt in their minds that David could have learned. He should have been made to do chores.

But difficult as he was, David was good-natured and amusing. While staying with George and Alexandria Keeshig, David took up reading newspapers and magazines, right side up, upside down, by lamplight or starlight.

"David! Go to bed! It's getting late and you're using up coal oil," Alexandria spoke sharply to David, and she turned the lamp down. At midnight she was awakened by some noise in the living room. She opened the door an inch, peeked out. There was David sitting next to the window still reading, holding the *Owen Sound Sun Times* upside down ... reading by the moonlight.

There were changes in the community, but little ones that scarcely attracted any attention. At the time they made hardly any impact on the life of the people on the reserve. Returned soldiers set the changes in motion. "Go to school!" they urged their sons and daughters. And young people flocked to high schools to get ahead, and neglected their language to get ahead. "Indian" would prevent them from getting ahead. "Getting ahead" was the slogan of the day.

Returned soldiers served as councillors: John Johnston, Barney Nadjiwon, Charlie Nadjiwon, Bryce Elliott, Ernest Akiwenzie, Howard Chegahno, and many others. In the beginning of their public service the new councillors were deferential. It was "Mr. Tuffnell ... Sir!" Not many months later, exasperated by the agent's dictatorial attitude and his inability and refusal to expedite decisions, they growled and snapped at him, "Tuffnell!" They were no longer deferential. Impatient, they badgered him. "Tuffnell! When can we expect a decision from Ottawa? Did you send the letter? Why can't you hurry them up? That's your job, isn't it? You're supposed to be helping us, are you not? ... Maybe we should have another agent."

Tuffnell stood his ground. He said nothing. His red face and quivering lips said it all.

Chief Jones, heartened by his councillors' support, took them to Ottawa to complain about their agent, and to find out why it took so long, a year and sometimes as long as sixteen years, to approve band council resolutions, the registration of deeds of possession, birth and death certificates, probates, loans, band membership records, enfranchisements, elections.

The delegates didn't receive much satisfaction from the Indian Affairs Branch executives, a variety of former servicemen, lieutenants, captains, majors, colonels, and a few old generals. They still retained their titles. They were crisp in dress, crisp in manner, crisp in speech, and crisp in temperament. "Why didn't the delegation make an appointment?" they crunched their words. "It is the civil way of doing business," they reminded the delegation. "Indians must follow protocol like everyone else." As for their complaint about Mr. Tuffnell, a hill of beans was worth more attention. "The man can't read? Can't write? Absurd! There've been no complaints from administration about the department representative's monthly reports." Tom Jones and his delegation were dismissed.

Outside the Indian Affairs Branch headquarters the Cape Croker band council, slighted and seething, held a war council to determine what to do next. After scratching their heads, they agreed that they should call on the member of parliament for their riding. The member was amiable, but there was little he could do for them, they being non-citizens, without voting rights. At least the honorable member listened to them and promised to look into their complaints.

This was the first of several trips that Tom Jones made to Ottawa over the next few years. He'd get rid of that miserable little tyrant if it was the last thing he'd do in his life. Chief Jones didn't have to extend his efforts to topple Fred Tuffnell beyond 1949. A heart attack felled the agent. His replacement, some say, was Adams; others say it was McGregor. Whoever it was didn't stay too long. On his departure the agent torched the office records, letters, journals, minute books, and reports. Edwin Akiwenzie, who was the janitor of the agency at the time, alarmed by the smoke coming from behind the agency, hurried to the building. Too late; most of the records were damaged beyond recovery, but he did manage to salvage some scorched papers that were deeds representing Cape Croker's ownership of certain islands. What was in the other documents no one could say.

Not too long after the incident, Tom Jones received a visit from officials from Ottawa who threatened to have him charged with theft of government properties—the documents. He countered by letting them know that he would press charges against the agent for destroying government documents. Tom Jones was never charged, and the matter was forgotten.

Tom Jones' work was done. He had fulfilled his dream. In 1956, six days after his reelection as chief, he died. But his aspiration for a greater role for chief and council in the management of their community did not die with him. The younger councillors took up Tom Jones' cause. They weren't happy with the status quo. They had fought in the White Man's war for equality and other principles. But after the war they were no better off than before. They were not citizens of the country; except for war veterans, Indians still could not vote. They were prohibited from receiving service in dining rooms where spirits were offered; they couldn't obtain mortgages for the purchase of homes; they couldn't secure bank loans; returned war veterans received smaller amounts of rehabilitation grants. The chief and councillors were largely figureheads. The real authority was vested in the agent, the regional director, and the superintendent general in Ottawa. The new and younger generations were itching for change. It was time for Indians themselves to take charge of their destinies. They had learned nothing from their agents.

In his home at the north end of the reserve David knew little of the events in the village. The residents knew little of David, except that he was a poor Indian, poorer than the rest.

In the fall of 1956, as he sat chewing his tongue and contemplating life at the end of his foot, David toppled to the floor. When Stanley came home from work he found his brother prostrate beside his brooding chair. A massive heart attack had finally released David from his human bondage.

In his eulogy Father Dwyer, S.J., Father Barker's replacement, said that David would go straight to heaven. He would not, as most would have to, spend any time in purgatory to purify his soul and render his being worthy of admission into the presence of God.

They buried David next to his mother, our grandmother. To her David would once more be united.

nce, in the summer of 1947, I ventured to the tip of the Little Port Elgin and Sidney Bay Bluff before I went back to school to try to pick up my education, which I had suspended two and a half years earlier. From my vantage point a thousand feet or so above sea level I saw the entire "Cape," as the locals knew and called Cape Croker. My eyes followed the shoreline from behind King's Point Bluff to the southeast, swerved toward and around King's Point, then swept into Little Port Elgin Bay before snaking out toward Lighthouse Point. From here the shoreline veered left and curved right before wheeling a sharp left at Cove of Cork Point, then curled into Little North Bay and on out to Benjamin's Point, the northernmost end of the reserve. It circled back at this terminus, meandered southward as far as Pine Tree Point, then hooked left. It weaved as far as The Little Point where it looped around McGregor Harbour as far as Partridge Point, then looped around Sidney Bay and out toward Hope Bay Point. There it bent to the left into Hope Bay, out of sight and beyond.

About half of the reserve, the northern portion, is almost an island. Between the east shore of McGregor Harbour and the west shore of Little Port Elgin Bay is a narrow neck of land, no more than a fifteen-minute walk from one side to the other, convenient for portaging. Our ancestors called Cape Croker Portage Point, or "Naeyaushee-winnigum-eeng."

When I looked on the home that Kitchi-Manitou had given us, it was then mid-August. The cicadas, according to legend, were carrying out their duties coloring leaves, berries, fruits, and vegetables with a variety of yellows, browns, and reds, and splashing on each a fragrance.

I saw the land with its hills, little valleys, meadows, swamps, muskegs, ridges, moraines, creeks, and spring overspread with woods; cedars, pines, spruces, balsams, maples, oaks, birches, poplars; meadows, fields, and glades awash with daisies, clover, grass, and hay.

This was Kitchi-Manitou's gift to my ancestors and to us, their descendents. As I stood there and gazed upon the land, my home, fifty-two years ago, I didn't think of it as I now do. Still, it drew me and would not let me go, so that it made me sad. "Do not leave. But if you must go, come back home. I have what you will not have elsewhere," it seemed to say.

And so I left to complete my high school diploma program in Spanish, Ontario, then went on to university in Montreal, Quebec. From 1948 to 1954 I returned home once a year, at Christmas. After I graduated and began working in "the big city," Toronto, I came home more frequently.

In 1958 I was smitten by love and charmed by Lucie Desroches, a glamorous farmerette from Penetanguishene. "Marry me," she commanded. Willingly I complied in 1959.

Soon after our marriage I took my wife home to Cape Croker. As we drove over the crest of Little Port Elgin Hill, Lucie caught a glimpse of the shoreline that trailed out toward the lighthouse; she glanced from left to right at the Niagara Escarpment bluffs that wedged into the reserve. "So pretty," she sighed. After I had taken her on a tour of Cape Croker she added, "So clean ... so tidy."

And indeed it was. About the only two places that were unsightly were Muggs' yard, where he repaired old cars and had an assorted collection of car parts, and Aesop's place, which sullied Cape Croker's natural beauty. On the side of the road that flanked his property were parked neatly three and sometimes four venerable old cars known as B29s during their operable years, a name derived from the year of their manufacture and from their roar, which was assumed to equal the roar of the famous World War II bomber, the B-29. This fleet of derelicts would be drawn off somewhere out of sight, there to wither away in dignity and to rust in peace.

By 1966 Lucie was thoroughly taken in by the community. She made up her mind that Cape Croker was heaven, where she and our children, Miriam, Tibby, and Geoffrey, would spend their weekends and summers. We bought a slice of land in Little Port Elgin Bay from Wellington Elliott in 1966, signed the papers, and delivered them to the Indian Affairs Branch in Chippewa Hill, Ontario, for registration. Silas Proulx, my brother-in-law, finished the log cabin that Charles Nadjiwon had started. This was in 1967. We waited, waited, and waited, called and called for our deed of possession. Sixteen years we waited for our deed, and when we received it, the slice of land that we had purchased was severed.

One morning two or three years after our log cabin had been built I was sitting outside on a picnic table on the beach drinking coffee and watching the sunrise. Norman Jones, otherwise known as "Josh," came along, sat down, and accepted my offer of coffee. After some chitchat we both lapsed into silence. I studied the horizon and the woods that capped the land. Behind us robins, sparrows, wrens, and warblers piped and whistled.

"Have you ever seen anything more beautiful or heard anything more cheerful?" Josh finally asked.

"No," I answered. I had, but could not recall that I had. I had indeed seen, heard, breathed in, tasted, felt, and sensed the beautiful every day, but I had paid little attention or didn't recognize it as such, otherwise I might have derived greater benefit for my soul and spirit.

Since that morning I have often thought about Josh's question and have tried, insofar as I am capable, to admire the beauties and wonders of the earth.

When Josh asked the question about thirty years ago there were several hundred people who still spoke the ancestral language, soft, rhythmical, and expressive, and the people who spoke it could do so with humor and gravity. They saw and valued the world and life from a native perspective. Grasses, flowers, and shrubs graced the roadside and scented the air. Beavers, bears, ravens, geese, ants, and bees still meant something, as creatures that gave their lives so our ancestors could survive.

An hour or two after sunset the whippoorwills piped up from behind our houses, and when they had finished their singing they settled into their nests for the night. It was time for darkness, silence, and peace to still the world and life. Only the owls and the wolves had permission to intrude upon the silence; only spirits and ghosts were free to roam the world.

In 1995 Lucie and I came to live in our newly constructed home to take in the beauty of creation in all its forms at Cape Croker; to listen to the chants and pipings of birds, to animals, insects, the winds, and the thunders.

But alas, Cape Croker is not what I wanted it to be. The changes, little ones that began thirty years ago, are now more pronounced. Rusted cars and heaps have displaced shrubs and bushes around some homes; beer bottles, tin cans, and plastic containers cast along the roadside have supplanted roses and dandelions; radios and stereos screech and blare, drowning out whippoorwills and intruding upon the silence. Like our neighbors outside the reserve, our people have grown to fear and hate silence. English has been adopted completely; instead of the soft, rhythmic Ojibway, people now speak English with its harsh d's, t's, f's, x's, b's, and ch's. A hundred of us still speak our language.

Even the Manitous and spirits have been disowned. Weendigoes, Little People, Nana'b'oozoo and their kin no longer dwell in the hills and swamps, nor in the hearts of men and women. In their place are imports, Venus, Hercules, and all that they represent. Spirits and ghosts of our departed ancestors no longer roam the roads at night to visit the village that was once theirs. They are strangers in their own home, unwanted by their descendents.

When I think of Uncle David and welcome his spirit into the inner sanctum of my own soul and spirit, he settles in, shakes a finger in my face. "Ook! Ook!" he says, and he talks on and on. I still don't understand.